When Stone Walls Cry

When Stone Walls Cry

The Nehrus in Prison

Mushirul Hasan

OXFORD
UNIVERSITY PRESS

OXFORD
UNIVERSITY PRESS

Oxford University Press is a department of the University of Oxford.
It furthers the University's objective of excellence in research, scholarship,
and education by publishing worldwide. Oxford is a registered trademark of
Oxford University Press in the UK and in certain other countries.

Published in India by
Oxford University Press
YMCA Library Building, 1 Jai Singh Road, New Delhi 110 001, India

First Edition published in 2016

ISBN-13: 978-0-19-946689-4
ISBN-10: 0-19-946689-0

Typeset in Adobe Jenson Pro 11/15
by Tranistics Data Technologies, New Delhi 110 044
Printed in India by Replika Press Pvt. Ltd

For Zoya

Contents

Acknowledgements

This book, *When Stone Walls Cry: The Nehrus in Prison*, and *Roads to Freedom: Prisoners in Colonial India* (2016) have grown out of my project on political prisoners in colonial India. I am extremely grateful to the Nehru Memorial Fund for appointing me as the Jawaharlal Nehru Fellow (2013–15). Work on these two books was completed during the course of the Nehru Fellowship.

Both books involved considerable archival work. I have relied on the goodwill and generous help of the librarians and staff of several libraries. I would like to record my thanks to the staff of the National Archives of India, New Delhi, and also the Uttar Pradesh State Archives, Lucknow, for their help in finding documents and materials for this book. I am indebted to the staff of the Nehru Memorial Museum and Library, New Delhi, and the India International Centre, New Delhi, library, for their constant help in finding materials and documents.

I am deeply grateful to Zafar Alam, Suranjan Das, Nitasha Devasar, Gyanesh Kudesia, Ranjit Nair, Bikas Niyogi, Mohammed Shakir, Babli

Parveen, Hari Vasudevan, and Nishat Zaidi for their generous encouragement and support in various ways for this project. I want to thank the Oxford University Press for its sympathetic and efficient handling of this book. I owe special thanks to the editors at Oxford University Press for all their help in facilitating the publication of the book.

I want to thank members of my family—Salma Rizvi, Mujeebul Hasan, Abida Hasan, Zakia Hasan, Naazli Naqvi, Samina Rizvi, Shaaz Hasan, Samir Rizvi, Shahzad Hasan, Abbas Kazim, Adil Abbas, Mohammed Tariq Siddiqi, Kahkashan Siddiqi, Khusro Siddiqi, Saadi Atiq Siddiqi, Sameen Siddiqi, Akif Siddiqi, Amman Siddiqi, and Mohammed Ateek—who have over the years given me great affection and support.

The book is once again dedicated to Zoya for her unfailing support over the years and also in making this book happen.

1 Introduction

The continuing saga of the Nehru family, of the vicissitudes of
Jawaharlal, Indira, Sanjay and Rajiv has been, for hundreds of millions
of us, an obsession spanning more than three decades. We have poured
ourselves into this story, inventing its characters, then ripping them
up and re-inventing them. In our inexhaustible speculations lies one
source of their power over us. We became addicted to these speculations, and they, unsurprisingly, took advantage of our addiction. Or,
we dreamed them, so intensely that they came to life. And now, as the
dream decays, we cannot quite bring ourselves to leave it, to awake.

Salman Rushdie*

Julia Brenda indicts intellectuals for treason to their destiny, and blames
them for betraying the very moral principles that made their existence
possible. The Nehrus were not cast in this mould; they were identified
with national life so closely that they came to personify the triumphs

of an entire nation.[1] According to Nayantara Sahgal, an accomplished writer, for the Nehru family, there was no such thing as a personal life that could be kept apart from the demands and duties of public life.[2] Indeed, the growing up of her elders was India's growing into political maturity—a kind of political maturity different from any that the world had seen before, based on an ideology inspired by self-sacrifice, compassion, and peace.[3] And so, her family story is, more often than not, 'a chronicle of sweat and toil, loneliness and suspense, personal anguish and political frustration', against which proud patriotism was the only defence.[4] Even though the argument is far-fetched, such boasting helped to keep the morale of the Nehrus high whenever they were put in prison. 'It is only the favoured few', observed Vijaya Lakshmi Pandit (1900–1990), 'whom prison cannot break because their vision and their passion for freedom enables them to soar beyond the locks and bars of jail and no physical restriction can take away their liberty.'[5]

Habits are inculcated by family and other social groups with the help of social agencies. Hence, Motilal Nehru had a coherent conception of the life of his family and of the stages of its growth. He gave exclusive importance to the meeting of national and family histories so that grandparents, parents, uncles, and aunts started a new life in the thrall to a country whose destiny they took to be their own. Then, sooner or later, came the next stage when the connection with the country's destiny became rooted, emotional, and permanent. Maybe those who made the connection missed the tune of both life and history, but Nayantara Sahgal had no doubt in her mind of what she and her sisters were told in all the years she was growing up: that 'history was ourselves and we were making it.'[6] Whether they were involved in so large a project as 'the making of history' is a questionable proposition, though the self-pride of the Nehrus would not allow them to think or act differently. 'We are an abnormal family', wrote the most distinguished of them, 'or rather force of circumstances has made us lead rather abnormal lives, and the emphasis of these lives is more and more cherished, though it is hidden from the public gaze.'[7]

Biographers have been generous to the Nehrus in drawing a picture of their sufferings and sacrifices, and of their ideals and their courage in facing the might of the British empire. The Nehrus renounced property and a livelihood, and spent months and years in jail, but did not make peace with the authorities. Nayantara Sahgal could, therefore, tell two stories at the same time: a fictional one that drew its material from her personal and political selves, and a 'national' one, about the making of modern India.[8] As a result, the Nehrus were counted not as mere individuals but as symbols and representatives of fellow Indians.[9] Mulk Raj Anand (1905–2004), the writer, asserted in *Apology for Heroism* that the creation of a new society would be the work of men and women 'who are sincere, disinterested and free, men who are willing to save the world ... men who are human, who represent humanity everywhere and seek a new way of life ... thereby becoming an example to other men.'[10]

Several theories attempt to correlate the rise of nationalism with the pre-eminent influence of the Nehrus. Sarojini Naidu (1879–1949), for one, believed that their history was both a living symbol and an integral part of the story of the Indian struggle for freedom.[11] 'Across the landscape of this moving family history', she added, 'fall the bright lights and the half lights, the dimmer and the deeper shadows inseparable from human destiny.'[12] As the very conception of the ascendancy of a family in these theories is vague, we must settle for the simple fact that the Nehrus were key figures in regional and local politics because they were represented in Allahabad in force, and their patriarch was no other than Motilal Nehru, born only a day earlier than Rabindranath Tagore—on 6th May. While he passed on his legacy to his son, 'the keeper of the nation's conscience,'[13] his daughters, cousins, and other relatives recovered the intellectual tendencies of an epoch with their writings. This theme itself is a subject of sufficient complexity to warrant book-length treatment. Since this is not practicable for our purposes here, we simply note some of the relevant facts.

The above, however, does not mean that the claims of Sarojini Naidu, a close family friend, are not exaggerated. But let us, nonetheless, now turn to the claims of political prisoners, which extend far back in time and will go on well into the future, writes Albie Sachs—a young South African barrister arrested in South Africa on 1 October 1963, under the 90-Day Act, which permitted the detention of a person without charge for this period.[14] The Nehrus were not the only people who had to go to the prison during the freedom movement; many preceded them and many more followed them. But then why are we interested in them as a group? Here it has to be added that the majority of the men in the Nehru family had the same language, mores, economic status, and occupation. They had a high proportion of talented men and women as well and performed, comparatively speaking, not as a disparate but a cohesive entity. Second, they had tangible relationships with the freedom struggle, which is manifested in their personal privations and indignities of incarceration: 'These constant pilgrimages to prison are, as a rule, deadening, and one cannot undergo the experience again and again without bearing the scars on one's soul.'[15]

The Nehrus navigated the political journey with such ease, and, in a certain fundamental sense, they managed to keep steadily in view the unity of national life. It remains to be said that no other family represented the pluralist values of the nation as well as they did, and that they are counted as individuals as well as symbols and representatives of their fellow Indians.[16]

My study is confined to the peaks of nationalist resistance and popular struggles, when the masses fought honestly and courageously to free India and faced imprisonment, torture, or death. Those who survived, freed themselves from the clasp of their fetters, and echoed the sentiments that Lieutenant Shmidt expressed in his last speech at his trial in the Soviet Union:

> For thirty years I have nurtured
> My love for my native land,
> And I shall neither expect
> Nor miss your leniency.[17]

There are grounds here of a detailed examination.

A discussion on the subject is not rendered any easier by the complex nature of India's encounter with British colonialism, but my study begins with two passionate and intrepid crusaders for freedom, who adjusted well to dreary prison life. One is the proud and truculent Motilal Nehru; he suffered in jail in his old age but hoped for better days and prepared for them. A man with an unusually wide range of interests, he raised the status of legal practice in Allahabad from a subordinate place to the dignity of an independent profession. The other is, of course, a robust and energetic individual who had a passion for freedom and a determination to battle in order to secure it whatever the cost to himself and his family. Jawaharlal spent almost nine years in colonial jails; the longest spell, a total of 1,040 days, being between August 1942 and June 1945. 'The days have passed,' he wrote, 'and the months and the years, but each day, each moment, has left its impress, and layer upon layer of these impressions and experiences lie embedded in the recesses of our mind.'[18]

Together, father and son unfold a great historical epoch—the four decades before Independence and seventeen long years afterwards. I hope the unparalleled moral prestige that lay in their hands would have its effect upon the younger generation, and their ideas on pluralism and secularism will find gradual acceptance in Indian society.

The Allahabadis could not think of the Nehrus without their women—their moral and intellectual fibre, and their intellectual attitude that gave rise to a wider outlook.[19] No one can read their writings without seeing that their mind was occupied with what they considered to be the fundamental issues facing the nation. Many of the Nehrus combined the benefits of privilege with the satisfaction that they had freed themselves from caste and religious conventions, and, instead, linked their eclectic world view to a long and proud tradition. Here it is appropriate to cast a glance at this aspect in the larger context of women's political activism.

The Nehrus conducted their personal and political lives from Anand Bhawan, a familiar landmark in the history of the nationalist struggle. Intimately connected with the freedom struggle, great events occurred and great decisions were taken within its walls.[20] It is full of memories for the Nehrus and is indeed part of their family—a very substantial part. Following are some typical examples that may corroborate such statements. In 1910, delegates to that year's Congress session—including President William Wedderburn (1838–1918)—had stayed in Anand Bhawan. Gandhi visited Anand Bhawan in 1940. Nayantara Sahgal was tasked with carrying garlic for him and she did so at arm's length (detesting its strong smell). Sarojini Naidu said to her, 'There is no need to be so snooty, young lady. If you want to have a complexion like the old man's when you're his age, you'd do well to eat some of it yourself!' It was also here that Vijaya Lakshmi had the time to ride with her brother and read George Bernard Shaw. Their reading habits did not change even amidst the hustle and bustle of political life. The children enjoyed the comfort of the place and a feeling of security and stability.[21]

With his hectic political life and the long years in jail, Jawaharlal Nehru asked a close family friend, Padmaja Naidu: 'Where is a home for any of us, for you, for me? We may find a shelter and even affection with people who care for us, if we are fortunate. But we wander still, in spirit and mind, if not in body, nomads with no fixed abode, exiles everywhere.'[22] Nehru wrote this from Badenweiler, where he was nursing Kamala. The elders did their bit to keep intact the character of Anand Bhawan, until Motilal Nehru, fired by the patriotic spirit, presented it to the nation on 27 March 1930.

The stories of the beginning of India's past filled Jawaharlal Nehru with wonder, and he sought to understand it in terms of the present and even of the future. Why should there be so much misery in the world? This question troubled him. Why do people argue and quarrel among themselves as a sect or a religious group? Why are they blind to the vision of freedom? To explore further his thoughts, I discuss his philosophy of history, his definition of culture, his appraisal of anti-colonial movements, and, above all, his *idea* of India. I also shed light on his uneasiness over the growing religious stimulus in the public domain. I analyse his comments on political affairs, many of which tend to corroborate or supplement, to a fair degree, the information that is available to us from some other sources.

There is sufficient cause to shield Jawaharlal Nehru's memory from the calumny of his detractors. As a result of new research in the field, we are better placed to pass on his truly heroic and tragic image to the readers, his largeness of vision, emotion, pathos, and tolerance. He dedicated his immense energies and intellectual powers to bring joy and freedom to his people, to build a 'modern' India, and to strengthen its democratic and secular foundations. As an optimist, he shared with others the joy of working and struggling for a great cause and, despite the dark spots around him, his ideals remained undimmed and his spirit undaunted. He would say that life would be dull and colourless but for the obstacles that one had to overcome and the fights one had to win. 'Real failure', he wrote, 'was a desertion of principle, a denial of our right, and an ignoble submission to wrong. Self-made wounds always took longer to heal than those caused by an adversary.'[23]

Jawaharlal Nehru's seriousness, courage, and unselfish devotion to India's liberation speak for themselves throughout the pages that follow.

Prison Studies: A Resumé

Scores of books and articles appeared on Jawaharlal Nehru in the 1950s and 1960s, underlining his role as the architect of modern India, the genius behind India's secular democracy, and the driving force behind the Non-Aligned Movement. His people loved him dearly and he loved them with equal passion. Marie Seton's abiding recollection was his expression as he heard an old peasant complain about officials making life intolerable for the villagers. Jawaharlal Nehru bowed his head in shame. 'That he did explains why India's nameless people relied on him.'[24]

Michael Brecher, the Canadian scholar, presented steadily before the reader the significance of an age pregnant with great issues.[25] He talked to the prime minister of the second-largest democracy in the world in June 1956 and read more than 250 of his unpublished letters. The end product excited great attention. It was not easy for a scholar to pick his way through a straggling jungle of incidents and episodes, but Brecher did just that. Interwoven with the pre- and post-Independence phases and with public and private lives, his narrative offers readers an objective scrutiny and analysis of both Nehru the individual and the events of the time. His caution is in striking contrast to the dash and certitude of other writers. 'There is, I believe', stated a reviewer, 'no better political biography of Jawaharlal Nehru and probably also no better introduction to contemporary India.'[26] Writing the book was a great achievement, one which owed a great deal presumably to the author being fascinated by of his subject.[27]

Frank Moraes, B.N. Pande, Rafiq Zakaria, Natwar Singh, and innumerable historians and journalists have expressed their admiration for Jawaharlal Nehru's patriotism and endurance, his character and statesmanship. Natwar Singh has recently written that he was mesmerized by the prime minister's courage and his penchant for living dangerously.[28] Nehru gave hope and pride to the young Indian Foreign Service officer. His ideas were not mere abstractions: 'He made them come alive—alive in our minds, inspiring us, shaping and influencing our lives.'[29]

Describing him as a man of intellect, of vision, and of essential goodness, B.N. Pande, the London-based historian, salutes Jawaharlal Nehru's intellect and wisdom: 'In believing that the truth would always win and in abstaining ... from returning evil for evil he excelled Gandhi.'[30] B.R. Nanda's admiration of Jawaharlal Nehru is unconcealed. Intoxicated by the brilliance of his hero, he failed to recognize the limitations of his own sympathies and understanding.

Stanley Wolpert began with political history but did not go further, and was hampered by his inability to let himself come through freely.[31]

Judith M. Brown, who handled the sources more critically, maintained the impetus given to Nehruvian studies by her predecessors, and supplied more advanced students in this field with much of what they needed. According to her, Jawaharlal Nehru's life was a window into the changing world of Indian politics, and he was central to the making of modern India.[32] Although amateur historians like Tariq Ali, M.J. Akbar, and Shashi Tharoor accepted and recorded events without challenging their veracity, they introduced the ideal and the methods of secular study. They painted a far more flattering picture of Jawaharlal Nehru, who had lived long enough to fear and to hear evidence of the dreadful destruction caused by the partition of India.

The three-volume biography by Sarvepalli Gopal is a useful corrective to the competing extravaganza of Nehru's other biographers. In lucidity of expression and freshness of style, it marks a breakthrough in biography-writing. Enriched by the personal knowledge of many of the actors in the political drama and based on meticulous research, Gopal's work occupies a place in the select class of Indian historical classics. The narrative is the work of a wholehearted admirer. 'To a whole generation of Indians', Gopal writes, 'he [Nehru] was not so much a leader as a companion who expressed and made clearer a particular view of the present and vision of the future. The combination of intellectual and moral authority was unique in his time.' This appreciation of Jawaharlal Nehru is also reflected in Gopal's scholarly essays, which have been recently reprinted.[33]

Prison studies have had a long career in Europe. Scholars like Michel Foucault have explored a corpus of knowledge, techniques, and 'scientific' discoveries entangled with the practice of the power to punish.[34] For the duration of her second and longest wartime imprisonment from July 1916 to 1918, Rosa Luxemburg's correspondence and writings became her sole emotional and intellectual outlet. She remembered her days in the Warsaw Citadel when her brother came to see her. She was weak and had to be carried into the visitors' room. She had to hold on with both hands to the wires of the cage. The cage stood in a dark corner of the room and her brother had to press his face against the wires. 'Where are you?' he kept on asking continually wiping away the tears that clouded his glasses. 'How glad I should be if I could only take Karl's place in the cage of Luckau prison, so as to save him from such an ordeal!'[35]

In South Africa, Nelson Mandela and some of his brave colleagues provided vivid impressions of the injustice, the unhappiness, and the brutality of the apartheid regime. In Kenya, Maina wa Kinyatti was arrested in June 1982 for his opposition to the unpopular Moi-Kanu regime. He wrote his letters from prison as an act of defiance to prove to his captors that bars, stone walls, chains, and guards with guns could not deter a determined patriot. He was able to break the siege and make friends with a few guards who secretly provided him with pens and writing paper and courageously took the risk of smuggling out all the letters.[36] Antonio Gramsci handwrote 2,848 pages of notes, which he left to be smuggled out of jail and out of Italy after death.

There are other telling accounts of men and women being pushed behind the Iron Gate, put in prison, and being chained to the wall. They felt the anguish of captivity, and heard the music of death but did not give up. Faith in Allah, clear conscience, and loyal friends provided peace and comfort to Mohammed Fadhel Jamali Baghdad, who was condemned to death when the revolution of 17 July 1956 broke out in Iraq. These three things made up the message that he carried from the vicinity of the gallows to those who sought a free and happy life, a life which did not terminate with physical death but was renewed thereafter.[37]

In South Asia, V.D. Savarkar has given us a shocking picture of hatred, bloodshed, exploitation, and treachery in his book *Majhi Janmathep* (My Life-term). The tone of this book is polemical, and a religious flavour permeates the text. Unlike him, Sri Aurobindo Ghose was unworldly, more at home with his books than among men.[38] Although his influence and the impression he made preceded the publication of his *Tales of Prison Life*, its strong spiritual content attracted serious attention. Its abiding interest lies in Aurobindo's evolution as a religious thinker. He is praised, as the following passage suggests, for his faculty of divination when he was giving reins to his imagination:

> When I was asleep in the Ignorance, I came to a place of meditation full of holy men and I found their company wearisome and the place a prison; when I awoke, God took me to a prison and turned it into a place of meditation and His trysting-ground.[39]

Among monographs, several books hold pride of place. I have discussed their arguments elsewhere, along with the enhanced historical value of prison memoirs, diaries, and proceedings of public trials.[40] Invariably, they expose the flaws of the penal system. On the other hand, the victims, mostly political prisoners, emerge from these sources as courageous and strengthened in mind and will. This is certainly true of Mohandas Karamchand Gandhi whose jail experiences are legendary, but who searched for new aspects of truth in harmony within the jail environment in South Africa and India. This was conceded by Justice Broomfield, who let Gandhi occupy the high moral ground all through the proceedings in 1922.

Indian politicians in jail wrote to their dear and near ones whenever they were allowed to do so. A letter in certain circumstances was much more than an ephemeral piece of scribbled paper. Its arrival in jail was a distinct event.[41] Govind Ballabh Pant's own letters from the Ahmadnagar Fort Prison are mostly 'personal', or they furnish details of his interest in the Upanishads, the Rig Veda, and books on ancient Indian history. To Laxmi Pant, his daughter, and son K.C. Pant, his advice was to read books, for no treasure was more valuable than knowledge and that nothing could give greater joy than a good book.[42] Thanks to Jawaharlal Nehru, Pant had a stream of recent publications and overseas periodicals pouring in steadily and there was no dearth of reading matter.[43]

The great wish of all incarcerated men and women was to write their memoirs. The same was the case with Manabendranath Roy, a commanding figure in the communist movement. He wrote about 3,750 pages in prison—a testament to the importance of the act of writing in defying the oppression of the prison cell. These were written between 11 November 1931 and 26 November 1936 in Kanpur, Bareilly, Almora, and Dehradun prisons, all in Uttar Pradesh.[44] They have not been much utilized, though there is no doubt that his wide-ranging scholarship, which latter-day Marxists rejected, is quite illuminating. Apart from the philosophical and sexual issues on which Roy held forth, he devoted his leisure hours in prison to unravelling many aspects of the Indian nationalist movement. His bitter and dogmatic critique of Gandhi and Jawaharlal Nehru was heeded in certain quarters, though his transformation into a 'radical humanist' lowered his prestige in the public eye.

Among the autobiographies I have utilized in this work is *The Days I Remember* by Kailash Nath Katju, who had argued the Meerut Conspiracy Case in 1933 in the Allahabad High Court. He wrote his account in the Naini Central Prison in the winter of 1942–3, when he was detained for his part in the Quit India Movement. He was released in April 1943 due to a very serious illness.[45] I have devoted a substantial part of the book to the significance and glory of the legal profession.

B.K. Nehru (1909–2001), a product of Allahabad University, rose to be the governor of Jammu and Kashmir, Assam, and Gujarat. He grew up in the Nehru household and witnessed the changes in their lifestyle. He profiled the social and cultural life of the Kashmiri Pandits and marked out the most important features of Motilal Nehru's character. What is extremely useful are the brief but informed narratives on the five sons of Motilal's elder brother Nandlal—Biharilal, Mohanlal, Shyamlal, Kishanlal, and Brijlal (father of B.K. Nehru)—who died in the cholera epidemic of 1887 at the age of forty-two.[46] Kishanlal and Brijlal were brought up entirely by Motilal Nehru. There is much less of this in T.N. Kaul's autobiography, a student of Allahabad University (1932–4), and a witness to the unfurling of the tricolour of independence at Allahabad in 1923.[47]

Then there is the autobiography of Kamaladevi Chattopadhyay, who spent five years within the grey walls of six different prisons (Yerwada Women's Prison, Arthur Road Jail, Hindalga Women's Jail, Belgaum, Women's Jail, Vellore, and Trivandrum Jail), two of them in the princely states.[48] Although she repeats the obvious that a prison brings out the worst in people, the fact is that the prison experience brought out the creative aspects of her personality. Her emotional responses were mature, and she took decisions with a sense of urgency. Her part in the Civil Disobedience Movement, for which she was jailed, was probably her finest hour.

The gaps in the historical accounts could be filled by the literary and poetic writings, which best convey the feelings of the age. Among the prose writers, the best-known works are on the ulama of Deoband, on the Wahhabi movement, and on the 'Silk Letter Conspiracy'.[49] Urdu poetry offers a vast array of insights into prison life as well. Although some lack distinction, the poems of Maulana Zafar Ali Khan (1873–1956) attracted attention.[50] In the 1920s, Mohammad Ali Jauhar (1878–1931) and Hasrat Mohani (1875–1951) wrote ghazals in jail. To read them is to measure the gulf that separates them from the poets of the last quarter of the nineteenth century. Progressive writers such as Josh Malihabadi (1894–1982), Faiz Ahmad Faiz (1911–1984), and Ali Sardar Jafri (1913–2000) were not free from grave faults, but they are nevertheless worthy of their privileged position in Urdu poetry.[51] This judgement proceeds naturally because of their conviction that independence, democracy, socialism, secularism, and faith in progress were requisites for the production of great literature. They used the symbolism of *qaidi* (prisoner), *qaidkhana* (prison), and *daar-o-rasan* (gallows) to lead mankind towards emancipation. Faiz wrote *Zindanama* (Prison Writings) to describe what the experience of imprisonment did for his development as a poet. Elsewhere, he writes,

> But the experience of imprisonment, like that of love, is in itself one of
> fundamental significance, and opens up new windows of thought and

vision. Thus in the first place, all one's sensations are again heightened, as they had been at the onset of youth, and the sense of wonder at the coming of day, the shades of evening, the deep blue of the sky, and the feel of the passing breeze comes back once more. Another thing that happens is that the time and distance of the world outside becomes unreal. Things that are near seem far away, and far away things seem near, and the distinction between tomorrow and yesterday vanishes so that sometimes a moment seems like an eternity and things that happened a century ago seem to have happened only yesterday. And thirdly, in the leisure of isolation from the world outside, one finds time for thought and study, and time to devote more attention to adorning the bride of poetry.[52]

Only those who know the miserable condition in which public records are kept in our repositories can realize the immense advance made by the *A Bunch of Old Letters* (1958), which reveals the various stages of Jawaharlal Nehru's public life and his world outlook, which conflicted with Gandhi but not so much with Rabindranath Tagore. The *Selected Works of Jawaharlal Nehru, Letters between Indira Gandhi and Jawaharlal Nehru* (1989), and *Two Alone, Two together* (2004) enhance the value of the 'Nehru Collection'.

When the young were lodged in prison, Jawaharlal Nehru wrote cheerful, affectionate, and optimistic letters to them. These letters were precious and eagerly expected. When in prison himself, Nehru would be worried when a letter did not come on the appointed day. And yet when it did come, he hesitated to open it for the fear of some tragedy or untoward incident: 'Letter writing and receiving in gaol were always serious incursions on a peaceful and unruffled existence. They produce an emotional state which was disturbing, and for a day or two afterwards one's mind wandered and it was difficult to concentrate on the day's work.'[53]

Even later in life, his exchanges with chief ministers reflect the spirit of sharing, advice, and consultation. Jawaharlal Nehru kept them posted about not only party affairs but also about complex arguments on capitalism and socialism. Realizing the benefits of a meaningful engagement with them, he inflicted the 'discursive monologues of an ardent and yet philosophic mind' on them to knit together his thoughts and comments on urgent issues as well as for long-term purposes.[54]

Jawaharlal Nehru found it amusing that the members of family felt a great urge to write their autobiographies and admitted that he himself had set the example in this regard. The books that the Nehrus wrote are closely woven into the fabric of family history. Motilal Nehru wrote and spoke enough to fill seven bulky volumes, which were published by the Nehru Memorial Museum and Library in New Delhi.[55] Although he gleamed across a decade, mainly with reflected glory, he expressed his deepest and most cherished convictions on various issues. In a not so dissimilar way, his daughter's autobiography is an essential contribution when dredged of its smirking domestic gossip.[56] Though Jawaharlal Nehru was dismissive of his sister's *Prison Days*, her story is like Susan Rosenberg's.[57] *Prison Days* is illuminated by a quiet dignity, insight, and, surprisingly, a sweet vein of hope. She details the bizarre realities of incarceration and describes the fetters that bound her country to the arbitrary rule of foreigners. Glowing with patriotic feelings, she writes about police bursting in to search her home at midnight, about arrests and imprisonment, forced separation from the family, and personal tragedies. She slept on a wooden cot in the pouring rain in prison yards, and on a pallet on stone in prison cells. Her husband, the Maharashtrian lawyer Ranjit Sitaram Pandit, shared two prison terms with Jawaharlal Nehru, one in Naini Central Prison, and the other in Dehradun Jail. No other woman in the Nehru family contributed so powerfully to the awakening and fostering of the spirit of a composite Indian nationality.

Literature must maintain close contact with contemporary affairs and be animated by an acute social consciousness. This consciousness was present in the simple-minded Krishna Nehru Hutheesing (1907–1967), the youngest sister of Jawaharlal Nehru and Vijaya Lakshmi Pandit, who 'speaks of her happy if wayward childhood in a home of wealth and beauty, of her somewhat difficult and some-times rebellious girlhood in surroundings strangely and unbelievably altered by the influence of the meek but mighty Mahatma, from a background of rich festivities to a battle-camp of austere conflicts and tremendous sacrifice.[58] Both she and her niece, Nayantara, were con-scious of and concerned about the events unfolding around them, for they were brought up 'to feel that freedom was one's undeniable right, and responsible people should take action to achieve it. Going to jail was most acceptable.[59] To them, nationalism expressed the people's life, growing by natural process out of their experiences and needs. In the spirit of constructive patriotism, they portray the sufferings they endured. Krishna Hutheesing does so with crystal clearness in *With No Regrets* (1944), a book she wrote following the Black Sunday of August 1942.[60] She was not a literary artist or a historian, but *We Nehrus* (1967) captured the atmosphere of that long-vanished era. We revisit that era in this book.

It would be neglectful to end this section without introducing *Prison and Chocolate Cake* (1954) and *From Fear Set Free* (1959) by Nayantara Sahgal. The first book is 'wholeheartedly about the tumult and exhilaration of political action and an intense commitment to it';[61] the second is equally autobiographical, with some telling comments on the Partition and its aftermath. In both the books, the author acknowledges her debt to Jawaharlal Nehru with respect to his early idealism, his cultured outlook, and his dedication to the people's uplift. Although many ideas and movements simmered or festered, she was mostly swayed by what her uncle said. When she writes on his capa-cious and subtle mind or his charisma and popularity, she is able to convey to the reader a genuineness and persuasive sincerity of tone. She is also able to represent the totality of his work and his remarkable and interesting personality. The people and their grievances, the lead-ers and their quarrels, all receive attention.

Taken together, both books have the glitter and glamour of romance, as well as the outlines of family histories set in the context of a nationalist struggle. The personal and political coalesce nicely, especially when Sahgal describes the excitement in Anand Bhawan. She does not dwell on historical themes because her imagination is fired by the political excitement around her. Even the so-called immediate experience was the part-product of conceptual frameworks, which were themselves a deposit of both individual and collective experiences.

What Sahgal writes on the growing fissures in the family is beyond my concern in this book. Let me, however, add that she wrote fiction as well, which won her both censure and further popularity at home and abroad. Ritu Menon's book, *Out of Line: A Literary and Political Biography of Nayantara Sahgal*, is fascinating, bringing so attractively to life the experiences of a key figure in the Nehru household.

With Nayantara Sahgal we shall finish our survey of the primary and secondary literature on the Nehrus. Now we shall pass to the subject of this monograph, which is one on which there are strong opinions but few primary works.

Notes

*   Quoted in Tariq Ali, *An Indian Dynasty: The Story of the Nehru–Gandhi Family* (New York: G.P. Putnam, 1985), p. xii.

1. Jad Adams and Phillip Whitehead, *Dynasty: The Nehru–Gandhi Story* (London: Penguin Books, 1997), pp. 3–4.

2. Nayantara Sahgal, *The Political Imagination: A Personal Response to Life, Literature and Politics* (New Delhi: HarperCollins Publishers, 2014), p. 4.

3. Nayantara Sahgal, *Prison and Chocolate Cake* (London: Alfred A. Knopf, 1954), p. 20. Nayantara Sahgal's uncle, Jawaharlal Nehru, was India's first prime minister; her mother was the country's first ambassador to the United Nations; Indira Gandhi was her first cousin. She was educated in Lucknow and Wellesly College (BA, 1947). She served as India's ambassador to Italy for a short while when Indira Gandhi was thrown out of power in the elections after the Emergency. Her upbringing informs both her fiction and her political writing, beginning with her memoir. Her novels, which are often

set against the backdrop of pivotal events in Indian history, include *A Time to Be Happy* (1958), *Storm in Chandigarh* (1969), *A Situation in New Delhi* (1977), *Rich Like Us* (1985), *Mistaken Identity* (1988), and *Point of View: A Personal Response to Life, Literature and Politics* (1997).

4. B.R. Nanda, *The Nehrus: Motilal and Jawaharlal* (London: Allen & Unwin, 1962), p. 10.

5. 1 January 1943, Vijaya Lakshmi Pandit, *Prison Days* (Calcutta: The Signet Press, 1945), p. 109.

6. Ritu Menon, *Out of Line: A Literary and Political Biography of Nayantara Sahgal* (New Delhi: Fourth Estate, 2014), p. 347.

7. 22 April 1938, *Before Freedom, 1909–1947: Nehru's Letters to His Sister*, edited by Nayantara Sahgal (New Delhi: Roli Books, 2004), p. 55.

8. Menon, *Out of Line*, p. 349.

9. Jawaharlal Nehru, *The Unity of India: Collected Writings 1937–1940* (London: Lindsay Drummond, 1948), p. 396.

10. Suresh Renjen Bald, 'Politics of a Revolutionary Elite: A Study of Mulk Raj Anand's Novels', *Modern Asian Studies* 8, no. 4 (1974): 487. Educated in Cambridge and University College, London, Mulk Raj Anand was one of the pioneers of Indo-Anglian fiction. He had an international readership. His personal collection is at the National Archives of India.

11. Sarojini Naidu, born Sarojini Chattopadhyay, is also known by the sobriquet 'the Nightingale of India'. She became the first woman to become the governor of an Indian state when she served as the first governor of the United Provinces of Agra and Oudh from 1947 to 1949. She was the second woman (and first Indian woman) to become the president of the Indian National Congress in 1925.

12. Sarojini Naidu, 'Foreword', in *With No Regrets: An Autobiography*, by Krishna Nehru Hutheesing (New Delhi: Oxford University Press, 1944), p. vi.

13. *Tribune*, 19 November 1944.

14. Albie Sachs, *The Jail Diary of Albie Sachs* (London: Harvill Press, 1966).

15. 1 January 1943, Pandit, *Prison Days*, p. 109.

16. J. Nehru, *The Unity of India*, p. 396.

17. Alexander Solzhenitsyn, *The Gulag Archipelago 1918–1956* (London: Collins & Harvill Press, 1974), p. 615.

18. J. Nehru to Indira, 27 March 1945, in *Two Alone, Two Together*, ed. Sonia Gandhi (New Delhi: Penguin Books India, 2004), p. 473; *Selected Works of Jawaharlal Nehru* [henceforward referred to as *SWJN*], vol. 13, ed. S. Gopal (New Delhi: Jawaharlal Nehru Memorial Fund, 1972), p. 596.

19. Manmohini Zutshi Sahgal, *An Indian Freedom Fighter Recalls Her Life*, ed. Geraldine Forbes (New York: East Gate Book, 1994). Ranjit S. Pandit, who married Vijaya Lakshmi Pandit, was one of them. Yet they have been forgotten and their enthusiasm is 'downgraded as sentiments of little value'. Chandralekha Mehta, *Freedom's Child: Growing Up during Satyagraha* (New Delhi: Puffin Books, 2008).

20. On 27 March 1930, Motilal gifted Anand Bhawan (thereafter named Swaraj Bhawan or Abode of Freedom) to the nation. The house, as erstwhile Anand Bhawan and later Swaraj Bhawan, flaunted its patriotism by flying the Congress flag: a saffron band for Hinduism and a green band for Islam, divided by a spinning wheel representing cottage industry on a white middle band denoting unity.

21. Mehta, *Freedom's Child*, p. 30.

22. J. Nehru to Padmaja Naidu, 23 December 1935, *SWJN*, vol. 12, p. 693.

23. Jawaharlal Nehru, *An Autobiography* (London: Allen & Unwin, 1936), p. 360.

24. Marie Seton, *Panditji: A Portrait of Jawaharlal* (New Delhi: Rupa & Co., 1967)

25. Michael Brecher, *Nehru: A Political Biography* (New Delhi: Oxford University Press, 1959).

26. Merrill R. Goodall, book review of *Nehru: A Political Biography* by Michael Brecher, *Cambridge Journal of Politics* 22, no. 3 (August 1960): 583.

27. W.H. Morris Jones, book review of *Nehru: A Political Biography* by Michael Brecher, *The Journal of Asian Studies* 19, no. 3 (May 1960): 369–70, available at http://www.jstor.org/stable/2943529, last accessed on 14 July 2016.

28. Natwar Singh, *One Life Is Not Enough: An Autobiography* (New Delhi: Rupa & Co., 2014), p. 108.

29. Singh, *One Life Is Not Enough*, p. 113.

30. B.N. Pande, *Nehru* (London: Macmillan, 1976), p. 440.

31. Stanley Wolpert, *Nehru: A Tryst with Destiny* (New York: Oxford University Press, 1996).

32.   Judith M. Brown, *Nehru: A Political Life* (New Delhi: Oxford University Press, 2003), pp. 243, 245.

33.   Srinath Raghavan, ed., *Sarvepalli Gopal: Imperialists, Nationalists, Democrats: The Collected Essays* (New Delhi: Permanent Black, 2013).

34.   Michel Foucault, *Discipline & Punish: The Birth of the Prison* (New York: Vintage Book, 1995).

35.   Mary-Alice Waters, ed., *Rosa Luxemburg Speaks* (New York: Pathfinder Press, 1970), p. 236.

36.   Maina wa Kinyatti, *Mother Kenya: Letters from Prison, 1982–1988* (New York: Vita Books, 1999), p. 28.

37.   Mohammed Fadhel Jamali, *Letters on Islam: Written by a Father in Prison to His Son* (London: Oxford University Press, 1965), pp. viii–ix.

38.   Mushirul Hasan, *Roads to Freedom* (Delhi: Oxford University Press, 2016).

39.   Sri Aurobindo, *Tales of Prison Life*, 2nd impression (Pondicherry: Sri Aurobindo Ashram Publications, 2002).

40.   Jawaharlal Nehru's first trial took place on 17 December 1921; the second was on 13 May 1922. The third trial was conducted in Nabha in September 1923. The fourth trial took place following his arrest on 14 April 1930. J.S. Grose sentenced him to six months' simple imprisonment in the Naini Central Prison. The fifth trial took place on 19 October 1930 (the charge related to the speech delivered on 12 October). For the sixth time, he was arrested and charged with various crimes. He appeared before a magistrate at Allahabad on 4 January 1932. He was sent to prison and was released on 30 August 1933. Nehru was re-arrested on 13 February 1934 for a trial before the Chief Presidency Magistrate of Calcutta, S.K. Sinha. He courted arrest once more on 6 November 1940 and was produced before E. De V. Moss. He passed another period of internment in Ahmadnagar Jail following his arrest on the passing of the Quit India Resolution on 8 August 1942.

41.   G.B. Pant to Chandradatt Pande, 12 June 1943, B.R. Nanda, ed., *Selected Works of Govind Ballabh Pant*, vol. 10 (New Delhi: Oxford University Press, 1998), p. 83. G.B. Pant was arrested on 9 August 1942 at Bombay, following the adoption of the Quit India Resolution. He was kept under detention along with nine other members of the Working Committee, including Jawaharlal Nehru, Vallabhbhai Patel, and Maulana Azad, in the Ahmadnagar Fort prison for nearly thirty-two months.

42. 23 January 1943, Nanda, *Selected Works of Govind Ballabh Pant*, vol. 10, p. 30.

43. G.B. Pant to Lakshmi Pant and K.C. Pant, 26 April 1944, Nanda, *Selected Works of Govind Ballabh Pant*, p. 318.

44. Kris Manjpara, *M. N. Roy: Marxism and Colonial Cosmopolitanism* (Routledge: New Delhi, 2010).

45. Kailash Nath Katju, *The Days I Remember* (Calcutta: New Age Publishers Pvt., Ltd, 1961).

46. B.K. Nehru, *Nice Guys Finish Second* (New Delhi: Penguin Books, 1997).

47. T.N. Kaul, *Reminiscences, Discreet and Indiscreet* (New Delhi: Lancers Publishers, 1982), p. 28.

48. Kamaladevi Chattopadhyay, *Inner Recesses Outer Spaces: Memoirs* (New Delhi: Navrang Publishers, 1986). I mention her because of her proximity to the Nehru family. In fact, her book has frequent references to Motilal Nehru and Jawaharlal Nehru.

49. Maulana Syed Mohammad Miyan, *Aseeran-e Malta* (Deoband: Kitab Khan Naimia, 2002).

50. Maulana Zafar Ali Khan, *Habasiyaat* (Lahore: Mansur Steam Press, n.d.).

51. In 1936, Ali Sardar Jafri presided over the first conference of the Progressive Writers' Movement in Lucknow. His literary career began in 1938 when his first collection of short stories, called *Manzil* (*Destination*), was published. *Parvaz* (*Flight*), his first collection of poems, was published in 1944. On 20 January 1949, he was arrested at Bhiwandi, for organizing a (then banned) Progressive Urdu Writers' Conference, although he had been warned against it by Morarji Desai, the chief minister of Bombay State; he was again arrested three months later. Fifty years after the Aligarh Muslim University expelled him, it awarded him a doctorate (D.Litt.) in 1986. This was a rather special honour, previously bestowed on Iqbal and Jigar Moradabadi.

52. Ralph Russell, *In Pursuit of Urdu Literature: A Select History* (Delhi: Oxford University Press, 1992), p. 236.

53. J. Nehru, *An Autobiography*, p. 349.

54. Sarvepalli Gopal, *Jawaharlal Nehru—A Biography*, vol. 2 (New Delhi: Oxford University Press, 1975), p. 316.

55.   I have discussed Motilal Nehru's political career in my other writings. It is worth noting that he led the swarajists in the central legislative assembly with distinction, and earned accolades for proposing a round table conference to draw up India's new constitution. He and Mohammad Ali Jinnah got on well. Both acted in unison on a number of critical issues until the Nehru Committee Report, which was associated with Motilal Nehru, created an unbridgeable gulf between the Congress and the Muslim League.

56.   Vijaya Lakshmi Pandit, *The Scope of Happiness: A Personal Memoir* (New York: Crown Publishers, 1979).

57.   Susan Rosenberg, *An American Radical: A Political Prisoner in My Own Country* (New York: Kensington Publishing Corporation, 2011).

58.   Sarojini Naidu, 'Foreword', in Hutheesing, *With No Regrets*, p. i. Krishna Nehru was married to Gunottam (Raja) Hutheesing, who belonged to a prominent Ahmedabad family that built the Hutheesing Jain Temple. She and her husband fought for India's independence and spent a great deal of time in jail while raising their two young sons, Harsha and Ajit. Krishna Hutheesing documented her own life as well as the lives of her brother, Jawaharlal Nehru, and niece, Indira Gandhi, in a series of books where history is intertwined with personal anecdotes. These include *We Nehrus* (1967), *Nehru's Letters to His Sister* (1963), and *Dear to Behold* (1969). Her husband also wrote books such as *The Great Peace: An Asian's Candid Report on Red China* (1953), *Window on China* (1953), and *Tibet Fights for Freedom: The Story of the March 1959 Uprising* (1960).

59.   Robert Hardy Andrews, *A Lamp for India: The Story of Madame Pandit* (London: A. Barker, 1967), p. 130.

60.   23 August 1942 was the Sunday on which Stalingrad was bombed by the Germans for the first time.

61.   Menon, *Out of Line*, p. 45.

2   Dynasty, Biography, and History

The Indian National Congress was founded by around eighty-three participants on 28 December 1885. Dadabhai Naoroji—whose intellectual prestige was guaranteed by his learned contacts within the Parsi community in Bombay—successfully steered this gathering through difficulties of every kind and watched it grow vigilantly, but not without anxiety; Pherozeshah Mehta, assured of a strong social position in the legal profession, was in full brilliance as a party member; Surendranath Banerjea, a brilliant lawyer representing the best of the Bengal renaissance, worked tirelessly to acquaint fellow delegates with the Congress' own campaign against the Vernacular Press Act (1878); Kashinath T. Telang lobbied for his resolution on free trade; Ananda Charlu, one of the founders of the Madras Mahajana Sabha, and the turbaned G. Subramaniya Iyer, editor of *Hindu* (1878–98), lent the Congress a more representative character; W.C. Bonnerjee, the president of the first session of the Congress in 1885, enjoyed being in the thick of things. When it was his turn to deliver the presidential address, he enumerated the government's good deeds, and tried to dispel the image of the Congress as 'a nest of conspirators and disloyalists'. He provided, writes his biographer, 'the wise head and firm hand, and took the helm when the good ship was launched'.[1]

Occupying the pride of place was the former civil servant Allan Octavian Hume. As somebody who always felt a warm attachment to the Indian people, 'he recognized the Bombay gathering [of the Indian National Congress] as a truly momentous occasion, much as the first sitting of the Continental Congress at Philadelphia in 1774 was for the United States'.[2] Badruddin Tyabji, the president of the Bombay Presidency Association, was conspicuously absent, but he became a member of the second session of the Congress along with Camruddin Tyabji, A.M. Dharansi, a Bombay corporator, and R.M. Sayani, sheriff of Bombay.

'All these men', the Congress boasted in 1885, 'assembled in the same hall, presented such a variety of costumes and complexions, that a similar scene can scarcely be witnessed anywhere except at a fancy ball.' According to the official report: 'Not only were all parts of India thus represented, but also most classes; there were barristers, solicitors, pleaders, merchants, landowners, bankers, medical men, newspaper editors and proprietors, principals and professors of independent colleges ... It is difficult to conceive any gathering of this restricted number more thoroughly representative of the entire nation.'[3]

City and civilization often go together, Jawaharlal Nehru wrote in *Glimpses of World History*. As cities expanded, learning and the spirit of freedom also grew. By the time the Congress travelled to Allahabad, the *Ghamkhwar-i Hind* of Lahore (15 December 1888) reported that 200 tents had been pitched for receiving delegates. A bazaar was opened in the midst of the camp, chairs were provided for delegates, and galleries erected for about 5,000 visitors.[4] Pandit Ajudhia Nath Kunzru, a leading pleader in the 1880s, set out the Congress' inclusive agenda. He involved Nawab Abdul Majid and Syed Abdul Rauf in order to garner Muslim support for the Congress.[5]

After Lucknow, Allahabad elected one-fifth of the Muslim delegates to the Congress. This group mainly comprised small zamindars from Daryabad—mostly Shias, poverty-stricken, and dependants of the old royal house of Awadh—a small group of lawyers and pleaders, and minor officials carrying their grievances against the local government.[6] In 1888, the Shia–Sunni schism widened with the onset of the Congress movement.[7] In another sphere, manifestations of Hindu revivalism in the land of Aryavarta made it tough for the Muslims to consort with the Congress.[8] These trends did not augur well for Allahabad's rich and composite tapestry of life.

Meanwhile, proliferation of the press brought news of the changing power relations in Asia and Europe. Japan's victory over Russia in 1905 stirred the youth even in Allahabad's conservative establishment. It was 'a great pick-me-up for Asia'.[9] For Jawaharlal Nehru, who was then a student in England, 'this trend perfectly matched his mood of rejoicing in a sense of liberation from the past, and he took great delight in the affront'[10] to a Western country that Japan's victory represented. He demanded a more aggressive and fighting attitude to foreign rule. What was the Congress doing in the course of the stirring days of 1906, 1907, and 1908? Not much, he said. The 'moderate' leaders did not contribute much either to the awakening of the national spirit or to the flaming enthusiasm of the Bengali bhadralok.

In Allahabad, the Congress was essentially a secondary organization for many local leaders. 'Their association with it derived from the need to pursue within the regional and all-India skeletal organization and aspiration the much more circumscribed local and sectional aims that derived from lower levels of politics.'[11] C.A. Bayly reminds us of the vitality of the patron–client relationship and the corresponding weakness of other forms of political associations. The most powerful patrons were wealthy bankers and traders, while their clients were priests, lawyers, and others who worked to maintain the family's ritual, social, and political status. Publicists and literati attached themselves to town magnates as hagiographers and propagandists, or in the hope of gaining support for wider religious or political projects.[12]

The *Awadh Punch* (Lucknow) of 3 January 1888 carried a cartoon in which a native lady called the Jumna and a European lady called the Ganges stood on high pedestals pouring water from vessels held in their hands into a reservoir to water a garden marked the Indian empire. The stream of water poured by the Jumna was marked loyalty, wealth, and greatness, and that poured by the Ganges was marked education, protection, and peace. The union of the two streams is labelled the National Congress. The letterpress below is, 'The new year's presents. The auspicious conjunction of Jupiter and Venus at Allahabad.'[13] However, the Home Rule Leagues altered the political landscape: 'Not only had the political leaders moved into a stance of greater hostility to government, but they were able to draw on resources of political organization created by interest groups deepening their own constituencies in the meantime.'[14]

C.A. Bayly argues that the national movement drew up and recast some patterns of social relations, sentiments, doctrines, and embodied memories that had come into existence before British rule was established in the subcontinent in the late eighteenth century.[15] Sentiments against the Raj had been violently expressed in 1857, and they stayed, without being coherently expressed, in the public conscience. In the following two decades, there was no great outburst of public anger, but there was, nonetheless, criticism of the government's total disregard for what was being put together as the collective interests and goals of 'Indians'. In each town and locality, local alignments and antagonisms largely shaped the nature and character of the opposition to the Raj.

The Congress grew, as Jawaharlal Nehru observed in his *Glimpses of World History*, but even faster than the Congress grew the idea of nationalism and the desire for freedom. Bal Gangadhar Tilak had expressed contempt for annual sessions, which he thought were 'like the croaking of frogs in the rain', although reports of his own activities, as indeed his conviction, spread far and wide. 'Almost without an exception', noted Jawaharlal, 'we were Tilakites or Extremists.'[16]

The line of cleavage, to which Jawaharlal Nehru and others alluded, was drawn between those who wanted to tread warily in the volatile political world and those who advocated militancy. Tilak exploited a great volume of anti-British feeling; Gopal Krishna Gokhale, on the other hand, pinned his faith in the arena of conflict within the Congress. They formed the nucleus of significant mobilization, and left behind structures and networks that Gandhi harnessed in his bitter encounters with the justice of British democracy till he reconciled to foreign domination as a transitional arrangement. Aurobindo Ghose, who secured a senior classical scholarship at Cambridge, was embittered after his return to India. The schism between the Home Rule Leagues and the Servants of India Society, and the Raj widened. Jawaharlal Nehru summed up the Congress history in *Glimpses of World History*:

> This organization, which you and every boy and girl in India knows well, has become in recent years great and powerful. It took up the cause of the masses and became, to some extent, their champion. It challenged the very basis of British rule in India, and led great mass movements against it. It raised the banner of independence and fought for freedom manfully. And today it is still carrying on the fight. But all this is subsequent history. The National Congress when it was first founded was a very moderate and cautious body, affirming its loyalty to the British and asking, very politely, for some petty reforms. It represented the richer *bourgeoisie*; even the poorer middle classes were not in it. As for the masses, the peasants and workers, they had nothing to do with it. It was the organ of the English-educated classes chiefly, and it carried on its activities in our step-mother tongue—English language. Its demands were the demands of the landlords and Indian capitalists and the educated unemployed seeking for jobs. Little attention was paid to the grinding poverty of the masses or their needs. It demanded the 'Indianization' of the services—that is to say, the greater

employment of Indians in government service in place of Englishmen. It did not see that what was wrong with India was the machine which exploited the people, and that it made no difference who had charge of the machine, Indian or foreigner.[17]

Kashmiri Pandits in Allahabad

Louis-Théophile Marie Rousselet, a French traveller, boarded a train from Kanpur that followed the right bank of the Ganges until it reached Calcutta, covering a distance of about 628 miles. The train covered the distance between Kanpur and Allahabad in six hours, passing through the Lower Doab, 'one of the finest and richest districts in India'. Impressed by what he saw, he could not understand why the British still persisted in ascribing such an important position to Calcutta, 'a city buried in the corner of their empire, in the midst of pestilential swamps, which the sea and the cyclones are constantly threatening to swallow up'.[18]

Lady Dufferin had noted in her journal, 'Allahabad is very uninteresting; there is nothing at all to see.'[19] She was wrong. Allahabad means 'City of God'. Pilgrims come from everywhere, especially for the course of the great Kumbh Mela held every twelve years. Annually, during the Magh Mela, pilgrims brave the heat and dust, looking forward to the prospect of cleansing away their sins in the holy waters of the Ganga and Yamuna. 'Brahmins installed under immense parasols receive the pilgrims and guide them through all the ceremonials of the great purification.'[20] Sustained by their unwavering faith and belief, they endure the resultant miseries without complaint.

Every year Jawaharlal Nehru's mother, Swarup Rani, and her elder sister, widowed in childhood, left home for a month to live in a reed hut on the bank of the Ganga. From here they had their dips on the prescribed holy days, listened to learned swamis, and met up with their cronies living in similar huts. The family *panda* (priest) accompanied them. Upon their return they found Jawaharlal Nehru in homespun khadi, smiling at them and asking them questions about their journey and their impressions of the miles they had travelled. Motilal Nehru did not approve: 'Pilgrimages', he said, 'should lead to the West—to Europe, to America, in search of the key to progress so that we can open the door to a fuller, richer life for ourselves.'[21] Nonetheless, the family hosted holy figures, such as the guru of the Maharaja of Kashmir.

Ceded to the East India Company in 1801, Allahabad served as a staging post on the Grand Trunk Road linking Delhi to Bengal. However, it was not considered important enough to merit a garrison of British troops; consequently, they were stationed there only in June 1857 when Colonel Neill secured reinforcements. The Muslim communities suffered the most after the takeover. They were suspected of conspiracy to overthrow British rule.

In November 1858, the rule of the British Crown was proclaimed in Allahabad and the town became the capital of the North Western Provinces and Awadh, usually known as the NWP. The rebuilt town had the High Court, the famous Muir College,[22] and a cantonment, the home of British families. The new railway line effectively divided Allahabad into two sides: the station on the northern side, and the bazaars and native town to the south. Immediately in front of the railway station lay the civil station. Mark Twain described the British section in the following words:

> It is a town of wide avenues and noble distances, and is homely and alluring, and full of suggestions of comfort and leisure, and of the serenity which a good conscience buttressed by a sufficient bank account gives. The bungalows stand well back in the seclusion and privacy of large enclosed compounds (private grounds, as we should say) and in the shade and shelter of trees. Even the photographer and the prosperous merchant ply their industries in the elegant reserve of big compounds, and the citizens drive in there upon their business occasions. And not in cabs—no; in the Indian cities cabs are for the drifting stranger; all the white citizens have private carriages; and each carriage has a flock of white-turbaned footmen and drivers all over it.[23]

Unlike the Bengali bhadralok who seized the opportunities offered by the new dispensation, the Islamic gentry in Allahabad fragmented after the British takeover. Having been tied to the nawabs, they gradually lost their monopoly in government service. The British gave to them—the *wasiqadars*—a small pension. The less privileged sections were gradually eased out of the professions because they paid little attention to Western education, for which Syed Ahmad Khan, the founder of the M.A.O. College in Aligarh, chided them: 'They recall the tales of their ancestors and conclude that no one is superior to them, and this blinds them to the garden which is now before their eyes and to the flowers that bloom in it.'

The Islamic gentry had strong cultural and intellectual links with the Awadh *qasbas* (small towns). Even though the fortunes of the Muslim zamindars and *taluqdars* (landed elites) in the region nosedived, they kept intact their *shurafa* (noble) values and had little contact or sympathy with the peasantry, the victims of their exploitation. In the adjoining district of Jaunpur, they did not give up their feudal lifestyle. They spent time enjoying music or dance, or in the company of courtesans in their havelis. Hunting (*shikar*) was their favourite occupation. Some of them read Persian, and most were fluent in Urdu. Like the nawabs of Awadh, whose lifestyle they imitated, they doled out patronage to Urdu poets, dancers, and musicians.

On the other hand, the Brahmins, the kayasthas, and the Kashmiri Pandits took advantage of Western education and availed of the openings created by British rule, the most important of which was the transfer of the High Court from Agra to Allahabad and the founding of the Allahabad University in 1887. The High Court exercised jurisdiction over thirty-six districts with a population of about fifty million. And the university became a major draw, more so because of its distinguished alumni—including Ajudhia Nath, founder of the Literary Institute; Pandit Sundar Lal; Munshi Hanuman Prasad; and Madan Mohan Malaviya, a graduate of Muir College in 1884, editor of *Hindustan* and *Indian Union*, and the founder of the Hindu Samaj.

Moreover, district boards and municipalities offered a break to Indians to bid for licences, contracts, and other local benefits.

Sections of the kayasthas, *prabasi* (non-resident) Bengalis, émigré Brahmins, and Kashmiri Pandits (their original name was 'Kaula'), benefited the most. One example of the success of the Kashmiri Pandits is the career of Pandit Ajudhia Nath, a 'glittering star of the Agra Bar' who 'shone so brilliantly in the legal firmament of Allahabad'.[24] Later on, Kailash Nath Katju entered the Muir College, a major draw for the Kashmiri Pandits. The Meerut Conspiracy Case worked a miracle for his professional career: it converted him from a civil lawyer into a criminal one.[25] His ancestors, settled in the princely state of Jaora in the Central Provinces, were drawn to Allahabad by the prospect of a lucrative career in the legal profession.

Unlike in provincial and feudal Lucknow, the mixing of different émigré groups with the local population turned an otherwise sleepy town of Allahabad into an urban and cosmopolitan centre. It was stratified on caste and class lines, but such divisions neither disturbed the city's overall equilibrium nor did they polarize society and politics. The foul communal atmosphere in the 1880s was conditioned by the local temper, and even though the people of Allahabad were influenced by Hindu and Muslim revivalism, they were not necessarily inspired by any distinct religious conviction. To be an Allahabadi was a matter of pride for its citizens; they defined their identity neither by Islam nor Hinduism but by their dialect/language and the existing cross-community networks.

After Lahore, Allahabad was the principal literary and intellectual hub in north India. The figure of Akbar Allahabadi (1846–1921) loomed large on its intellectual horizon.

This gifted Urdu poet elevated satire to a fine art. He possessed the skills to distort words, twist their meanings, and to resort to pun, and idiom-based or verbal jugglery. Satire and cynicism ran through much of his poetry, especially when he directed his verses against the materialism of the West, the idiocies of his society, the quaint customs that came with Western learning, and the naiveté of those who considered themselves emancipated. Today, Akbar Allahabadi's poetry survives not because of its relevance to our times but because of the fine blending of satire with humour.

When he appeals to the young boys to go to the prayers, they say, 'Look at this man! Even at such an old age, Akbar has not ceased to be humorous.'

Or

'What words of mine can tell the deeds of men like these,
Our nation's pride?
They got their B.A., took employment, drew their pensions and then died.'

Or

'My rivals have repeatedly gone to the police station to report That Akbar worships God in this Age.'[26]

Asghar Gondvi and Raghupati Sahay—better known under the name Firaq Gorakhpuri, who was appointed to the Allahabad University in 1930—were some of the other noted Urdu poets. Both Firaq and Harivansh Rai Bachchan taught English. In this literary Hindi heartland, Munshi Premchand, Mahadevi Varma, Sumitranandan Pant, Suryakant Tripathi, Subhadra Kumari Chauhan, and Upendra Nath 'Askh' flourished.[27] Kitabistan, owned by the Rehman brothers—Kaleemur Rehman and Obaidur Rehman—published thousands of books and became the first publishers from India to open a branch in London in 1936. Around this time, Allahabad's literary milieu was a melting pot, teeming with Urdu poets and writers. A natural outcome of mingling sensibilities was new themes and approaches towards one's literary tradition.[28] For many, 'this was largely a happy story, in which a heroic vanguard of poets, writers, and journalists [led] the readers out of a world of dull, cautious, standardized prose into a home of freshness, variety, and some degree of sophistication.'[29] Besides offering delightful reading, good amusement for leisure hours, and spiritual counsels for various moments, they make life brighter, happier, and worth living.

The *Pioneer*, for which Rudyard Kipling worked as an assistant editor and overseas correspondent, the *Leader*, the *Independent*, and *Bhavishya* appeared from Allahabad. 'Public life was richer in Allahabad than in any other place in north India,'[30] writes D.P. Mishra, who studied at the Muir Central College and turned a non-cooperator. The men who contributed to this rich public life were Madan Mohan Malaviya, C.Y. Chintamani, Purushottamdas Tandon, the Nehrus, the Saprus, the Katjus, and the Kunzrus. Many of them distinguished themselves in the profession of their choice—law. Many of them, if not all, valued pluralism and stuck to their belief in communal harmony. Students and teachers fluttered around Tej Bahadur Sapru's residence at 19 Albert Road where he held a durbar at the end of the day. Iswara Dutt, editor of the Allahabad-based *Twentieth Century*, writes that Sapru used to

> throw out an idea, summon to his aid a master-mind—maybe anybody from Plato to Passfield—and read with animation from a well-thumbed book, or just give a fascinating exposition of democracy as 'a way of thinking and a way of living' or merely linger a trifle sadly on India's lost causes and Britain's lost opportunities. One loved to hear his voice and revel in the presence of a man who was an illustrious representative of a noble tradition.[31]

The Nehrus were no different. Once upon a time, they used to live in Lahore and Lucknow before they migrated to Allahabad. Little is known of their ancestors, who had undertaken the long trek from Brij Bihara, a small village in the Kashmir valley, to the Gangetic plains. One of them, Pandit Raj Kaula (a word used in medieval Kashmiri texts for a devotee of Shakti, the goddess of power and energy), received a boost to his career at the hands of Farukhsiyar, the Mughal emperor (1714–19). He learnt Persian, built a house along one of Delhi's canals (*nehr* in Farsi), and took 'Kaul-Nehru' as his surname.[32] His family's fortunes remained steady for a while until the *jagirs* (land grants) bequeathed to his grandsons—Mausa Ram and Sahib Ram—dwindled gradually into nominal rights. But Pandit Lakshmi Narayan, son of Mausa Ram, did well to serve as the first *vakil* (lawyer) of the East India Company at Delhi's Mughal court, a comfortable position for any new aspirant to the local bureaucracy. He quickly recognized where his true worth lay. In 1857, his son, the blue-eyed, red-bearded, Pandit Gangadhar, served as Delhi's *kotwal* (chief of police). In a little painting, he is seen wearing the Mughal court dress with a curved sword in his hand. His wife learnt Persian and quoted from its poets.

The Pandit had three sons of whom the middle one was Nandlal (d. 1887). Nandlal and his young bride fled the city of Delhi in 1857 through Delhi Gate into the desert village of Raisina, which is now the flourishing city of New Delhi. They stayed in Agra, once the seat of the Mughal emperors and renowned for its Taj Mahal, 'a leitmotiv in the great Indian symphony'. Bansidhar, the Pandit's eldest son, became a subordinate judge. Nandlal became a vakil of the High Court and the dewan of Khetri for sixteen years. The third son, Motilal, was born in 1861, a few months after his father's death.

Unlike some of the elite Muslim families that faded away, the Kashmiri Pandits found their way into almost all vocations in life. Something else also occurred: they set great store by education and learning. The starting points of their careers were, indeed, Delhi College and the Muir College in Allahabad. When Bishambhar Nath Pande enrolled at the Delhi College after 1857, he became a part of a Kashmiri group that already included Ajodhia Prasad Gurtu 'Hairat', assistant professor at the college, Motilal, Katju, Dharam Narain Haksar, Sarup Narain Haksar, first professor at Meerut, and Ram Kishen Haksar. They had a healthy attitude to life, their manners were refined and they had a delightful sense of fun. They ate well, being better at appreciating whenever possible the good things of this life than at accumulating merit for another.

Some other Kashmiri Brahmin service communities performed equally well. Pandit Ajudhia Nath Kunzru's father settled in Agra, the site of the Sadr Diwani Adalat. His fortunes improved in 1866, when this court became the High Court. A year later when the court moved to Allahabad, Ajudhia Nath rose to become a leading pleader. He edited the *Indian Herald* (1879–82), and took a prominent part in the local Congress movement.

In an era of limited physical mobility, the enterprising Kashmiri Pandit families did not hesitate to move from one city to the other. Take the case of Tej Bahadur Sapru's grandfather. He taught mathematics at the Delhi College before the family moved to Agra. Sapru practised in Moradabad before moving to Allahabad in 1898. Likewise, following the movement of B.K. Nehru's family from his mother's side, we learn that it was extremely mobile since the eighteenth century. Starting with the career of Pandit Kishen Das, who lived in Banaras, his son rose rapidly in the services of Ranjit Singh. So did his adopted son, Ajodhya Prasad.[33]

Bishan Narain Dar, who later became Congress president, committed the sin of travelling overseas. For that he was made to eat cow dung as repentance. Dar submitted, but a section of the *biradari* (fraternity) would still not eat in his company. The result was that at biradari dinners there were two sections with a mud partition between the two. On one side sat the people belonging to the 'Bishan Sabha', which meant those who had agreed to forgive Bishan Narain for his sin, and on the other sat those of the 'Dharam Sabha', who held that no amount of penance—eating cowdung or drinking cow urine—could ever wipe out the sin of having eaten with infidels.[34]

However, the well-educated amongst the Kashmiri Pandits followed the triumphant, rationalist, humanist 'Enlightenment' of the eighteenth century. Despite the ban on crossing the seas, Pandit Prithi Nath, the leader of the District Bar at Kanpur and the chief patron of

Kailash Nath Katju, travelled widely, and his sons read for the Bar in London. Pandit Bansidhar went overseas; Shridhar, his youngest son, and Jawaharlal Nehru went to England more or less at about the same time; Sridhar studied in Cambridge and Heidelberg before entering the Civil Service in 1912; Brijlal studied at Oxford before entering the government finance department; Kishanlal obtained a medical degree from Edinburgh. These men reached the pinnacle of success with the help of Western education. Their daily lives were a seamless blend of tradition and modernity, and, as a result, they left the imprint of their enquiring and assimilative ethos. In the long run, hard work, intelligence, and intellect served them best. Maybe, this was one of the reasons why they appreciated the good things in life. This is evident from what Krishna Hutheesing writes: 'We ate very daintily, with the tips of our fingers.... We washed our hands sitting down and dried them on fine linen towels before eating desert—with a spoon.'[35]

Were the Kashmiri Pandits a trifle arrogant? Vijaya Lakshmi Pandit claims that Bijju, her cousin, said to her with a twinkle in his eye, 'But of course, and why the hell shouldn't we be!' However, Bijju contested her version of this.[36] Put a little differently, was the claim of aristocratic descent justified? Ram Manohar Lohia, probably the most trenchant critic of the Nehrus, once said in Parliament, 'I can prove that the Prime Minister's grandfather was a *chaprasi* [junior worker] in the Mughal court.' Jawaharlal Nehru replied: 'I am glad the Hon'ble Member has at last accepted what I have been trying to tell him for so many years—that I am a man of the people!'[37] That he was. Until the 1960s, parliamentarians often exchanged jibes, jokes, and sallies that were directed against politicians, religious preachers, publicists, and the elites. Word-play, in particular, was a source of great joy.

Those Other Moments

In his boyhood, Motilal Nehru studied at the feet of Muslim teachers,[38] secured a law degree with distinction, cultivated a taste in literature, and developed a positive outlook towards life, an exquisite code of manners, and a great sense of humour. He laboured hard to build his life, for one day of which there is a record, dated 9 November 1905: he got up at four in the morning, worked at his briefs till eight, saw clients till nine, and was in court on his feet throughout the day. The secret of his success, he boomed, was simple: 'I want money, I work for it and I get it.'[39]

The legal fraternity recognized his work to be of the highest value in Allahabad. In January 1896, he was admitted to the Allahabad High Court, one of only four appointments that year. The pinnacle of his career was in August 1909, when he appeared and pleaded at the Bar of the judicial committee of the Privy Council. In the early 1930s, he earned nearly 2,000 rupees a month (equivalent to around a million rupees and 20,000 pounds a year in the 1990s). His clients included begums and ranis, who came to Anand Bhawan in curtained cars or elaborate horse carriages and entered his study to sit behind a screen. The retinue that travelled with Motilal to Lucknow when he visited that city was second to no prince's. The house at 1 Church Road, which Motilal Nehru called Anand Bhawan, was purchased by him from a high court judge for 19,000 rupees.

The Nehrus did their very best to zealously guard their cultural frontiers, and preserve their *Kashmiriyat*.[40] M.R. Jayakar, Bombay's lawyer and legislator, asked Motilal Nehru about the tilt in his khaddar cap, as it sat on his forehead, and the why it looked different from that of other wearers. To this, Motilal remarked, 'You have to be born a Kashmiri to know this, a rugged Maratha like you can hardly understand this business.'[41] On the occasion of marriages, the entire Kashmiri biradari feasted. Kashmiri Pandits prepared and served the food. True to their *rasm* (custom), they came from faraway places to attend Jawaharlal Nehru's wedding to a Kashmiri Pandit bride, Kamala Kaul (b. 1899), who possessed the typically fair skin of Brahmins of Kashmiri decent. The sixteen-year-old bride had lived in Old Delhi before she was married on 8 February 1916. It was *Vasant Panchami* that day—the festival which heralds the coming of spring.

Besides the elaborate wedding ceremonies, the Kashmiri Pandits observed the major rituals of *mundan* (shaving the head of a child during the first or third year of their life) and *janeu* (thread-bearing ceremony) to reinforce their biradari networks. So, when the *upanyan* or janeu ceremony of Bijju (Braj Kumar Nehru) and his brother took place in 1925 in Allahabad, the whole Nehru clan was present.[42]

In 1935, Bijju visited Jawaharlal Nehru in jail with Fori (Shobha Nehru). When she had earlier come to India and stayed with her future in-laws, Fori was demure, dressed in a sari and learning to speak Hindi, but when she saw the tub in the bathroom, she cried out in delight 'Hallelujah'.[43] While the visitors spoke with Nehru, the warder came in and laid a hand on the prisoner's arm to take him back to his cell. Fori could not bear this and began to cry. Jawaharlal Nehru looked back and said to her, 'No tears. In this family we keep a stiff upper lip'.[44] The first and last time his iron discipline was breached was the outpouring of grief he could not control when he knelt behind Gandhi's blood-covered body on the evening of 30 January 1948.[45]

Motilal Nehru's instincts were based on the confidence that all things were possible for an aristocratic family like his.[46] Hence, he endeavoured to promote a sense of togetherness so that each member of the clan was loved and respected by the other.[47] He celebrated his nephew's entry into the ICS,[48] claiming that no single Indian family could boast of such a galaxy of intellectuals among its scions— B. Nehru M.A. (Oxon) of the Inner Temple Esq, Dr K. Nehru M.B., Ch. B., B.Sc. (Edin.), J. Nehru M.A. (Cantab). 'Why', he added, 'we should conquer the world with these and their descendants who I am sure will go on adding fresh lustre to the family name as the years go by'.[49] Motilal Nehru spoke for the Nehrus with a sense of pride:

Allahabad is doing splendidly. My wife is altogether a changed being since the incarceration of Jawahar—she is all activity—takes part in processions, meetings, salt-making and shows no sign of tiring—Kamala and Krishna have thrown themselves whole heartedly in the campaign and so has my niece Uma [Mrs Shamlal]. Ranjit [son-in-law] was hesitating while Jawahar was free but immediately took the final plunge the moment he was arrested. Sarup [Vijaya Lakshmi Pandit] poor girl is not at all well but manages to attend meetings and make stirring speeches.[50]

Having been bequeathed with this fusion of professional commitment and family pride, Motilal Nehru's kinsmen saw one another as members of one family living together in the manner of those days. Motilal Nehru attended to the needs of Mohanlal, who lived a short distance from Anand Bhawan on Hamilton Road; Shyamlal, son of Nandlal and Motilal Nehru's nephew, and his wife Uma; and Kala Masi and her husband Triloki Nath Madan. He regarded Ladli Prasad Zutshi as one of his own children, arranged her marriage, and incorporated his nephew's family into the larger extended clan.[51] There was continuous contact between the residents of Anand Bhawan and the families of the nephews so that Motilal Nehru's thought, behaviour, and manner of living influenced them all.[52] Any form of success brought a smile on his face.[53] Overjoyed that three generations of the Nehrus were jailed, he was in seventh heaven at the time of his grand-niece Manmohini Zutshi's arrest in 1930.

Jovial, easy-going and generous, it was hard to imagine the Motilal lonely, bored, or despondent. He was the hero of most of the intellectual people in his youth, who turned to him for advice and guidance. The effect of one of his anecdotes on them would be to make his listener warm to humankind and its failing. Inviting Bansidhar to share the good life, he wrote: 'Indeed you have not seen the younger generation of Nehrus which came into existence after you left Allahabad [for Agra]. They should have a chance of seeing the head of the family and it goes without saying that you will be right heartily welcome to all.' Braj Kumar Nehru or Bijju was, in fact, born in Anand Bhawan.[54]

Good eating and good drinking were always, in Motilal Nehru's view, proper adjuncts to civilized living. In the course of a tour to the Central Provinces, D.P. Mishra and Motilal Nehru were together. One of their conversations began on this note: 'You [Misra] seem to be exceedingly wise. Someone must have told you that I am a drunkard, and so you slipped out of the room, to enable me to drink to my heart's content. Yes, I do drink, but I am not in the habit of doing things secretly.' After dinner, he poured out a small drink, and raising it to Mishra he said, 'See, how I make myself drunk!' Mishra broke his silence: 'But Panditji, this must be the quantity which doctors prescribe by way of medicine.' Motilal Nehru told him that the Deshbandhu (Chittaranjan Das) used to drink regularly but under Mahatmaji's influence he had suddenly stopped it. 'Haven't you seen what happened to him? If you people want me to live for a few years more you have to tolerate this medicinal dose.'[55]

Motilal Nehru owned the first automobile in Allahabad, a Model T Ford, and a motor boat, on which he used to take friends and family out for rides and picnics. Swarup Rani Thussi, a shy Kashmiri girl, often heard the tinkle of ice cubes as her husband sat next to a low wooden lamp holding gin and tonic in his hand. In almost four decades, he had seldom missed a drink for eleven months in each year. He abstained for a month every year simply to avoid getting enslaved to the habit.[56] 'I know you will feel polluted if you eat at my table', he said to one of his uncles, 'but it won't hurt you to drink a whisky-and-soda with me.'[57] When Gandhi chided him for his drinking habits, he responded angrily with the remark that he simply could not bring himself to yield to Congress' puritanism. He continued: 'If there are idiots in the world who still think that after all I have gone through during the last four years and am going through now, I can be capable of selling my soul to the devil for party purposes, let them think what they like.'[58]

Nayantara Sahgal once remarked, 'It used to be said that wherever he [Motilal Nehru] sat became the head of the table because he was such a tremendous personality.'[59] Motilal Nehru led a social life with a fine clutch of interesting persons living nearby and a constant stream of others attached to the high court and the university. They dropped by to sit around the tiered fountain in the centre of the courtyard, or take a dip in the indoor swimming pool in a great, cavernous, damp-smelling room. At one end of the pool there was a large carved stone crow's head from whose mouth fresh water poured to fill it. Sapru could not swim; hence, he would not move from the first step in fifteen inches of water. Manmohini Zutshi's mother recounted an incident when one of the women lost her gold ring in the pool. Jawaharlal Nehru dived in and got it out. How he teased his sisters-in-law! They had to beg and plead with him before he retrieved the ring.[60] The swimming pool was reserved for the use of his family even after Motilal Nehru formally presented the Anand Bhawan to the nation.

When Motilal Nehru was about, he filled the scene; there hardly seemed to be room for anyone else.[61] But for a man with bubbling warmth it required no effort to draw people to Anand Bhawan. The guest list had everyone who was anyone in Allahabad—politicians, journalists, poets, and British administrators. 'Strange as it may seem to some I have found the "sundried bureaucrat" to be the most charming fellow in the world once he puts off the bureaucratic mask.'[62] Harcourt Butler (1869–1938), United Province's (UP's) lieutenant governor and a lover of music, dance, and good food, was a welcome guest.[63] As knives and forks appeared on the dining table, social conversation with him veered around Shakespeare and the nineteenth-century Romantic poets. After dinner, guests took their turn on the *takhtposh* (low bed) chewing *pan* (betel leaf) from the *pandaan* (pan box), and listened to ghazals or *thumri* and *dadra* (varieties of Indian classical music). On a wintry night, they would move into the large living room with the tabla and *sarangi* (string instrument). Come Muharram and they'd put away their musical instruments in memory of the martyrdom of Imam Husain, the grandson of the Prophet of Islam. These gestures survived well until the 1930s, when Shia–Sunni animus, along with Hindu–Muslim conflicts, began to disturb Awadh's composite ambience.

Motilal Nehru's guest list included Mohammad Amir Ahmad, the Raja of Mahmudabad. He addressed him as 'Bhai Sahib'.[64] His affection for Hakim Ajmal Khan was like that of real brothers. He loved him for his searching, lucid, and incisive mind. Dr M.A. Ansari was his family doctor, and Nehru respected his standing in the Congress. Tej Bahadur Sapru, an eminent lawyer, shared their outlook. In addition, Motilal Nehru placed his knowledge and experience at the disposal of young lawyers, journalists, and college teachers. He recognized the good everywhere, however unexpected its source might be, and his encouragement went out to help any man or woman, old or young, cultivated or callow, who worked honestly and diligently. Generous and indulgent, he had a kind, somewhat whimsical manner, and was blessed with a large capacity for affection.

Motilal Nehru also had his dark moods and cold sulks. He was arrogant as well, and he was condescending towards those who did not belong to his class. Once, when a Hindu Sabha leader entered the central assembly after getting his teeth extracted, he remarked to the member sitting next to him: 'His fangs are out and we will now be safe.' About one member he complained that 'he never soaps his beard', and about another that 'his mouth smells like [the] gutter'. At the same time, he dispensed patronage with unrivalled dignity amongst his colleagues.[65]

John Locke, the British philosopher, stated that wit lies most in the assemblage of ideas, and in putting these together with quickness and variety. He was right. Every generation has its own standard of critical judgement, but there is no denying that humour introduces a tenderness and loftiness of feeling. Without that, speech would be insipid and company frightfully dull. The more advanced a language, the greater its ability to express wit and humour. 'Now the pen has on its tongue some witty tales, which it lays out for the friends' sake', wrote the Urdu poet Mir Taqi Mir (1723–1810). Motilal Nehru captivated his generation with his aristocratic manner, his humour tempered with good taste in poetry, and his sophistication, which under no circumstances degenerated into 'showing off'. Though some judged him to be too worldly, domineering, acerbic, and wilful, the flaws in his character were redeemed by his gracious and courteous bearing. People knew that he was egotistical, self-important, and impatient, and yet they relied on his urbanity, high poetical feeling, and elegant tastes. Indeed, in days of affluence or in days of hardship, his own family remembered both his awe-inspiring temper and infectious laughter.

If an outsider had seen the family talk, joke, and laugh, he would not have thought that the Nehrus had many cares or worries to trouble them, much less that they were mentally anguished. There was little sleep those days. The younger ones were simply delighted with this excitement and riotous living. Motilal Nehru regaled his daughters with stories of his travels. Jawaharlal Nehru narrated old and new stories, joked, and laughed. And whenever Sarojini Naidu was in town they turned to her scintillating wit, irrepressible vivacity, and joie de vivre.[66] Motilal Nehru was 'papaji'; Kamala Nehru, 'mammaji'; and Krishna, 'betti'. On the occasion of Krishna's wedding, the *Bulbul-i Hind* (Nightingale of India) congratulated her: 'You are bringing as your share in that comradeship some wonderful personal gifts, enhanced by all the richness and nobility of tradition that belong to your family, as the integral part of the existing traditions, ideals and achievements which are an example and an inspiration to the nation.'[67]

People flocked to Anand Bhawan to meet Sarojini Naidu, and some, who knew she was a gourmet, brought special kebabs or other Mughal delicacies.[68] Music flowed from her lips, as it did from her pen. Charming, kind-hearted, and friendly, she had a generous disposition.

There was no mistaking the euphoria at Anand Bhawan, 'the steadfast symbol it had been before, brazenly flaunting the tricolor and defying defeat'.[69] The Congress drafted the Memorandum of Reform at Anand Bhawan, and revised its constitution in 1920; Gandhi laid the first foundations of the Non-Cooperation Movement at Anand Bhawan; it was also the venue of the final sittings of the Civil Disobedience Committee. Even after Motilal Nehru handed over Anand Bhawan to the nation, relatives, friends, and comrades lived in the spacious and specially furnished rooms for weeks and months. 'We are full up here', Jawaharlal Nehru informed Indira Gandhi on

6 April 1936. Among the guests were: Bapu and Kasturba Gandhi, Mahadev Desai, Vallabhbhai Patel and his daughter, Sarojini Naidu, and Padmaja Naidu. Many more came streaming into Anand Bhawan for fairs and exhibitions. On one such occasion, a group of young boys and girls from the nearby school sang the Ramadhun:

> Thou art the purifier of the fauen,
> Iswar and Allah are Thy names,
> Do Thou grant right understanding to all men,
> Krishna and Karim are Thy names,
> So are Rama and Rahim,
> Do thou grant right understanding to all men.

Notes

1.   William Wedderburn, *Allan Octavian Hume, C.B.* (London: T. Fisher Unwin, 1913), p. 58.

2.   Mushirul Hasan, 'Indian National Congress', *Oxford Islamic Studies Online*, available at http://www.oxfordislamicstudies.com/article/opr/t343/e0164?_hi=0&_pos=3574.

3.   Balmiki Prasad Singh, *The Indian National Congress and Cultural Renaissance*, 2nd edition (Lucknow: Allied Publishers, 2007).

4.   Government of India, 'Reports on the Native Newspapers, Punjab' (New Delhi: Nehru Memorial Museum and Library, microfilm, January–December 1889), pp. 21–2.

5.   *Tribune*, 21 February 1888, 23 January and 6 February 1889.

6.   *Akhbar-ul Momineen* 21 May 1890 (Lucknow: United Provinces Newspaper Reports).

7.   C.A. Bayly, *The Local Roots of Indian Politics: Allahabad 1880–1920* (Oxford: Clarendon Press, 1975), p. 130.

8.   Bayly, *Local Roots of Indian Politics*, p. 147.

9.   Jawaharlal Nehru, *Glimpses of World History* (London: Lindsay Drummond Limited, 1942, reprint), p. 441.

10.   Ray Monk, *Bertrand Russell: The Spirit of Solitude, 1872–1921*, vol. 1 (New York: Simon and Schuster, 1996), p. 54.

11.   Bayly, *Local Roots of Indian Politics*, p. 4.

12.   Bayly, *Local Roots of Indian Politics*.

13.   Report on the Native Newspapers, Punjab, January–December 1888.

14.   Bayly, *Local Roots of Indian Politics*, p. 209.

15.   C. A. Bayly, *Origins of Nationality in South Asia: Patriotism and Ethical Government in the Making of Modern India* (New Delhi: Oxford University Press, 2001), p. 1.

16.   J. Nehru, *An Autobiography*, p. 21.

17.   Jawaharlal Nehru, *Glimpses of World History Being Further Letters to His Daughter, Written in Prison, and Containing a Rambling Account of History for Young People with 50 Maps by J. F. Horrabin* (New Delhi: Jawaharlal Nehru Memorial Fund, Teen Murti House, Distributed by Oxford University Press, 1982), p. 439.

18.   Louis Rousselet and Charles Randolph Buckle, *India and Its Native Princes; Travels in Central India and in the Presidencies of Bombay and Bengal* (London: Forgotten Books, 2013, first published in 1882), p. 556, available at http://www.forgottenbooks.com/readbook_text/India_and_Its_Native_Princes_1000693522/575.

19.   Harriot Georgina Blackwood, Marchioness of Dufferin and Ava, *Our Viceregal Life in India: Selections from My Journal, 1884–1888*, vol. 1 (London: Forgotten Books, 2013, first published in 1890), pp. 89–90, available at http://www.forgottenbooks.com/readbook_text/Our_Viceregal_Life_in_India_v1_1000425571/117.

20.   Rousselet and Buckle, *India and Its Native Princes*, pp. 556–7, available at http://www.forgottenbooks.com/readbook_text/India_and_Its_Native_Princes_1000693522/575.

21.   Vijaya Lakshmi Pandit, *The Scope of Happiness: A Personal Memoir* (New York: Crown Publishers, 1979), p. 39.

22.   William Muir founded the Muir Central College in 1872. The buildings were designed by William Emerson. Initially affiliated to the University of Calcutta, it became a part of the Allahabad University in 1921 under the Allahabad University Act. Its graduates did well as professionals and government servants, with some rising to eminence as teachers, journalists, publicists, and government servants. With scholars like Amarnath Jha setting

high standards of learning, the Allahabad University became a premier centre of education.

23.   *The Writings of Mark Twain*, vol. 6, *Following the Equator: A Journey around the World* (New York: Harper and Bros, 1809), p. 160.

24.   M.L. Bhargava, *Hundred Years of Allahabad University* (New Delhi: Ashish Publishing House, 1987), p. 30.

25.   Katju, *The Days I Remember*, p. 366.

26.   Mushirul Hasan, 'Where's the Punch of Yesterday?', available at http://indiatoday.intoday.in/story/humour-and-satarical-phrases-mirza-gharib/1/217347.html.

27.   B.K. Nehru, *Nice Guys Finish Second*, pp. 69–71.

28.   Mehr Afshan Farooqi, *The Postcolonial Mind: Urdu Culture, Islam, and Modernity in Muhammad Hasan Askkari* (New Delhi: Oxford University Press, 2012), p. 5.

29.   Hasan, 'Where's the Punch of Yesterday?'

30.   D.P. Mishra, *Living an Era: India's March to Freedom*, vol. 1 (New Delhi: Vikas Publishing House, 1975), pp. 24–5.

31.   K. Iswara Dutt, *The Street of Ink* (Masulipatam: Triveni Publishers), p. 102.

32.   B.K. Nehru, *Nice Guys Finish Second*, pp. 8–9.

33.   B.K. Nehru, *Nice Guys Finish Second*, pp. 12–13.

34.   B.K. Nehru, *Nice Guys Finish Second*, p. 17.

35.   Krishna Nehru Hutheesing, *We Nehrus* (Bombay: Pearl Publications, 1967), p. 6.

36.   B.K. Nehru, *Nice Guys Finish Second*, p. 15.

37.   B.K. Nehru, *Nice Guys Finish Second*, p. 15.

38.   *Legislative Assembly Debates*, February 1934, vol. 10, no. 14 (Delhi, 1934), p. 784.

39.   Nanda, *The Nehrus*, p. 69.

40.   Krishna Nehru Hutheesing, ed., *Nehru's Letters to His Sister* (London: Faber and Faber, 1963), p. 11.

41.   Mushirul Hasan, *The Nehrus: Personal Histories* (London: Mercury Books, 2006), p. 49.

42.   B.K. Nehru, *Nice Guys Finish Second*, p. 55.

43.   Mehta, *Freedom's Child*, p. 10.

44. Mehta, *Freedom's Child*, p. 10; Nayantara Sahgal, *Jawaharlal Nehru: Civilizing a Savage World* (New Delhi: Penguin Books India, 2010), p. 17.

45. N. Sahgal, *Civilizing a Savage World* p. 19.

46. Like a true patriarch, he told his son on 20 October 1905:

> You must bear in mind that in you we are leaving the dearest treasure we have in this world and perhaps in other worlds to come.... It is not a question of providing for you as I can do that perhaps in one single year's income. It is a question of making a real man of you which you are bound to be. It would have been extremely selfish—I should say sinful—to keep you with us and leave you a fortune in gold with little or no education. I think I can without vanity say that I am the founder of the fortunes of the family. I look upon you, my dear son, as the man who will build upon the foundations I have laid and have the satisfaction of seeing a noble structure of renown rearing up its head to the skies.

(Hasan, *The Nehrus: Personal Histories*, p. 55.)

47. Krishna Hutheesing, 'My Brother—Then and Now', *A Study of Nehru*, edited by Rafiq Zakaria (Delhi: Rupa, 1989), p. 131.

48. Shridhar, son of Bansidhar, was one of them. Educated in Allahabad, Cambridge, and Heidelberg, he joined the Civil Services in 1912 and held several key positions in the United Provinces.

49. M. Nehru to Bansidhar Nehru, 9 October 1912, *Selected Works of Motilal Nehru (SWMN)*, vol. 3, edited by Ravinder Kumar and D.N. Panigrahi (Delhi: Vikas, 1984), p. 175.

50. M. Nehru to Gandhi, 19 April 1930, *SWMN*, vol. 7, p. 198.

51. For a brief profile, see Mehta, *Freedom's Child*, pp. 8–9.

52. B.K. Nehru, *Nice Guys Finish Second*, p. 79.

53. M. Nehru to Bansidhar Nehru, 9 October 1912, *SWMN*, vol. 1, p. 175.

54. Son of Brijlal and Rameshwari Nehru, who edited a Hindi women's magazine, *Stri Darpan*.

55. Mishra, *Living an Era*, p. 93.

56. Motilal Nehru to Gandhi, 10 July 1924, *SWMN*, vol. 4, p. 47.

57. Hutheesing, *We Nehrus*, p. 21; M.C. Chagla, *Roses in December: An Autobiography* (Mumbai Bharatiya Vidya Bhavan, 2012), p. 67.

58. N. Sahgal, *Civilizing a Savage World*, p. 4.

59. Adams and Whitehead, *Dynasty*, p. 10.

60. M.Z. Sahgal, *An Indian Freedom Fighter Recalls Her Life*, p. 6.

61. Chattopadhyay, *Inner Recesses Outer Spaces*, p. 119.

62.   M. Nehru to Mohamed Ali, 23 January 1926, *SWMN*, vol. 5, p. 8.

63.   His uncle, Henry Montagu Butler, had been headmaster of Harrow and was still Master of Trinity when Jawaharlal Nehru went to Cambridge.

64.   M. Nehru to Mohamed Ali, 23 January 1926, *SWMN*, vol. 5, p. 26.

65.   The notable beneficiaries were: Manzar Ali Sokhta, Syed Mahmud, T.A.K. Sherwani, Choudhry Khaliquzzaman, the scholar Amarnath Jha who later became the vice chancellor of the Allahabad University, and Firaq Gorakhpuri, the English teacher and Urdu poet. Puran Chandra Joshi (1907), the future communist leader, was more 'a friendly member of our family than a friendly visitor'. Acc. No. 1161, Nehru Memorial Museum and Library (NMML) Manuscripts.

66.   Pandit, *Scope of Happiness*, p. 59.

67.   Pandit, *Scope of Happiness*, p.104.

68.   Mehta, *Freedom's Child*, p. 40.

69.   N. Sahgal, *Prison and Chocolate Cake*.

3 'Who Rides a Tiger Cannot Dismount'*

Life in prison is not meant to be exciting—it is about as uneventful as the existence of the average turnip—and if some exciting event does take place once in a while, the veil of mystery must not be removed and no whisper of it must percolate to the outside world. Inside the jail— and outside—the massive gates and the high walls of the jail separate two worlds. Almost one might say that it is like one living world and the hereafter—but few, if any, want to rush to the hereafter, and none love the jail so much as to wish to remain here. Two worlds! You could also compare the two to the animal and the vegetable kingdoms. The object of jail appears to be first to remove such traces of humanity as a man might possess and then to subdue even the animal element in him so that ultimately he might become the perfect vegetable! Soil-bound, cut off from the world and its activity, nothing to look forward to, blind obedience the only 'virtue' that is instilled, and spirit considered the great sin—is it any wonder that the prisoner approximates to the plant? Of course this does not apply to the likes of me who come for short periods, but the others who spend years and years here, wherein do they differ, I wonder, from the plant? And if after long years they are let off how do they feel in the strange new world of bustle and activity?[1]

It was a March day in Allahabad. A parcel had just arrived for Nayantara's father from Motilal Nehru, and standing on the verandah beside him, examining the stamps on it, Nayantara asked him if the King of England's pictures would also be on stamps. 'Not always', he had said, adding with vehemence, 'One day it won't.'[2]

The Raja of Mahmudabad once commented that Motilal Nehru had the manner and the polish of a man both born to authority and with the right to exercise it.[3] A photograph taken in 1899 shows him in his formal cutaway coat of English broadcloth and grey striped trousers, with a stiff shirt, high collar, and satin tie. His rather full face had a handlebar moustache—which he soon cut off. Artists portrayed him as a vigorous man with the clear-cut and domineering mask of a Roman senator, his bearing irresistibly youthful till the very end. M.R.A. Baig's abiding impression was of 'an imperious Roman Senator in a snow-white toga presiding like a patriarch at a table.... He loved a "court" round would flow back and forth interrupted every now and then by a guffaw of laughter from the host as he scored off someone, either present or absent [sic]'. His impact on Baig, the future diplomat, 'remains the greatest of the great.'[4]

Like many other influential men in the 1890s, Motilal Nehru had joined forces with the Indian National Congress. He attended its session in 1888, joined the subjects committee in 1892, chaired one of G.K. Gokhale's lectures in Allahabad in early February 1907, presided over the first Provincial Conference of the United Provinces in March that year, and attended the Congress at Allahabad in 1910 where he seconded a resolution proposed to Congress president William Wedderburn (1838–1918), Scottish civil servant and president.

Meanwhile, the Swadeshi Movement came up with some of the emotive lyrics and songs in Allahabad; *Bande Mataram* became a common form of salutation. Motilal lost sleep. Like so many other *ashraf* or elite families in Awadh, he did not accept the dhoti and chaddar culture in place of English-manufactured goods. As a person whose views were 'even more moderate than those of the so-called moderates', he found it distasteful that Muir College students heeded B.G. Tilak's 'wild and revolutionary propaganda'.[5] That this attitude did not involve hatred may be true, but the mentality in any case was a typically aristocratic one. Motilal Nehru would not stoop to encourage authoritarian tendencies as a curb upon popular enthusiasm. On the contrary, he held fast to the hope that men would prove amenable to reason.

Motilal Nehru occasionally professed allegiance to the Raj, but he also blamed the Morley–Minto Reforms (1909) for creating enlarged councils that would be no more than a collection of *jee-huzoors* (sycophants). From the earliest years he manifested a horror for violent change, and detested revolutionary methods, and this feeling was deepened by his knowledge of a sermon 'Against Disobedience and Wilful Rebellion' (included in 1574 in the official *Book of Homilies*). He, therefore, declined to attend in May 1907 a meeting at Allahabad in protest against Lala Lajpat Rai's arrest and deportation.[6] He spent sleepless nights over the consequence of 'terror' and violence. He chided Manzar Ali Sokhta, son of Mubarak Ali and his ward, for associating himself with people whose methods he disapproved of.[7]

With his self-imposed constraints, Motilal Nehru remained a rather marginal figure for at least a decade after 1892, the year of the Congress assembly in Allahabad. There is little sign of anyone wooing him into becoming more closely involved, and equally little indication that he wanted to become so. Besides his own work, he had no overpowering impulse to get embroiled in the great political issues of the day. He liked to believe that his nature was too noble for the world. But the consequences of the Swadeshi Movement in Bengal and the 'Surat Split' between the mild and soothing moderates and the direct and truculent extremists were profound and were to affect all parts of Motilal Nehru's life. With his emotional investment in his abandonment of militancy, he chose to remain 'most immoderately moderate'. But the slow and steady march of history made him revisit his own theories. As the political barometer rose, Gandhi shot up for the first time in the Indian firmament. A glimmer of hope appeared, 'a whisper of better times and lighter burdens'.

Gandhi's name had an unfamiliar and uncanny sound in the beginning:'When the peasant and the worker and all who were down-trodden saw him and heard him, their dead hearts woke to life and thrilled, and a strange hope rose in them, and they shouted *Gandhi Mahatma ki jai* [victory to Mahatma Gandhi] and they prepared to march out of their valley of suffering.'[8] Doubtless it was that in Gandhi Jawaharlal Nehru found his happiest moments. Sometimes in the evening of a busy day he would sit alone, or with some old and trusted friends, and reveal to them how Gandhi was like 'a powerful current of fresh air that made [them] stretch [themselves] and take deep breaths; like a beam of light that pierced the darkness and removed the scales from [their] eyes; like a whirlwind that upset many things, but most of all the working of people's minds'.[9] Jawaharlal Nehru would have added that there was nothing of consequence that escaped Gandhi's attention in the long run, and there were few moves he had ever missed for the good of his people. He emboldened people to eliminate all restraints from politics, and to use their moral and intellectual resources to rid the country of British rule.

This was the Gandhi Age in India. To live through a stirring period of history and to let the mind play with the problems of authority and subordination was a unique event for sections of the intelligentsia. It was good to be alive and to take one's share in it, even though the share consisted of solitude in the Dehradun Gaol.[10] Nayantara and her sisters felt stimulated 'by the spark with which Gandhi illumined our country'. It touched their lives in innumerable small ways and penetrated their consciousness gradually.[11]

Motilal Nehru, who was invited to attend the Delhi Durbar during the visit of George V, took a while to understand the growing resentment to British rule. The transformation was not to be completed overnight, but the Jallianwala Bagh incident on 13 April 1919 made it clear to him that law and order, English education, roads, railways, and telegraph wires were signposts of a modernity that did not include racial equality.[12] Filled with wrath and dread, he applauded Gandhi for pleading with the men in power to be worthy of themselves. The Inner Light glimmered: 'My blood is boiling', he thundered. This was more than letting off steam. He knew that no return to the past was possible and also that the past was not worth returning to. We can see in his exchanges a contrast between a conservative ideal and a humanitarian, social, democratic ideal to which Motilal Nehru gave pride of place in the interest of the nation, that is to say, of the human beings composing it.

The British in India extended their legal privileges to the breaking point, and General Dyer misused them to mock people gathering for a non-political assembly. The disappointment of fervent expectations had shaken moderates like Motilal Nehru, whose own view was that law assumes a broadly moral and human sense and is tempered by mercy and love. Therefore, his ideal had been orderly development by process of law. After Amritsar's gruesome happenings, if his stand nevertheless showed sharp contrast with his earlier views, which he had stated some years earlier, it was but a sign of the incomparable depth of Gandhi's political authority. At any event, he expressed national self-confidence, no less than aversion to rebellion. With one fierce bound of enthusiasm, he thought, the entire Indian nation had shaken off its chains.

So we see Motilal Nehru as a son of his country and of his age. A newly awakened national consciousness was an infinitely stronger consideration than those of wealth and professional laurels. A most remarkable character, he renounced his worldly gains, and took no cases, except in defense of the Congress members arrested under the black bills.[13] Once a client came with one lakh rupees as fees for a case in which he wanted Motilal Nehru to appear. 'Well Beti', he asked Krishna Nehru, 'do you think it would be right for me to accept this case?' 'No, Father, I don't think you should', said the daughter.[14] Shakespeare would have said,

> ... all men idle, all;
> And women too, but innocent and pure;
> No sovereignty—

In an age marked by prudence and calculation rather than adventure, Gandhi brought the non-cooperation issue before the Special Session of the Congress in Calcutta in September 1920. Once matters came to that pass, there was no holding him back. Motilal Nehru showed singleness of vision by backing non-cooperation. Cynics have interpreted his change of heart in terms of his self-interest. How different was the reality! There was a time when he exhorted his son not to precipitate a family crisis. He had once dreaded the thought of his son languishing in prison, but he was now determined to fight for his freedom to his last breath. He was, under the changed circumstances, a faithful representation of a 'radical', and his speeches were an eloquent and sincere testimony of early twentieth-century liberal idealism. To Shudha Mazumdar of Bengal and others he came across as strong-willed, energetic, and proud.[15]

Enough is enough, said the local government, which was keeping a close watch on the activities taking place in Anand Bhawan. After a while, the police department lost its patience and stepped in to arrest Motilal Nehru and his son. Alexander Solzhenitsyn writes that arrest 'is a breaking point in your life, a bolt of lightning which has scored a direct hit on you'. It is 'an inassimilable spiritual earthquake not every person can cope with, as a result of which people often slip into insanity'.[16] The Nehrus kept their cool. When the trial began on the seventh of December, the next day, the father looked at ease sitting in court 'with his toga-like white garments, with his little granddaughter on his knees'.[17] The judge showed no mercy; he sentenced Motilal Nehru to six months' imprisonment for being a member of an 'illegal' organization. Without seeking legal remedies, the proud patrician declared from prison:

> It is now my high privilege to serve the motherland by going to prison with my only son. I am fully confident that we shall meet again at no distant date as free men.... Continue nonviolent noncooperation without a break until Swaraj is achieved. Enlist as volunteers in your tens and thousands. Let the march of pilgrimage to the only temple of liberty now existing in India—the jail, be kept in an uninterrupted stream, swelling in strength and volume as each day passes. Adieu.[18]

With this, he entered through the fateful gates of the Lucknow prison. On the other hand, Anand Bhawan turned into a house of sadness, as though the light had gone out of it.[19] 'That's what arrest is', Alexander Solzhenitsyn said, 'it's a blinding flash and a blow which shifts the present instantly into the past and the impossible into omnipotent actuality.'[20]

At all times, Motilal Nehru kept his head high up, and appeared to the wardens to be remarkably buoyant. His primary loyalty was to his co-prisoners, and he avoided any appearance of being favoured by the authorities. Even in the depths of Lucknow's district jail, life turned out to be a touching period of discovery for father and son. They understood each other's point of view in a state of extreme loneliness in a manner which the demands of a busy public life had made difficult earlier.[21] Even though solitude and inaction ate deeply into their spirit, they radiated the aura of optimism, energy, and adventure in their combined pursuit of nationalist goals. Motilal Nehru kept his cool, calm, and collected style, settled in solitary splendour with his 'nose touching the Eastern wall of the jail & the back rubbing the wall'.[22] 'I may land in your jail some day; will you give me champagne?' he had asked his friend Harcourt Butler, who had enjoyed the hospitality of the Nehrus at Anand Bhawan. Butler said yes to his request. On Motilal Nehru's first morning in prison, an A.D.C. from Government House arrived at lunchtime with a half bottle of champagne wrapped in a napkin, and every single day of his imprisonment this was repeated. On another occasion, he mentioned to the prison superintendent his typical meals—based, of course, on his Anand Bhawan habits. His colleagues were amused; the younger Nehru was to be served 'grass-like' things.[23]

Every morning doors were unlocked and doors were slammed. Every morning new batches of prisoners, young and old, men and women, were brought in and terrorized by the guards. Many were undertrials who were utterly dependent on the jail establishment. The law as they knew was not represented by the judge or magistrate, defending counsel or prosecutor, but by the police and prison. Many others were unwelcome visitors because they could connect with life outside their cell. They had friends, who mounted pressure on the government to either secure release or make their living conditions a little better. The 'revolutionaries', in particular, had the satisfaction of being counted as 'martyrs'. Legends of all kind developed around their torture, flogging, and shuffling around in vanloads.

Ahmad Kathruda spent twenty-six years in prison in close proximity to both Nelson Mandela and Walter Sisulu. His experience of meeting political prisoners was one of warmth, fellowship and friendships, humour, and laughter; of strong convictions and a generosity of spirit and compassion, solidarity, and care.[24] Making communal life richer and more profound was, apparently, one of their chief goals. In India, likewise, Motilal Nehru belonged to an unusually gregarious group and developed to a high degree the art of cooperation with each other. Supreme in the lighter sphere of anecdote and romance, he talked and laughed, and read the verses of the great fourteenth-century Persian poet, Hafiz Shirazi (1325/26–1389/90).[25] He also played gilli-danda (a game played with a large stick called a danda, used to hit another small stick, the gilli) as well. Khaliquzzaman and Maulana Salamatullah of Firangi Mahal, also known as Dulare Mian, were his companions. When Dulare Mian went to jail, a song was written in which, speaking in the name of his nephew, Hamid, the songwriter said:

Bole Hamid Dulare chacha se
Jail jana Mubarak ho tum ko.
[Hamid said to Uncle Dulare,
Congratulations on going to jail.][26]

We have an admirable description of Motilal's jail life in B.K. Nehru's autobiography:

We arrived at the jail in the afternoon and ... were admitted straight-away and escorted to the ward where the four Nehrus were imprisoned. It was a long way to go and we went through several yards enclosed by many walls and gates. We then heard from a long distance away the sound of Dadaji's *qahqaha*. It was a very heavy laugh the sound seeming to come directly from his belly.... In a few moments we arrived in the ward which contained the Nehrus alone ... I do recall that Dadaji was sitting very comfortably on a *dari* covering the floor which itself was partially covered with a *chandni*. Spread before him were not only a tea-pot and tea cups and other accessories for tea but also a large variety of fruits to which was added the contribution we had brought with us ... It seemed to me that the best afternoon tea available in Lucknow was the District Jail! The grandfather and the uncles all seemed comfort-able, happy, and relaxed.[27]

Of the influences which combined to mould Jawaharlal's mind and character, the earliest and the deepest was his father. Yet, they did not see eye to eye. When they were free, they spent tortured days and nights trying each in his own way to convince the other. Visitors enjoyed the heated arguments between father and son at the dining table. In the wordy combats, the son held his own.[28] 'These were most unhappy days for all us', recalled Krishna Hutheesing, 'especially for Mother and Kamala, who could not bear to see father and son torn by politics and endless arguments. The atmosphere was tense all the time and one hardly dared to utter a word for fear of rousing Father's anger or irritating Jawahar.'[29]

One of the many examples of Motilal Nehru's outbursts took place in Anand Bhawan in the presence of guests. Motilal Nehru recited some Persian couplets and asked his son to translate them. He hesitated, but eventually came up with a poor translation. Motilal criticized him for not knowing the difference between two similar Persian words. The angry son made the most penetrating and the most balanced comment, 'At least I know the difference between dominion status and independence!' Motilal Nehru jumped up in fury and overturned the entire table in front of the invited guests.[30]

Motilal Nehru's decision to throw in his lot with Gandhi did not put an end to his differences with his son. In December 1927, the Congress in Madras had declared that its goal was national independence, but the Nehru Committee, chaired by Motilal Nehru, favoured dominion status. Following this, the Lahore Congress adopted complete independence as its goal. The Congress Working Committee met in Ahmedabad early in 1930 to finalize the blueprint for 'direct action'. Kamaladevi Chattopadhyay heard of the plan from Jawaharlal Nehru: launch Salt Satyagraha. Is that all Gandhiji could devise? she asked. Jawaharlal Nehru smiled and went on to suggest, 'You have yet to learn his ways. We cannot always grasp his ideas in their entirety. But rest assured there is a method in what people think is madness.'[31] As Gandhi's march from Sabarmati started, Kamaladevi 'felt elated as part of one of the most spectacular dramas in India's political history, pulsating every moment, to its subtlest nuances'.[32]

Gandhi's civil disobedience pushed Motilal Nehru and other leaders into jail yet again. He had been unhappy with the ways of the Mahatma, but to Ansari, his great friend, he said, 'Nothing but a deep conviction that the time for the greatest effort and the greatest sacrifice has come would have induced me to expose myself at my age with my physical disabilities and with my family obligations to the tremendous risks I am incurring. I hear the clarion call of the country and obey.'[33]

The one major event in jail was Motilal's and Jawaharlal's interview with Sapru and Jayakar who had sought the viceroy's permission to break the political impasse resulted from the Salt Satyagraha. They met the Nehrus on 27–8 July,[34] but the meeting did not produce any fruitful result: the Nehrus spurned the viceroy's offer. When someone suggested that civil disobedience should be toned down as a gesture towards the British prime minister, Ramsay MacDonald, Motilal Nehru 'sat up in bed and declared he would not compromise till the national objective had been gained, and that he would carry on the struggle, even if he was the sole person left to do so'.[35]

Duniyata Jeno Badley Galo (The World Seems to Have Suddenly Changed)[36]

Gandhi believed that the freedom struggle attended by violence entailed the ruin and waste of much that was good and noble in it. There was, by contrast, a school of thought, vocal and animated by the consciousness of having a significant message to pass, according to which the revolutionaries, though misguided and ill-advised, had to be defended. Motilal Nehru belonged to that school. Armed with copious learning, he performed brilliantly in the legislative assembly. In 1924, he demanded the holding of a round table conference and a resolution to this effect was passed but it did not receive any response from the government. On 8 March 1926, he masterminded the Swarajist walk-out. He entered upon an almost untrodden path of speaking against the Public Safety Ordinance in May 1929, challenging the sedition law that led to the arrest of communists in the Meerut 'conspiracy' case; he also contributed to the Meerut 'conspiracy' case defence fund. On 4 August 1929, he condemned the treatment of political prisoners in the Lahore Jail, and disputed the force-feeding of Bhagat Singh and Madhusadan Dutt in the context of their fifty-two-day hunger strike. Motilal Nehru warned that the harsh treatment of political prisoners would cause agitation.[37] Painting a clear picture of the political issues at stake, he hoped that the government would initiate remedial steps. Pointing to the European group in the legislative assembly, he recited a Persian verse with the following meaning:

Thou, oh pigeon of the roof of Haram [Kaaba in Mecca]
What dost thou know of the agonies of birds
With their feet tied.[38]

'This is the position,' he said, 'you are the pigeons on the roof of Haram. We are the pigeons with the string round our feet.'[39] He enjoyed speaking as heartily as his hearers, and he looked back on the years in the course of which he spoke as the happiest of his life. As a matter of fact, when he entered the lobbies of the assembly in his immaculate dress and leonine gait, every one stood up to show respect to him; ladies in Delhi and Simla idolized him.[40]

The gay and carefree chitchat of yesteryears was over. The Spode china and Venetian glass, the stock of choice wines, and the prized horses and dogs disappeared. Carriages and horses were dispensed with. Bank accounts, securities, and so forth, were transferred to Manmohini Zutshi's father so that Swarup Rani and the immediate family would not face any financial crunch.[41] The Nehru men and women wore khadi; household linen, sheets, and towels were made of khadi.[42] Gandhi himself spun Vijaya Lakshmi Pandit's wedding sari. When an Indian policeman first made his way to Anand Bhawan to arrest the two Nehru men, the women knew that they had to contend with a life of uncertainty, sacrifice, heartache, and sorrow. They had thoroughly assimilated Gandhi's methods and results, and it was in large measure from him that they derived the confidence that Swaraj was attainable. Aware of the revolution he had ushered in, they gave a positive response to him, 'not for the moment only, but for our entire lives.'[43] The following account sums up the atmosphere in the Nehru household:

Our home where life had run so smoothly before was now always in a state of chaos. Numerous Congress workers came from all parts of the country to stay a few days and discuss matters. Meetings were held almost daily and there was a never-ending stream of people in and out of the house. I had always been used to a great many people visiting my parents, but they were of a different type. They came in smart cars or carriages drawn by lovely horses each vying with the other in showing off their pomp and splendor. After the movement, quite a few of our wealthy friends kept away, and where one saw riches and wealth before, one now saw khadi-clad men and women, simple and humble. Each one bore within his or her heart an unconquerable determination, an undaunted courage to serve and free the country and, if need be, die for it.[44]

Hari (d. 1961), a Dalit boy who was Motilal Nehru's personal attendant, saw it all happen—the police raids, search for banned literature, and the confiscation of cars and furniture in lieu of the fines imposed on the Nehrus. When he appeared before the English magistrate who asked his age, he did not know what to say. But this much he knew: 'I had started shaving daily when Panditji [Jawaharlal] returned from college in England.' His freedom was taken away for a year. When it was restored, the Nehrus awaited his return at Anand Bhawan. 'At last a tonga clattered into the portico and an unrecognizable roly-poly form bounced out of it. The spare, sprite-like little man had disappeared and in his place emerged a prosperous-looking substitute. All through his enforced idleness, Hari had gained two stone', which he was not destined to lose again. Prison had been 'a happy holiday for him'. His rotundity became a joke and all the other servants in the Nehru household declared that they too wanted to spend a few months in jail if such was the result of martyrdom!'[45]

What was Motilal Nehru's greatest quality? Gandhi replied: 'Love of his son.' Was it not love of India? the Mahatma was asked. 'No', he replied, 'Motilal's love for India was derived from his love for Jawaharlal.'[46] The son had strong feelings for his father. He nursed him in jail, washed his clothes, and swept and dusted the barrack. Motilal Nehru wished there were many fathers to boast of such sons.[47]

An ailing Motilal was released on 8 September 1930. Philip Herbert Measures (1893–1961), the Superintendent of Police, drove him to Anand Bhawan. Motilal Nehru was taken to Calcutta on

17 November to consult his physicians and thereafter motored to Radha Swami Santholia's house on the banks of the Hooghly, very close to the Dakshineshwar Kali temple. When asked how he felt, Motilal Nehru said: 'Very bad, if one is to judge from the faces of my doctors. But I have been a fighter all my life, and I mean to fight against this illness. I am not afraid of death, and I have had enough of life, but I am determined to live till I have seen the birth of a Free India.'[48] Charles Tegart, a police officer who had initially refused to let Jawaharlal Nehru visit Calcutta, relented after a while.[49]

Before his death on 6 February 1931, Motilal Nehru uttered the Gayatri mantra. It seemed typical that a passionate believer in reason, intellect, and human agency should invoke a prayer that centred on the concept of enlightenment rather than on mercy.[50] Motilal Nehru was cremated on a pyre of sandalwood; and Gandhi gave an inspiring funeral oration to a man who gave an incalculable impetus to the nationalist movement in Allahabad and the United Provinces. Women do not usually attend funerals, but the silent, dry-eyed, and daring Swarup Rani turned up at the cremation. The stars were out and shining brightly; the Nehrus returned lonely and desolate after lighting the funeral pyre.

Writers invoke Muhammad Iqbal (1877–1938) to denote men of wisdom and sagacity:

> For thousands of years the yellow eyed
> Narcissus laments its
> Sightlessness!
> 'Tis had indeed in the garden
> to be born with discerning eyes![51]

Motilal had more than a discerning eye. Whatever else he may or may not have been, he was one of the great Indian liberals of the first half of the twentieth century. His lack of understanding of humble folk, or his aversion to them, seriously detracted from his greatness. To his credit, however, he was a man of fearless, pungent, clear-cut speech, and receptive to other people's points of view. Contemporaries recalled in addition, his forbearance, his great intellectual abilities, and his burning patriotism.[52] Till the very end, his bearing was irresistibly youthful. Those who knew him well remembered the animated sparkle of his eyes, and the vitality of his mind and senses. He had a thorough knowledge of men and a capacity to awe them into submission. Choudhry Khaliquzzaman, who wrote from the vantage point of Pakistan in the early 1950s, recollected:

> The loss was not only that of a great son of India who was possessed of a towering personality, extraordinary strength of character, ability and sincerity of purpose, but also of an affectionate friend and guide with his charming manners, jovial temperament, sweet humour and wide sympathy. It is sad to find that in India he is remembered as the father of Jawaharlal. What an irony! If his politics had been allowed by the Congress to be pursued without let or hindrance, India would perhaps not have been partitioned.[53]

This is a faultless judgement.

Biographies end with the subject's death. The story of Motilal Nehru has no such natural termination. If he had lived until the stroke of midnight on 15 August 1947, he would have been proud of his son unfurling India's tricoloured flag. Sapru, for one, grasped the event's significance. He wrote, 'I must be prepared for the end soon. I must bless my stars that I have seen the freedom of India with you at the helm.'[54] He blessed free India's first prime minister with the following couplet of Mirza Ghalib:

> *Tum salamat raho hazar baras*
> *Har baras ke hon din pachas hazar.*
> (May you live a thousand years
> May each year have fifty thousand days.)

In this chapter I have concentrated on the coming together of some of the qualities of Motilal Nehru—his intelligence, his eloquence, and his proper patriotism. But this is only the tip of an iceberg in the story of a man who not only did good but who was also truly good himself.

Notes

*   Chinese proverb

1.   J. Nehru to Vijaya Lakshmi Pandit, 25 June 1930, *SWJN*, vol. 4, p. 361.

2.   Nayantara Sahgal, *From Fear Set Free* (New York: W.W. Norton & Co., Inc., New York, 1963), p. 8.

3.   C.H. Philips and M.D. Wainwright, eds, *The Partition of India: Policies and Perspectives 1935–1947* (London: George Allen and Unwin, 1970).

4.   M.R.A. Baig, *In Different Saddles* (London: Asia Publishing House, 1967), p. 66.

5.   M. Nehru to J. Nehru, 24 January 1907, *SWMN*, vol. 1, p. 117.

6.   M. Nehru to J. Nehru, 17 May 1907, *SWMN*, vol. 1, p. 2.

7.   M. Nehru to Manzar Ali, 27 May 1907, *SWMN*, vol. 1, p. 125.

8.   J. Nehru, *Glimpses of World History*, p. 428; Manmathnath Gupta, *They Lived Dangerously: Reminiscences of a Revolutionary* (New Delhi: People's Publishing House, 1969), pp. 2–3.

9.   Jawaharlal Nehru, *The Discovery of India* (Bombay: Asia Publishing House, 1960), p. 138.

10.   J. Nehru, *Glimpses of World History*, p. 690.

11.   N. Sahgal, *Prison and Chocolate Cake*, p. 18.

12.   N. Sahgal, *The Political Imagination*, p. 28.

13.   Justice Rowlatt headed the sedition committee, based on whose recommendations two bills, known as the 'black bills', were introduced in the central legislature in February 1919. These provided the police with great powers to search a place and arrest any person without warrant.

14.   N. Sahgal, *The Political Imagination*, p. 31.

15.   Shudha Mazumdar, *Memoirs of an Indian Woman*, edited with an introduction by Geraldine Forbes (New York: An East Gate Book, 1989), p. 154.

16.   Solzhenitsyn, *Gulag Archipelago*, p. 3.

17.   Hutheesing, *We Nehrus*, p. 52.

18.   Frank Moraes, *Jawaharlal Nehru: A Biography* (Canada: The Macmillan Company, 1956), p. 83.

19.   Moraes, *Jawaharlal Nehru*, p. 54.

20.   Solzhenitsyn, *Gulag Archipelago*, p. 4.

21.   Ravinder Kumar, 'Introduction', *SWMN*, vol. 1, p. 39.

22.   M. Nehru to Jawaharlal, 24 May 1922, *SWMN*, vol. 3, p. 220.

23.   Syed Mahmud, 'In and out of Prison', *A Study of Nehru*, edited by Rafiq Zakaria (Delhi: Rupa, 1989), p. 181; Brecher, *Nehru: A Political Biography*, p. 160.

24.   Ahmad Kathrada, *No Bread for Mandela* (Delhi: National Book Trust, 2008), p. xiv.

25.   Choudhry Khaliquzzaman, *Pathway to Pakistan* (Pakistan: Longmans, 1961), p. 62.

26.   Nasim Ansari, *Choosing to Stay: Memoirs of an Indian Muslim*, translated from Urdu by Ralph Russell (Karachi: City Press, 1999), p. 16.

27.   B.K. Nehru, *Nice Guys Finish Second*, pp. 40–1.

28.   Chattopadhyay, *Inner Recesses Outer Spaces*, p. 119.

29.   Hutheesing, *We Nehrus*, p. 124.

30.   Tariq Ali, *The Nehrus and the Gandhis: An Indian Dynasty* (London: Chatto & Windus, 1985), p. 136.

31.   Chattopadhyay, *Inner Recesses Outer Spaces*, p. 119.

32.   Chattopadhyay, *Inner Recesses Outer Spaces*, p. 149.

33.   M. Nehru to M.A. Ansari, 7 February 1930, *SWMN*, vol. 7, p. 180.

34.   While the Mahatma agreed to attend the Round Table Conference on certain conditions, the Nehrus rejected the idea altogether.

35.   Mishra, *Living an Era*, p. 177.

36.   Remark attributed to Rajen Lahiri, the revolutionary, when he heard his death sentence.

37.   *SWMN*, vol. 7, p. 479.

38.   Motilal Nehru, *Voice of Freedom: Selected Speeches*, edited by Kavalam Madhava Panikkar and A. Pershad (Asia Publishing House, 1961), p. 428.

39.   *SWMN*, vol. 7, pp. 379–80.

40.   Mishra, *Living an Era*, p. 104.

41.   M.Z. Sahgal, *An Indian Freedom Fighter*, p. 29.

42.   Mehta, *Freedom's Child*, p. 50.

43. Hutheesing, *With No Regrets*, p. 18.

44. Hutheesing, *With No Regrets* p. 20.

45. N. Sahgal, *Prison and Chocolate Cake*, p. 88; Seton, *Panditji*, p. 113.

46. Nanda, *The Nehrus*, p. 343.

47. Nanda, *The Nehrus*, p. 39.

48. *SWMN*, vol. 7, p. 357.

49. Initially there had been fears that Jawaharlal Nehru would get drawn into nationalistic politics in Calcutta. Even if he gave an undertaking to not get involved in any political activity, officials thought that he would not be allowed to carry it as the local leaders would drag him into politics. *SWMN*, vol. 7, file no. 32 (III), 1931.

50. Uma Vasudev, *Indira Gandhi: Revolution in Restraint*, vol. 1 (Gurgaon: Shubhi Publications, 2011), p. 8.

51. Mushirul Hasan, *India Partitioned: The Other Face of Freedom*, vol. 1 (New Delhi: Lotus Collection, 1995), p. 58.

52. Rajendra Prasad, *Autobiography* (Bombay: Asia Publishing House, 1957), p. 328.

53. Khaliquzzaman, *Pathway to Pakistan*.

54. Rafiq Zakaria, ed., *A Study of Nehru* (New Delhi: Rupa & Co., 1989), p. 21.

4 Destiny as It Was

The Story of an Enlightened Family

Time crept on inexorably. Like many others, the Nehrus adapted themselves to the new ways. The life-motto of the head of the family, Motilal Nehru, was Major Barbara's great cry: 'Let God's work be done for its own sake: the work he had to create us to do because it cannot be done except by living men and women.'[1]

What about the ticklish problem of religion and Hindu–Muslim relations? Like any other mid-sized city in north India, Allahabad had its share of *sabhas* (assemblies) and *anjumans* (assemblies in Urdu), *madaris* and pathshalas, cow-protection societies, and *jamaats* (congregations), which set the reactionary tone and temper of their faithful adherents. The atmosphere in municipal politics was vitiated; competing groups and factions allowed full-flooded communalism to grow. While any generalization about 'communalism' must sound like the definition of an elephant in the fable in which five blind men describe the animal in consonance with the portion of the creature traced by each with his finger, the fact is that separate electorates laid the foundation of communitarian politics; Motilal reported that out of the twenty-one electors from twenty-one different districts, eight were Muslims who would on no account vote for a Hindu.[2] As a person who expressed his deepest and most cherished convictions on Hindu–Muslim amity, the danger he saw as immediately threatening was that of a reaction against the principle of separate electorates and communal representation.

All through the 1920s, Pandit Madan Mohan Malaviya buttressed the causes of Hindi, the Hindu University, cow protection, *sangathan* (organization), and the All-India Hindu Mahasabha. All through the period, he raised the spectre of Muslim aggression, though the 'lurid pictures of an all-devouring Muslim leviathan conjured up' by him bore almost no relation to the Muslim position in India.[3] He showed a very conservative temper in religious matters. Brahmin orthodoxy in the matter of *chhoot* (untouchability) was carried to extremes by Malaviya and his immediate family.[4] In 1910, Sarla Chaudhurani, granddaughter of Debendranath Tagore, set a few mantras from the Veda to music to be sung at the Congress session in 1910. The mantras dealt with the benefits of union and cooperation, but Malaviya interdicted the song on the ground that the Shastras prohibited their singing in the hearing of non-Hindus.[5] He again crossed swords with the provincial government in 1924 over bathing rights on a particular occasion on the banks of the Ganges in Allahabad.[6] As the head of the All India Independent Party, he used communal weapons to discredit his Swarajist rivals in the 1925 municipal elections, and in the 1926 provincial legislative councils elections.[7] In the Central Provinces, the All India Independent Party was led by Malaviya and Lajpat Rai, 'whose inclination was somewhat to the right as well as towards a more communal orientation,'[8] and the election battle ran on clearly communal lines. Once more, the Hindu Mahasabha stigmatized Motilal

Nehru as a beef-eater, but Malaviya, who knew that its charges were false, did nothing to stop the vilification campaign.[9]

For the Hindu sabhas, a policy of concession to the Muslims was incompatible with the exploitation of communal fears for political ends, and for Lajpat Rai, in particular, there was the added danger that any concession would involve the permanent subordination of Punjabi Hindus to a Muslim majority by separate electorates.[10] Malaviya wanted something more 'to the right and greater latitude, both politically and communally, and he got this in a new party, of which he was the founder and leader'.[11] As a result, however variously and attractively he disguised himself, his speeches were as bitter and dogmatic as the pathetic and high-flown pronouncements of Muslim Leaguers.

Yet the Cambridge historian C.A. Bayly does not find evidence of active anti-Muslim behaviour on Malaviya's part. That is because he is unable to see through his anti-Muslim proclivities. It was said about Malaviya that his heart was often in the Congress camp, but his head was in other camps.[12] This explains why he could represent the Hindu communalist point of view at the Second Round Table held in London and, at the same time, return to India to chair the annual Congress session.

Malaviya and Purushottam Das Tandon, another leading figure of the political scene in Allahabad, showed an unusual degree of intolerance towards religious minorities, passed the impulse of Hindu revivalism from locality to locality, and switched into political articulation along a variety of more traditional means of communication.[13] There was nothing modern about their politics, which preached inflexible morality, and which was hostile to minority rights. In Malaviya's schematic view of Indian history, all that we can see is sluggish conservatism feeding on self-interest. On the series of communal incidents that took place in 1924 in Allahabad, David Page, the Oxford historian, has provided circumstantial evidence against the Malaviyas and established how the family, indeed, did its best to stir up the Hindus and prevent the restoration of normal relations.[14]

In a certain sense, it is instructive to compare Malaviya with Motilal Nehru, although in innumerable details they were so different. There is a struggle here that is of the essence of the freedom struggle, a struggle to create a political constituency that would promote their respective world views. Both lived in the same city; both had the same Brahminical upbringing; both were flaming with patriotic and republican zeal after the Jallianwala Bagh episode. But here the comparison ends. Unlike Malaviya, Motilal Nehru adhered to his expansive and culturally liberal attitudes, and carried the richness and appealing quality of his personal outlook. And in nothing does the modern quality of his mind appear more clearly than in his acceptance of toleration and compromise on the one hand, and his aversion to the Hindu Mahasabha and hidebound traditionalism on the other. Motilal Nehru shared this dislike with many of the greatest minds of the twentieth century, but he was more vocal and consistent than the others.

The Hindu Mahasabha was founded in 1910, but Motilal Nehru stayed away from its activities on the ground that it would minimize all chances of Hindu–Muslim unity, sap the foundation of the Congress itself, and come in the way of cultivating a pluralist point of view. The same year, he and Pandit Ganganath Jha, an Indologist and professor of Sanskrit, censured the 'obscenities' practiced during the Holi celebrations in Allahabad. This offended orthodox Hindus, who petitioned against them. Motilal Nehru defended the Civil Marriage Bill, introduced in the viceroy's council, for which he was reprimanded. 'At times one is ashamed to call himself [sic] a Hindu', he remarked.[15] Motilal Nehru, who detested the Hindu Mahasabhites as fanatics and disturbers of public peace, frowned upon the 'Malaviya–Lala gang', and made some disparaging remarks against G.D. Birla for joining them.[16] He asked for the meaning of 'mahamana'—an epithet used for Malaviya—and when he was told that it meant high-minded, he smiled and remarked: 'High-minded, indeed!'[17]

After the Non-cooperation Movement, Motilal Nehru worked for Hindu–Muslim unity. In March 1923, he visited Punjab in an effort to reconcile Hindu–Muslim differences before the elections that year. When the communal temperature rose in 1926, he suggested that (*a*) recipients of honours belonging to riot-ridden districts should have their names removed and (*b*) anybody belonging to the area should be excluded from public service. Hindu–Muslim unity was a plank of his platform.[18]

In his view of religion, the dogmatic contrasts within Hinduism receded into the background. He did not believe in divine revelation, mocked the Hindu adoration of 'mother cow', and looked doubtfully at *Ram Rajya*.[19] Anand Bhawan had no *purohit* or guru unlike other Kashmiri families who had gurus of Kashmiri descent. There were no poojas in the family, not even on Diwali. The only ceremony was the one held at the time of the beginning of the Kashmiri year, known as Nauroz. The only major ritual that B.K. Nehru went through was his mundan, which took place in Rae Bareli. Motilal Nehru was also prepared to have the horoscope of Jawaharlal, his new-born baby, made by the court astrologer of Khetri State, where his brother had been influential. On the other hand, Motilal rejected irrational behaviour and institutions. Watching a butler serve a dish of eggs to Motilal Nehru, an orthodox Hindu visitor remarked in horror, 'Panditji, you are not going to eat those eggs!' 'I most certainly am', Motilal replied, 'and in another few moments I am going to eat their mother too.'[20]

Such stories prompted Malaviya and others to castigate Motilal Nehru as a beef-eater and disrespectful of cows.[21] The journal *Citizen* attacked him as a *bideshi* (foreigner), a *tamashawala* (performer), and so on.[22] Motilal Nehru, in turn, reacted to the affair with calmness: this was one of the many qualities that raised him many notches in public estimation. 'The greater the opposition', he informed the son, 'the merrier it is for me.'[23] Amid rising religious tensions, he declared at the Calcutta Congress (1928) that religion placed barriers and prevented the development of a cooperative national life. He called for separating religion from politics, a theme that figured in a report that was drafted under his chairmanship.[24] This was nothing new. Quite early in public life, he turned the picture of Hindu nationalists upside down.

Kailash Nath Katju, the lawyer, belonged to a very orthodox community, which observed the most rigid restriction about inter-dining. When he lived with Sapru before setting up his own legal practice, he would cook his own food.[25] Motilal Nehru was quite out of sync with these habits. He had shown early signs of stubborn independence by not indulging in the tomfoolery of *prayaschchit* or purification after returning from Europe in 1899. 'No,' he said, 'not even if I die for it.' 'I know what your biradari is and if necessary in self-defence I will ruthlessly and mercilessly lay bare the tottered fabric of its existence and tear it into the minutest possible shreds.'[26] This was not all. He had scandalized his community by taking his midday meals in public at the High Court. This was in contempt of the strict dietary rules for a Brahmin.

This kind of crusading fervour came to Motilal Nehru naturally, and he was not prepared to abandon his entire *Weltanschauung* (world view) or keep silent on the deepest and most cherished of his convictions. When a British magistrate asked for his parentage, caste, and previous convictions, he flatly refused to specify.[27] He had been arrested and tried on 1 July 1930. Earlier, he took lightly the news of his excommunication from his caste. After all, he was Motilal, the first to adopt 'Nehru' as a surname. The lesson that he extracted from history was an eclectic outlook on life with a commitment to uphold its decent values.

Swarup Rani, married at fourteen, went along with her husband's decision not to perform a prayaschchit or purification ceremony. She even agreed to the invocations at Jawaharlal's wedding being sung by a group of young girls rather than the pandits. Later in life, she stood by Indira when some people condemned her proposed marriage to Feroze Gandhi, a Parsi.[28] 'My grandmother said that since neither Feroze nor I were much concerned with religion, she did not see that it mattered what either of us were. If we were religious, then it might matter, but not being so, it did not.'[29] At the same time, she was deeply religious, and made sure that her food was cooked by a Brahmin in a separate kitchen. She also made sure that her granddaughter Nayantara learnt passages by heart from the Gita and Tulsidas' *Ramcharitmanas* and also from Bernard Shaw, Roger Casement's trial, and Paul Robeson's biography. In other words, there was a good-humoured co-existence in Anand Bhawan of the deep religiosity of the women—Jawaharlal Nehru's mother, his fragile and often ailing wife, and his sisters—'and the light-hearted agnosticism of the men'.[30]

Jawaharlal Nehru on Syncretism

Jawaharlal Nehru learnt stories from Hindu mythology and from the Ramayana and the Mahabharata from his aunt, and embarked upon a study of theosophy under his Irish tutor, Ferdinand T. Brooks. He accompanied his mother or aunt to the Ganga for a dip and sometimes visited temples. He was attached to the Ganga and Yamuna in Allahabad ever since his childhood. In his will and testament he mentions how he 'watched their varying moods as the seasons changed, and ... often thought of the history and myth and tradition and song and story that have become attached to them through the long ages and become part of their flowing waters'. The Ganga, in particular, figures as a symbol and a memory of India's past, running into the present, and flowing on to the great ocean of the future.[31] At heart a sceptic, Jawaharlal Nehru clarified that his desire to have a handful of his ashes thrown into the Ganga had no religious substance. Proud of his inheritance, he wanted India to 'rid herself of all shackles that bind and constrain her and divide her people, and suppress vast numbers of them, and prevent the free development of the body and the spirit'.[32]

The Indian national movement for independence appropriated the powerful spiritual legacy bequeathed by Swami Vivekananda. Annie Besant and the Home Rule Leagues, which had inspired Jawaharlal Nehru after his return from London as a student, introduced theosophy with great effect. But Gandhi beat them all with his profoundly religious outlook that was conditioned by the Gita and attuned with his times. He was concerned with Truth, Reason, Belief, Ethic, and with practical matters on the state of the contemporary world. *My Experiments with Truth* indicates the character of his early inclinations, which were greatly modified though not altogether reversed. By contrast, Jawaharlal Nehru talked of the old days of blind and unquestioning faith, and the overpowering faith of the architects and builders of wonderful temples, mosques, and cathedrals.[33] He warned that certain beliefs, faiths, and customs that had some use in earlier days were singularly unsuitable in his age.[34] During his prolonged illness in the autumn of 1923, he moved away from the religious outlook on life and politics. The 'spectacle of what is called religion' filled him with horror, and he 'frequently condemned it and wished to make a clean sweep of it'.[35] Whenever Mohamed Ali, the Khilafat and Congress leader, referred to religion in Congress resolutions, he would protest. The self-styled Maulana would, in turn, shout at him for his irreligion and remind him that he was fundamentally religious.[36]

In most cases, the jail made people turn to their religion, to discover its virtues, and to seek comfort in and inspiration from its great figures. We have given examples of Gandhi, Aurobindo Ghose, Maulana Azad, and Mohamed Ali, to name just a few. Jawaharlal Nehru was an exception. Religion or religiosity eluded him in jail as it did outside of it. If he emerged stronger after serving short or long terms in prison, it was because of his unwavering political and social commitments.

Nehru did not have much faith in spiritualism either as its séances and its so-called manifestations of spirits seemed absurd to him and inadequate in unravelling the impertinent ways and mysteries of the afterlife. The complex ideology of custom, convention, and superstition enchained people under the guise of religion, whereas organized religions, besides being one of the principal impediments to freedom,[37] produced narrowness and intolerance, credulity and superstition, emotionalism and irrationalism.[38] As a man who spoke his mind with terrifying honesty, Jawaharlal stated that 'the blight of religion, with its glory of our past, like the old man of the sea, crushes us'. He recounted:

For about eight years now the Ram Lila has not been held in Allahabad, and the greatest festival of the year for hundreds of thousands in the Allahabad district has almost become a painful memory. How well I remember my visits to it when I was a child! How excited we used to get! And the vast crowds that came to see it from all over the district and even from other towns. It was a Hindu festival, but it was an open-air affair, and Muslims also swelled the crowds, and there was joy and lightheartedness everywhere.... And now, for eight or nine years, the children of Allahabad, not to mention the grownups, have had no chance of seeing this show and having a bright day of joyful excitement in the dull routines of their lives. And all because of trivial disputes and conflicts! Surely religion and the spirit of religion have much to answer for. What kill-joys they have been![39]

Muslim countries like Turkey were developing along national lines and there was, in actuality, no room for a foreign policy based on religion. Their domestic policy had little to do with religious dogmas.[40] Even though Jawaharlal Nehru borrowed doctrines that led him to delve into Eastern mysticism, he endorsed 'collective representation'— experienced in the collective consciousness of the groups to which they belonged—but was not in favour of communitarian identities being foregrounded.

Like bourgeois liberals, Jawaharlal Nehru believed that human society and individual men could be perfected by the application of reason. When Nayantara was young, he told her 'to keep all the window[s of the] ... mind open and not to become bigoted and closed to reason.'[41] For the duration of the Khilafat Movement (1919–22), he disapproved of the statements of swamis and maulvis, and found their history, sociology, and economics to be wrong. Nor was he impressed with the outward ways of religion. When C.R. Das grew a beard in jail, Jawaharlal wrote to his father, 'It is bad enough for the Maulanas to insist on beards. I hope Hindu–Muslim unity does not mean that we should also grow beards to match.'[42] He endorsed neither Ram Rajya as a golden age nor the imageries and illustrations from the Hindu scriptures. Fasts and penances, vows and renunciations did not interest him either.[43] He believed in khaddar as an economic doctrine, but not as an offshoot of religion.

In a modern India, Jawaharlal Nehru envisaged inter-caste and inter-community marriages taking place on the basis of common sense and upon the widest intermingling of the social classes. Therefore, he welcomed a 'wide breach of custom' when his sister Krishna married Gunottam 'Raja' Hutheesing, a non-Brahmin. He took a shot at the 'petit-bourgeois vices' of the Kashmiri community to emphasize that he was not particularly interested in a person being a Brahmin or a non-Brahmin or anything else.[44] For overriding caste allegiance, Halide Edib, the Turkish author visiting India, complimented the Nehrus on their broad-minded outlook, a compliment from a very remarkable woman, whose secularity and revolutionary credentials acquired legendary proportions in Turkey and India.[45]

The Nehrus saw the high and low points in their struggles: Krishna Hutheesing describes the train journey (with mother and Kamala) to the Ahmedabad Congress in 1921 when she marvelled at the great love the masses showered on them.[46] At other times, the golden glow faded into the light of common day. Yet the Nehrus hardly ever compromised on the essentials of their beliefs and convictions. They believed in reiterating the old Indian outlook on religion and life, which was always one of tolerance, experiment, and change,[47] and reminded the people of an Asokan edict: 'All sects observe reverence for one reason or another. By thus acting a man exalts his own sect and at the same time does service to the sects of other people.'[48] With a very few exceptions, the Nehrus harmonized their religious beliefs with a strong commitment to north India's (Ganga–Jumna) composite values. The world from which they came was completely shaped by the creative interplay between the worlds of Hinduism and Islam.[49]

Neither man nor nation, Fyodor Dostoyevsky (1821–1881) had written, can exist without a sublime idea. He was right. Injected freely into the flow of history were Jawaharlal Nehru's ideas. Inherently the most rational and constructive possibility in a profoundly troubled world, they reflect Nehru's commitment to the nineteenth-century modernist traditions: the use of reason and science as the means to profess towards a perfectible world. He not only underlined the importance of patriotism and nationalism, but stood like a rock in a stormy sea in the midst of the mad whirlpool of violence and decay. While harnessing his studies to his politics, he prepared his countrymen for the momentous changes in the offing. 'Your whole education, your upbringing, and the makeup of your mind cannot permit you to think in terms of caste, creed, or colour', Sapru reminded him a year before Independence.[50] This flattering remark came from a person who himself epitomized, both in his private and public persona, north India's composite culture.

Jawaharlal Nehru talked of growing up in North India with its complex cultural life and was never tired of admiring the different castes and communities living together in peace.'When kings quarrelled and destroyed each other, silent forces in India worked ceaselessly for a synthesis, in order that people might live harmoniously together and devote their energies jointly to progress and betterment.' Hindus and Muslims lived with each other in peace in tens and thousands of towns and villages, and there was no communal trouble between them. New styles of architecture were introduced. Music developed with Amir Khusrow and Tansen, the court musicians in the court of Mughal emperor Akbar. Reformers like Ramananda, Kabir, and Nanak laid stress on the common features in religion and attacked rites and ceremonials. The Urdu language originated and flourished in India. These bear ample testimony to the fact that synthesis and composite living were integral aspects of Indian society for many hundreds of years.[51]

B.K. Nehru (Bijju) was born in Anand Bhawan. He recalls that his mother, Rameshwari, was educated at home. A maulvi taught her Persian, a pandit Hindi, and an Indian Christian governess, English. The children lived in the western wing of Anand Bhawan. They did not recall hearing discussions among the grown-ups about religion or religious duties. Bijju was not taught to say any daily prayers or perform any acts of worship, and there were no caste rules about inter-dining. 'The environment at Anand Bhawan', he writes, 'was one of rationalism and agnosticism.'[52]

Nayantara saw it all: a tradition of serene and symmetrical archi-tecture, an elegant school of dance, Hindi and Urdu prose and poetry, and accomplished excellent cuisine.[53] Cultural identification affected political outlook and vice versa. Krishna went to the nearby Anglican Church of the Holy Trinity with Miss Hopper on Sundays. Long before, in July 1940, Sapru had reminded the young Kashmiri Pandits in Srinagar that their forefathers and compatriots in other parts of India owed a great deal to a composite culture. Summing up this story of cultural fusion, he stated that the Kashmiri Pandits carried with them their keen intellect, their remarkable sense of adaptability, and their character into a larger and competitive world, and so long as Persian was the official language at the courts of Delhi and Lucknow, the Kashmiri Pandits shared with the kayasthas some of the highest offices in Mughal times. As a matter of fact, their lives came to be char-acterized by a certain discontinuity between their public and private worlds. 'Elements of the Mughal culture which they absorbed became part of their private environment as that culture became associated exclusively with Muslims and the price of public commitment to it by Hindus [became] higher.'[54]

These words are not less relevant in our own times in India. For what they point to is a vibrant cultural inheritance that is under criti-cal scrutiny. One would be a considerable optimist to answer in the affirmative that the cultural inheritance Nayantara and Sapru speak of can actually be recovered in our times.

Like his father, Jawaharlal Nehru did not submit to irrational authority, be it religion or any dogma. He was, for this reason, angry with Gandhi for invoking religion and religious symbols in his mobi-lization campaign. At the same time, he was more austerely religious than the majority of those who declared or believed themselves to be so, and accepted, more out of convenience rather than conviction, a few social and religious customs. Thus, he happily took part in the marriage ceremony—performing the seven rounds of the ceremonial fire that the bride and groom make. He did not believe in the chanted prayers and the sacred fire, but recognized the sanctity of marriage and family, and the value of traditional Indian culture and customs. He took part in his father's *shraddh* (funeral) ceremony as a mark of respect for his mother's religious susceptibilities.

Jawaharlal Nehru once said that India's spirit was in the depth of his conscience while the mind of the West was in his head by virtue of his education in Harrow, Cambridge, and all over London.[55] He may have felt alien in his own society—'a Hindu out of tune with Hinduism'— but did not want old established traditions to be scrapped or dispensed with. He once said, 'A Brahman I was born, and a Brahman I seem to remain whatever I might say or do in regard to religion or social custom.'[56] Driven or dominated by the urge to see reason in thought and action, he explained his explicit disavowal of interest in religions:

> I am becoming more and more hostile to the religious idea. Exceptions apart, it seems to me the negation of real spirituality and only a begetter of confusion and sentimentality. I should like to keep myself away, as far as possible, from all religious rites and ceremonials, all the hallmarks of religion—indeed to be wholly non-religious. Regard for mother and a desire not to hurt her feelings at this time of life, occasionally make me agree to participation in some ceremony. But even so it is an unwilling and ungracious participation and I am not sure if it is not better to do without it.[57]

Jawaharlal Nehru's travels and readings of European writers brought with them a whiff of the unorthodox. He found in them an exhilarating confirmation of his inner beliefs. Marxism lightened up many a dark corner of his mind; its essential freedom from dogma and the scientific outlook appealed to him. Moreover, the great world crisis and slump seemed to vindicate Marxist theories.[58] This was the time the Communist Party of India (CPI) became favourably disposed towards the Congress, exhorted the people to join it, and entered its local executives. A few communists were elected to the All India Congress Committee (AICC) chiefly because of the system of voting by means of proportional representation (single transferable vote), which enabled small minority groups to be represented.

In the world of art and literature, Jawaharlal Nehru's sympathies were similar to those of Ernst Toller, who had told his fellow German citizens that the artist was responsible for cultural values, and that it was his duty to arouse the spontaneous feeling for humanity, liberty, justice, and beauty, and to deepen it.[59]

Science and the secularization of Europe hardened Jawaharlal Nehru's sceptical dissent, and he began to see religion less as an alternative to the attractions of a modern life. In June 1926, he visited the Duomo (Cathedral) in Milan, which was a delightful experience. He went there repeatedly and attended service on Sunday too. In 1939, however, his host arranged a dinner at the Kathinesan temple in Colombo. Jawaharlal Nehru yelled: 'What? Temple! Why?'" He was then told that he was being taken to the hall attached to the temple.[60] Back home, however, he tried 'to conjure Bharat Mata as the body politic, composed of the bodies of millions of Indians, as an image that can convince and carry both himself as the speaker and the crowds that he addresses into a future of independent nationhood.'[61] For the benefit of his daughter, he translated a verse from the Bhagwad Gita: 'I desire not the supreme state of bliss with its eight perfections, nor the cessation of re-birth. May I take up the sorrow of all creatures who suffer and enter into them so that they may be made free from grief.'[62]

Jawaharlal Nehru criticized fellow Indians for their desire to look back and not forward, for their nostalgia for the past, and for obeying anyone who chose to order them about instead of getting to move on. But he was himself prone to celebrate the past and allowed his pen to run on the glories of ancient India. Once he received a picture of a famous old statue of Buddha at Anuradhapura in Sri

Lanka. He kept it on the table; it soothed him, gave him strength, and helped him overcome depression. While Buddhism or any other dogma did not interest him as such, he found Buddha to be an attractive figure and considered Asoka to be the paradigmatic ruler. For him, the Buddhist period was a veritable golden age, marked by a unique internationalism, tolerance, compassion, and a vigorous openness to outside influences and ideas. It is to Asoka that he constantly harks back, be it regarding the adoption of the chakra in the national flag or *Panch Shila* (five principles of Buddhist politics). The chakra or the wheel symbolized India's ancient culture and all that the country had stood for through the ages.[63] 'It is moving to think of this agnostic', writes one of Jawaharlal's many biographers, 'gaining strength to endure his loneliness through contemplation of the Buddha's serenity.'[64] To Nehru's disappointment, however, the divisive ideology of communalism replaced religious toleration and freedom of conscience, the marked features of old Indian life. He characterized the All India Hindu Mahasabha as 'communal, anti-national and reactionary'. 'It not only hides the rankest and narrowest nationalism but also desires to preserve the vested interests of the group of big Hindu landlords and princes.... The policy of the Mahasabha is a betrayal of the freedom struggle.'[65] He did not spare his own Congress colleagues who, he thought, masqueraded as 'nationalists'. Paradoxically, the national movement accommodated them and gave them a voice in arriving at major political decisions. Jawaharlal Nehru had a taste of what it meant to be communal from his father's experience in Allahabad in the course of an election campaign.

> It was simply beyond me to meet the kind of propaganda started against me under the auspices of the Malviya–Lala [Lajpat Rai] gang. Publicly I was denounced as an anti-Hindu and pro-Mohammadan but privately almost every individual voter was told that I was a beef-eater in league with the Mohammadans to legalise cow-slaughter in public places at all times.... Communal hatred was the order of the day.... In the present state of communal tension my voice will be a cry in the wilderness.[66]

Like John Maynard Keynes, the English economist, Jawaharlal Nehru was 'as aware of the faults of his fellow citizens as he was of their virtues; but he always attempted to devise policies and to design institutions which would enable them, if they so wished, to be able to live better, while at the same time fitting his and their society into an international order in which there could be desirable outcomes for all'.[67]

Notes

1.   George Bernard Shaw, *Major Barbara*, in *The works of Bernard Shaw*, vol. 11 (London: Constable, 1938), p. 349.

2.   9 May 1907, *SWMN*, vol. 1, p. 124.

3.   David Page, *Prelude to Partition*, in *The Partition Omnibus* (Delhi: Oxford University Press, 2002), p. 84.

4.   B.K. Nehru, *Nice Guys Finish Second*, p. 55.

5.   M. Nehru to J. Nehru, 23 December 1910, B.K. Nehru, *Nice Guys Finish Second*, p. 156.

6.   J. Nehru, *An Autobiography*, pp. 121–3.

7.   Page, *Prelude to Partition*, pp. 128, 135.

8.   J. Nehru, *An Autobiography*, p. 158; Page, *Prelude to Partition*, pp. 121–2.

9.   Mishra, *Living an Era*, pp. 92–3.

10.   Page, *Prelude to Partition*, p. 121.

11.   J. Nehru, *An Autobiography*, p. 158.

12.   J. Nehru, *An Autobiography*, p. 157. However, Nehru paid warm tribute to Madan Mohan Malaviya in his *Glimpses of World History*, p. 440.

13.   Bayly, *Origins of Nationality*, p. 17.

14.   Page, *Prelude to Partition*, pp. 82–4.

15.   M. Nehru to J. Nehru, 10 March 1911, *SWMN*, vol. 1, p. 159.

16.   M. Nehru to J. Nehru, 2 December 1926, Jawaharlal Nehru, ed., *A Bunch of Old Letters*, centenary edition (Delhi: Oxford University Press, 1989), p. 52.

17.   Mishra, *Living an Era*, p. 94.

18.   1926, file no. 13/1, AICC Papers.

19.   According to traditional Hindu lore, Ram Rajya began when Lord Ram became the King of Ayodhya upon his return from his fourteen-year exile. To M.K. Gandhi, Ram Rajya meant principled rule or ideal governance.

20.   Andrews, *A Lamp for India*, p. 25.

21.   V.S. Srinivasan to D.V. Gundappa, 15 December 1930, *Letters of V.S. Srinivasa Sastri*, edited by Jagadisan (Asia Publishing House: 1963), p. 203.

22.   M. Nehru to J. Nehru, 21 February 1907, *SWMN*, vol. 1, p. 120.

23.   M. Nehru to J. Nehru, 21 February 1907, *SWMN*, vol. 1, p. 121.

24.   *Congress Presidential Addresses, 1911–1914*, New Series (Indian National Congress), p. 864.

25.   Katju, *Days I Remember*, p. 11.

26.   M. Nehru to Prithi Nath Chak, 22 December 1999, *SWMN*, vol. 1, p. 53.

27.   Bomford, the district magistrate, charged him under Section 17 (1) of the Criminal Law Amendment Act and also under Section 117, IPC.

28.   Jawaharlal Nehru thought well of him, entrusted him with family and other errands, and commended his dynamism in running the *National Herald*. After Independence, the voters of Pratapgarh and Rae Bareli elected him to the first Lok Sabha. He died prematurely on 8 September 1957. By this time, he had separated from his wife, who played in Jawaharlal Nehru's life the role that Kamala had played with such endurance and dignity.

29.   Seton, *Panditji*, p. 103.

30.   Seton, *Panditji*, p. 27.

31.   For the text of the testament, see Zakaria, *A Study of Nehru*, pp. 612–13.

32.   Zakaria, *A Study of Nehru*, pp. 612–13.

33.   He added that 'the days of that faith are gone, and gone with them is that magic touch in stone. Thousands of temples and mosques and cathedrals continue to be built, but they lack the spirit that made them live during the middle ages'. (J. Nehru, *Glimpses of World History*, p. 952.)

34.   J. Nehru, *Glimpses of World History*, p. 951.

35.   J. Nehru, *Glimpses of World History*, p. 374.

36.   J. Nehru, *An Autobiography*, p. 118.

37.   Halide Edib, *Inside India*, with an introduction and notes by Mushirul Hasan (New Delhi: Oxford University Press, 2002), p. 204.

38.   J. Nehru, *Glimpses of World History*, p. 951.

39.   J. Nehru, *An Autobiography*, pp. 140–1.

40.   13 September 1927, *SWJN*, vol. 2, p. 361.

41.   J. Nehru to Nayantara Sahgal, 24 November 1942, *SWJN*, vol. 13, p. 33.

42.   J. Nehru to M. Nehru, 17 August 1922, *SWJN*, vol. 1, p. 330.

43.   J. Nehru, *An Autobiography*, p. 72.

44.   Pranay Gupte, *Mother India: A Political Biography of Indira Gandhi* (New York: Charles Scribner's Sons, 1992), p. 193.

45.   Edib, *Inside India*, p. 203.

46.   Hutheesing, *With No Regrets*, p. 27.

47.   J. Nehru, *Glimpses of World History*, p. 112.

48.   J. Nehru, *Glimpses of World History*, p. 65.

49.   Ravinder Kumar, 'Jawaharlal Nehru and Contemporary India', in *Nehru Revisited*, edited by M.V. Kamath (Mumbai: Nehru Centre 2003), p. 6.

50.   Henriette M. Sender, *The Kashmiri Pandits: A Study of Cultural Choice in North India* (Delhi: Oxford University Press, 1988), p. 264.

51.   J. Nehru, *Glimpses of World History*, p. 263.

52.   B.K. Nehru, *Nice Guys Finish Second*, p. 26.

53.   N. Sahgal, *From Fear Set Free*, p. 31.

54.   Sender, *The Kashmiri Pandits*, p. 275.

55.   Mohamed H. Heikal, 'A Dialogue with Jawaharlal Nehru', file no. 1097, misc., AICC papers.

56.   Brecher, *Nehru: A Political Biography*, p. 94.

57.   J. Nehru to M.K. Gandhi, 25, July 1933, *SWJN*, vol. 5, p. 491.

58.   J. Nehru, *An Autobiography*, pp. 363, 364.

59.   14 December 1936, Joachim Oesterheld, ed., *Jawaharlal Nehru, Ernst Toller: Documents of a Friendship 1927–1939*, translated by Susanne Thurm (Leipzig: Mittledeutscher Verlag Halle, 1989), p. 128.

60.   Hiral M. Desai papers, Acc 1329, NMML.

61.   Ananya Vajpeyi, *Righteous Republic: The Political Foundations of Modern India* (Cambridge: Harvard University Press, 2012), p. 179.

62.   J. Nehru, *Glimpses of World History*, p. 37.

63.   J. Nehru, *Glimpses of World History*, p. 190.

64.   Beatrice Pitney Lamb, *The Nehrus of India: Three Generations of Leadership* (New York: Macmillian Company, 1967), p. 113.

65.   J. Nehru, *An Autobiography*, p. 276.

66.   M. Nehru to J. Nehru, 2 December 1926, J. Nehru, *A Bunch of Old Letters*, pp. 51–2.

67.   Geoffrey Harcourt, 'John Maynard Keynes', in *Cambridge Minds* by Richard Mason (Cambridge: Cambridge University Press, 1994), p. 72.

5   'And Never the Twain Shall Meet'[*]

Immediately after landing at the Gateway of India on 17 November 1921, the Prince of Wales drove through the business and administrative centres of Bombay to the Governor's residence. Almost that very moment Gandhi stood up to address more than 60,000 people in an open space adjacent to the Elphinstone Mills at Dadar. But an otherwise spectacular mobilization ran into trouble even before the day drew to a close. Non-cooperating nationalist 'Hindus' and 'Muslims' faced loyalist 'Parsis' and 'Anglo-Indian' communities whose visible sartorial affluence identified them as a class apart. In retaliation to the physical assault on them, armed groups of middle-class Parsis patrolled their neighbourhood and, with shouts of *Gandhi topiwallah ko pakro* (catch the Gandhi cap wearers) and *maro salah ko* (beat them up), they exacted physical retribution on individual Hindus and Muslims whom they identified as non-cooperators.[1] The spark was a 'communal address of welcome' offered to the Prince of Wales; many

Parsis spoke out against this, and worked very closely with Gandhi in the months beforehand, but Gandhi's address and the Parsis' presence at the welcoming ceremony at Apollo Bandar damaged inter-community relations.[2]

'Action is the end of thought', said Romain Rolland, Gandhi's biographer.[3] True to the French scholar's advice, the boycott of the Prince of Wales in Allahabad was more complete than in any other Indian city. The agitation spilled over to the university campus. More and more people wore homespun and 'Gandhi topis'; some students gave up their studies, some lawyers their practice, and some government servants their jobs. They echoed whatever Gandhi said; then news of miracles spread—Gandhi was seen speaking simultaneously in several places or cotton had been found growing on neem trees, and the public believed such rumours.[4] Nayantara writes:

> When the speaker was Mamu, the speech would start on a reflective note but soon flash fire, sending a thrill through its audience. If Gandhiji was the leader of the struggle, Mamu personified its romance, its spirit of high adventure, its appeal to the patriotic young. In Allahabad the student body had a special claim on him. Living as he did just down the road from the university.[5]

Between December 1921 and January 1922, an estimated 30,000 were imprisoned for non-cooperation. Those were brave days, the memory of which endured and became a cherished possession for all the political actors. They did not fear death. Of the many messages Jawaharlal Nehru sent from prison to Congress workers, the one sent to fellow Indians on 8 December 1921 stated:

> Friends, I go to jail with the greatest pleasure, and with the fullest conviction that therein lies the achievement of our goal. Forget not that there is a complete hartal on the 12th instant, and that it is the duty of every man to enrol himself as a volunteer. The most important thing is to preserve complete peace and an atmosphere of non-violence. In your hands is the honour of Allahabad, and I hope it is quite safe therein.

I trust you will always be in the firing line in the battle of Swaraj and make the name of our city immortal.[6]

In his *Autobiography*, Jawaharlal Nehru traced the deep gulf that divided the British and the Indians, their mutual distrust and dislike. 'The Indians', he wrote, 'saw the Englishman function only as an official with all the inhumanity of the machine and with all the passion of a vested interest preserving itself.' In his trial on 17 May 1922, he had moved from the general to the specific:

I have said many hard things about the British Government. For one thing however I must offer it my grateful thanks. It has given us a chance of fighting in this most glorious of struggles. Surely few people have had such an opportunity given them. And the greater our suffer-ing, the more difficult the test we have to pass, the more splendid will be the future of India. India has not survived through thousands of years to go down now. India has not sent twenty-five thousand of her noblest and best sons to the jails to give up the struggle. India's future is assured. Some of us, men and women of little faith, doubt and hesitate occasionally. But those who have vision can almost see the glory that is to be India.

I marvel at my good fortune. To serve India in the battle of freedom is honour enough. To serve her under a leader like Mahatma Gandhi is doubly fortunate. But to suffer for the dear country; what greater good fortune could befall an Indian unless it be death for the cause or the full realization of our glorious dream.[7]

Motilal Nehru was a happy man. He told his son, 'On reading your statement I felt I was the proudest father in the world.'[8]

The people's enthusiasm remained unabated in 1930–1. Writing on mobilization in the United Provinces, the historian Gyanendra Pandey linked the various castes, classes, and individuals to a political ideology—nationalism—which symbolized for all of them the chance of a better future.[9] District after district applied to the high command for permission to start civil disobedience. Volunteers enrolled themselves to break the salt laws. The non-political prisoners looked upon the coming political prisoners as messiahs and as their 'natural allies' in their fight for prison reforms. Every time political prisoners entered the prison, they raised slogans and in return they were greeted with slogans from inside the prison.[10] As Jawaharlal Nehru sat with pen and paper in barrack no. 6 of Naini Prison, he remembered 26 January, the day of celebrating Independence Day. It was a year of struggle and suffering and triumph.

The Congress paid particular attention to Rae Bareli in the United Provinces, where it encouraged the non-payment of enhanced rents. The intelligence report warned of Jawaharlal Nehru's visit to Gujranwala on 6–7 April and the prospect of jathas meeting him.[11] The 'brutal sentences' passed on Bhagat Singh and the other accused in the Lahore Conspiracy Case heightened patriotic sentiments. Motilal Nehru chaired meetings at which appreciative references were made to the deep sense of patriotism which prompted these men to commit acts of violence.[12]

The government banned the associations under the Criminal Law Amendment, made newspapers furnish security under the Press Ordinance, and convicted thousands of activists. Volunteers of Hindustani Seva Dal and Desh Sevika Sangh were arrested for carrying Congress flags to the Esplanade Maidan. Jawaharlal Nehru's trial took place in Naini Prison, where so many of our 'near and dears spent years as guests of George V and VI'.[13] Known as a *bhangi* jail (the Bhangi are a Scheduled Caste in India, segregated on the basis of their occupation of sweeping and cleaning), the prisoners were tortured so much that they agreed to cast aside all the inhibitions of the caste system and become cleaners of the latrines.[14] Jawaharlal Nehru was sentenced to two years' rigorous imprisonment. In his absence, the women in the Nehru household were emotionally involved in the no-rent campaign, took part in hartals and processions.

Swarup Rani was profoundly stirred by the political events around her and immersed herself in them. Observing the National Week from

April 6 to 13 to commemorate Jallianwala Bagh and the other massacres, she was lathi-charged and hurt. When the police came to Anand Bhawan, she gave an interview to a journalist in which she rejoiced in the great privilege of sending her dear husband and only son to jail.[15] Having suffered because of her son's long absences in prison, she endured not only this agony but the physical pain of a police lathi charge. Sarojini Naidu writes, 'She who was carefully cherished and jealously guarded like a jewel in an ivory casket throughout her fragile youth and middle-years, transformed herself in her frail old age into a gem-like flame of inspiration to guide those whose feet were set irrevocably on the steep and perilous paths of freedom.'[16]

When the police arrested Vijaya Lakshmi Pandit, Chandralekha broke the silence. 'Don't worry, Mummie. I'll look after the girls. Bye Mummie darling! We shall keep the flag flying!' She added, 'Any way, we'll show the blinking British government that we can be happy in jail as anywhere else, can't we?'[17]

Krishna Nehru gave up her job at a Montessori school, volunteered to picket foreign cloth shops, organized processions, and did such other as work allotted to her. Once, she put on military uniform and picketed the cloth dealers in Allahabad. An old man with a long beard came up to her and mistaking her to be a son of Motilal Nehru, addressed her: 'Sahibzada! It does not behove Motilal's son to move about in the hot sun like a street boy.'[18]

Krishna and Shyama Kumari Nehru (daughter of Shamlal Nehru, a first cousin of Jawaharlal Nehru) were sent to Lucknow's Central Prison on an icy winter morning, and made to sleep on the floor. She recounted: 'It was one thing to be a cheerful martyr in the high excitement of being arrested for love of our country, and quite another to spend night after night in a filthy cell full of insects crawling about the grim walls.'[19]

Frequent controversies erupted between Jawaharlal Nehru's first and second imprisonment.[20] What, he thought, were the beneficent achievements of the Non-Cooperation Movement? What were its unfulfilled aspirations? These questions gave rise to differing views. He resented the fact that some of his colleagues basked in the sunshine of official favours, though he was not at all surprised that the Knights or Companions of the Order of British Empire (CIEs) and Rai Bahadurs kowtowed before and worshipped at the feet of their masters from across the seas. His interest was in institutions, and not individuals. For this reason, he tried to broker peace between rival Congress factions to ensure that they did not work against the established authority or engage in cloak-and-dagger work of outright subversion, but this turned out to be a damp squib in a year of strife, dispute, and mutual recrimination. This brings to mind Rousseau's first sentence in *Emile*: 'God makes all things good; man meddles with them and they become evil.'[21]

Jawaharlal Nehru's faults and failures were a talking point then and later, but that did not alter the fact that Gandhi's mentoring and his own skills established his fame as a statesman. Those who shared his great dream for the future of their country, and there were many who did so, saw a new man of some resolution and resource, tenaciously attached to the legacy of Dadabhai Naoroji and Gopal Krishna Gokhale. He gathered up the aesthetic and emotional sensibilities of the age, used language with dignity and enthusiasm, and drew upon a fund of resounding phrases which owed to both feeling and reason. A British intelligence officer in 1928 recorded:

> Jawaharlal Nehru is an energetic and capable leader, whose influence among subversive elements in this country has rapidly increased. His association with professional agitation in Europe, and the persistent propaganda conducted by him on behalf of the League against Imperialism, render him potentially dangerous. Though still a young man, he has already an unenviable record in Indian revolutionary affairs, and there is at present no reason to believe that his political conduct will be any the less disreputable.[22]

A year earlier, Jawaharlal Nehru had returned to India and reached Madras in time for the Congress session in December 1927 in which M.A. Ansari presided. Here the delegates jostled to secure a vantage point in the pandal. Tempers frayed between those who made dominion status the pivot of the settlement and those demanding complete independence. Gandhi suspected that the left, led by Subhash Chandra Bose, whom he regarded as his bête noire, had conspired against him and the Congress Working Committee. He even censured Jawaharlal Nehru for encouraging 'mischief-makers' and 'hooligans' to carry through the independence resolution.[23] The fact is that the younger Nehru reinforced the antagonisms created by the Western political and cultural domination; hence, he insisted on achieving complete independence as an instrument to achieve social and economic justice for fifty lakh beggars and five crore agriculturists sitting idle for a portion of the year, sufficient to break the back of any country.[24] According to an eyewitness: 'On the bitterly cold morning of 1 January 1930, under the deep blue Indian sky, tens of thousands of people gathered on the banks the Ravi River, while Bhai [Jawaharlal Nehru] solemnly read to them our Declaration of Independence of 1776, with a definite Gandhi–Nehru twist.'[25]

It was too serious a matter to be taken lightly;[26] yet, Gandhi did not go against Jawaharlal Nehru, but clarified, 'My point is not that you have not thought out any of your resolutions, much less the Independence one, but my point is that neither you nor anyone else had thought [through] the whole situation and considered the bearing and propriety of the resolutions.'[27] Pushed hither and thither, Nehru's compromise enabled the Congress to accept dominion status if the government extended a definite offer within a year. Without this, he left open the option of a non-violent civil disobedience. He threatened to resign, but Gandhi assured him that the ideal of independence did not conflict with greater freedom.[28] He had an abiding faith in Jawaharlal Nehru's 'incorruptible sincerity and passion for liberty'.[29]

Jawaharlal Nehru's robust energy and commitments kept him going. After visiting Russia in 1927, he saw the first proletarian revolution, the first regime in history to set about the construction of the socialist order, the proof both of the profundity of the contradictions of capitalism, and of the possibility—the certainty—that a socialist revolution would succeed. With this first-hand experience, he returned home with the conviction that modern industrial techniques rather than hand-spinning and hand-weaving would solve India's poverty and rural backwardness.

India, he said, would have to adopt a full socialistic programme if it was to end poverty and inequality. This was easier said than done. His initiatives were, as it turned out after Independence, half-hearted. The bureaucracy suffered from inertia, corruption was rampant, and the top echelons of the Congress leadership were not sufficiently committed to changes and innovation. Rajendra Prasad, a tall figure in the Congress Working Committee, 'had as little understanding of socialism as faith in it'.[30] The socialists' ways gave him anxiety. Convinced that they had set out to undo all that the Mahatma had done, he and his right-wing colleagues were willing to carry on with Jawaharlal Nehru but not with his socialist friends.[31] To break away from him was unthinkable, wrote Rajendra Prasad. The older generation had great admiration for Jawaharlal's sincerity, integrity, capability, profound thinking, and sacrifices in the country's cause.[32]

Standing at the crossroads of history, Jawaharlal Nehru thought of his chequered life, the many a summer and winter India, the land of adventure, and the long journey ahead of him. The brave gallant adventure beckoned and the flag called him. He would dream and think of friends and of all the fine things in the country. 'To act history', he said to Indira, 'is far more exciting than to write it or read it.'[33]

Notes

*   From Rudyard Kipling's the 'Ballad of East and West', first published in 1889.

1.   Sandip Hazareesingh, *The Colonial City: Urban Hegemonies and Civic Contestations in Bombay (1900–1925)* (Bombay: Orient Longman, 2008), pp. 160–2; A.D.D. Gordon, *Businessmen and Politics: Rising Nationalism and a Modernizing Economy in Bombay 1918–1933* (Delhi: Manohar, 1978),

pp. 49–50; Ravinder Kumar, *Essays in Social History* (Delhi: Oxford University Press, 1983), pp. 258–60.

2. See Richard Newman, *Workers and Unions in Bombay 1918–1929: A Study of Organization in the Cotton Mills* (Canberra: Australian National University, 1981), p. 99, for a different interpretation of the cause of the riot.

3. J. Nehru, *Glimpses of World History*, p. 953.

4. Harivansh Rai Bachchan, *In the Afternoon of Time* (New Delhi: Penguin Books, 1998), pp. 91–2; Gupta, *They Lived Dangerously*, p. 53.

5. N. Sahgal, *From Fear Set Free*, p. 70.

6. Sarvepalli Gopal and Uma Iyengar, eds, *The Essential Writings of Jawaharlal Nehru*, vol. 1 (Delhi: Oxford University Press, 2003), p. 212.

7. Sarvepalli Gopal, ed., *Jawaharlal Nehru: An Anthology* (New Delhi: Oxford University Press, 1980), p. 125.

8. M. Nehru to J. Nehru, 24 May 1922, Gopal, *Jawaharlal Nehru: A Biography*, vol. 1, p. 67.

9. Gynanendra Pandey, 'Mobilization in a Mass Movement: Congress "Propaganda" in the United Provinces (India), 1930–34', *Modern Asian Studies* 9, no. 2 (1975): 205–26, 225.

10. Gupta, *They Lived Dangerously*, pp. 32, 38.

11. UP, fortnightly report for the second half of March 1930, Home Department, Political, file no. 18/I, 1930.

12. G.F.S. Collins to W.W. Emerson, 16/19 October 1930, fortnightly report for the month of October 1930, Home Department, Political, file no. 17/xi, 1930.

13. Mehta, *Freedom's Child*, p. 4.

14. Gupta, *They Lived Dangerously*, p. 238.

15. Nanda, *The Nehrus*, p. 196.

16. Naidu, 'Foreword', in Hutheesing, *With No Regrets*, p. vii.

17. Mehta, *Freedom's Child*, p. 138.

18. Mahmud, 'In and Out of Prison', p. 178.

19. Hutheesing, *We Nehrus*, p. 103.

20. There was much mutual acrimony among those urging a reversal of Gandhi's ban against council entry. With the 'no-changers' turning down the vigorous plea for council entry, the Swaraj Party, formed on 1 January 1923, finally turned the tide in its favour in September 1923 when the Congress allowed them to breach the bureaucratic citadel from inside and outside

the legislative councils. The period of Jawaharlal's imprisonment was from 6 December 1921 to 3 March 1922; the second lasted from 11 May 1922 to 31 January 1923.

21.   Jean-Jacques Rousseau, *Emile*, available at https://books.google.co.in/books?id=yWadCgAAQBAJ&pg=PT7&dq=Emile+runs:+%E2%80%98God+makes+all+things+good;+man+meddles+with+them+and+they+become+evil.&hl=en&sa=X&ved=0ahUKEwjY87KCssfLAhWHPQ8KHSOiDJIQ6AEIMjAE#v=onepage&q=Emile%20runs%3A%20%E2%80%98God%20makes%20all%20things%20good%3B%20man%20meddles%20with%20them%20and%20they%20become%20evil.&f=false.

22.   Note by O. Cleary, L/P & J/12/292, India Office Records, British Library.

23.   Bapu to J. Nehru, 4 January 1928, J. Nehru, *Bunch of Old Letters*, p. 59.

24.   *SWJN*, vol. 3, p. 245.

25.   Hutheesing, *We Nehrus*, p. 82.

26.   M.K. Gandhi to J. Nehru, 17 January 1928, J. Nehru, *Bunch of Old Letters*, p. 61.

27.   M.K. Gandhi to J. Nehru, 11 January 1928, *Together They Fought: Gandhi–Jawaharlal Correspondence, 1921–1948*, edited by Uma Iyenger and Lalitha Zackariah (New Delhi: Oxford University Press, 2011), p. 53.

28.   M.K. Gandhi to J. Nehru, 8 November 1929, *The Collected Works of Mahatma Gandhi* (CWMG), vol. 42, p. 116. Iyenger and Zackariah, *Together They Fought*, 4 November 1929; J. Nehru, *Bunch of Old Letters*, p. 76.

29.   Sarojini Naidu to J. Nehru, 29 September 1929, J. Nehru, *Bunch of Old Letters*, p. 75.

30.   Prasad, *Autobiography*, p. 417.

31.   Prasad, *Autobiography*, p. 420.

32.   Prasad, *Autobiography*, p. 420.

33.   J. Nehru to Kamala Nehru, 23 July 1930; J. Nehru to Padmaja Naidu, 22 October 1930, *SWJN*, vol. 12, pp. 653, 658.

6 'Being Guarded Like a Jewel in a Casket'

Prisoners were restless souls, the creatures of moods and senses. They chafed and fretted at their surroundings, felt helpless at the many pinpricks of captivity before settling down in a resigned mood to take things as they came their way.[1] They lived up to the ideals of self-rule that were constantly on their lips, assuming that their sufferings would possibly bring relief from the chronicle of defeat, indifference, and dishonour.[2] They performed in the arena of life another chapter in the history of justice and good deeds. Maulana Abul Kalam Azad smiled when M.D. Swinner sentenced him to rigorous imprisonment on 9 February 1922, and said, 'It is much less than what I had expected.' His wife complained of the 'mild' punishment awarded to her husband.[3] Jail became the gateway to freedom for both of them.

Jawaharlal Nehru lived the most vivid part of his existence quite apart from his family, while the part of his life spent in the company of friends was in jail. In other words, from the age of thirty-two to fifty-six, he spent the best part of life behind iron doors. While truth, mercy, and love stopped at the gate, the silver lining was that the authorities could not keep God and His nature out of jail.[4] Prisoners lived, as Auguste Comte had said, dead men's lives encased in their pasts, and they found some sustenance for the starved and locked-up emotions in memories of the past or fancies of the future.[5] Otherwise, prison was the true home of that dreadful thing ennui, and yet, oddly enough, it taught some brave men and women to triumph over it. With *Inqilab zindabad, Inqilab zindabad* (Long live revolution) resounding, they felt that India was on the threshold of a revolution. Ali Sardar Jafri echoed this sentiment in one of his eloquent poems:

> Resistance grows
> Alongside oppression
> Even cruelty cries
> At the deeds of the cruel
> But they never speak a word;
> Their heads are never bowed.
> Instead of sighs,
> Their lips resound with
> Long live revolution.[6]

Albie Sachs talked of the officers of the law as inhuman agents of retribution, who work on certain assumptions, one of which is that, by virtue of their positions, they were entitled to demand absolute submission from those in custody. He continues,

> All prisoners are evil and deserve to be punished, the assumptions proceed, and all prisoners must share responsibility for those who assault and kill policemen and those who escape from custody. Policemen are good by virtue of the fact that they are policemen while prisoners are wicked by virtue of the fact that they are prisoners.[7]

Much before Albie Sachs, Jawaharlal Nehru talked of the unbearable oppressive atmosphere: 'The very air of the [gaol] was full of violence and graft and untruth; there was either cringing or cursing.'[8] He linked prison with the colonial project of enforcing conformity on the convicts, some of whom became warders or overseers because of fear and in anticipation of reward and special remissions.[9] To an innocent reader, this was uncomplicated business. But it was not. Jawaharlal Nehru exclaimed indignantly that the object of all prisons was to remove such traces of humanity as a man might possess, and then to subdue even the animal element in him so that ultimately he might become the perfect vegetable! He added: 'Soil-bound, cut off from the world and its activity, nothing to look forward to, blind obedience the only "virtue" that is instilled, and spirit considered the great sin—is it any wonder that the prisoner approximates to the plant.'[10] Like Albie Sachs, he was stung by reports of the destruction of young lives and the humiliation of families and friends before brute force.[11] Again, like Albie Sachs, he became painfully aware of the entrenched race prejudices. Sounds came from beyond the walls, the screaming of orders, and the caning of youths. Wardens and jail superintendents shouted at prisoners. He felt sorry for those who were still in their narrow cells deprived of the sight of the sea and the land and the horizon. A beleaguered prisoner watched abjectly, felt bottled up and repressed, and, inevitably, took a one-sided and rather distorted view of happenings.[12] Albie Sachs had aptly remarked: 'The law never sleeps; just as women give birth to babies day and night with complete impartiality, so the police bring in prisoners throughout the twenty-four hours. The wheels of justice are in perpetual motion.'[13]

Jawaharlal Nehru was much more comfortably placed than any other political prisoner, but he made it a point not to seek or accept any obligation, concession, or favour at the hands of the tormentors.[14] As a matter of fact, he asked his father not to send him dainty articles of food, such as the Mau melons.[15] Moreover, he disapproved of the special facilities (in regard to diet) extended to the accused in the Meerut Conspiracy Case, with the exception of Messrs. Benjamin Bradley (1898–1957), a British communist, and Philip Spratt (1902–1971), also a British communist, jailed with a short break from 1929–34.[16] On the other hand, he set up a Civil Liberties Union with Tagore and Sarojini Naidu in the quietude of Santiniketan.[17] The Union condemned the deaths of J.M. Adhikari, brother of G.M. Adhikari of the Meerut Conspiracy Case, and Rajni Kanta Pramanick, a pleader.[18] Around this time, the country observed 'Political Prisoner's Day' demanding a stop be put to the government sending prisoners to the Andaman islands.

Until 6 June 1932, Jawaharlal Nehru was in Izatnagar Central Prison in Bareilly, which was surrounded by a wall twenty-four feet high, which cut off all sight and sound of the outside world, and a great deal of life-giving sunlight as well. When on that day he bade goodbye to his companions of the barrack where he had lived for four months, he took a last look at that very wall under whose sheltering care he had sat for so long. He was being transferred to a jail in Dehradun. The other jails he went to were as bad as the one in Dehradun. The small cell in Naini Jail had holes in the roof and a broken stone floor. Bedbugs, mosquitoes, flies, and hundreds of wasps surrounded its inmates. By then, Nehru had become accustomed to the language of the prison. 'It is the life of a vegetable', he wrote on New Year's Day in 1933, 'rooted to one place, growing there without comment or argument, silent, motionless.'[19] Sometimes he felt bored and fed up and angry with the jail staff, with people outside for something they had done or not done, with the British empire, and above all, with himself.[20] And sometimes he was bewildered by the activities of the outside world, which appeared distant, and unreal—a phantom show. 'So we develop two natures, the active and the passive, two ways of living, two personalities, like Dr. Jekyll and Mr. Hyde.'[21]

'All roads in India in these days sooner or later lead to one destination; all journeys, dream ones or real, end in prison', an aggrieved

Jawaharlal Nehru wrote on 16 February 1934,[22] serving his seventh prison term. Meanwhile Gandhi, having called off civil disobedience, laid stress on the removal of untouchability, propagation of hand-spinning, and progress towards Hindu–Muslim unity. 'Suddenly', writes a revolutionary, 'I felt that from my exalted position of a fighter for freedom I had been degraded into the position of an ordinary convict, who is not in jail of his own accord, but is kept in prison by force.'[23] Motilal Nehru was disappointed: 'Why should a town at the foot of the Himalayas be penalized, if a village at Cape Comorin failed to observe non-violence?'[24] Jawaharlal Nehru protested from prison, just as he had done after the Chauri Chaura incident in mid-February 1922. The protest was a cry in the wilderness; Gandhi was not one to retrace his steps. Jawaharlal Nehru knew this, and so he felt bitter and estranged from the man he revered. Heads wagged and tongue clacked, and yet the Gandhi–Nehru friendship was rock solid: Gandhi was a loved and cherished member and an irreplaceable solace to the Nehru family unit through its trials and tribulations as long as he lived.[25]

The War and the Quit India Call

In terms of non-violence, Quit India was a healthy, potent cry of the soul. It is not a slogan. It means the end, through means truthful and non-violent, of foreign rule and domination.[26]

Hitler invaded Poland on 1 September 1939, and two days later, Britain and France declared war on Germany. Within a few hours, the viceroy announced India's participation on the side of the allies. He did this without consulting the provincial governments or the people's representatives in the legislatures. In the dominions of Canada and Australia, on the other hand, prior consultations were held with the elected representatives. Jawaharlal Nehru declared on 21 March 1939: 'India will not submit to any form of exploitation to further Britain's war effort. But how can India fight for democracy if she herself does not have it?'[27]

The war declaration was followed by an amendment to the Act of 1935, which granted the viceroy the power to override its provisions for coordinating the activities of the central and provincial governments in prosecuting the war. He was also empowered to direct the provincial governments to exercise their executive authority, including the enactment of laws. And because such an amendment struck at the very root of responsible government and rendered provincial autonomy ineffective, the Congress asked its members not to attend the Central Assembly's next session.

Realizing the gravity of the situation arising out of Congress' intransigence, the viceroy and the secretary of state agreed to set up a consultative group of representatives of all political parties and of the Indian princes. The viceroy declared that dominion status was the goal of British policy, but the Congress Working Committee on 22–3 October 1939 described the proposals as an unequivocal reiteration of the old imperialist policy. It called upon the government to declare its war aims with regard to democracy and imperialism, and also to announce its aims vis-à-vis India. Importantly enough, the Congress demanded that India be freed from colonial bondage.

Now, the Congress could either resign or continue in power at the provincial level. After much debate and disagreement, the ministries resigned. Thereafter, in November 1939, the Congress High Command convened a Constituent Assembly to determine the country's democratic constitution. Meanwhile Jawaharlal Nehru continued his work with the National Planning Committee, though his arrest on 31 October 1940 stalled its activities. Put on trial on 3 November 1940 in the Gorakhpur Prison, he was sentenced to four years' imprisonment. Gandhi commended his loyalty and said that he prized it beyond measure.[28]

Jawaharlal Nehru passed most of this prison sentence back in Ahmadnagar Fort; he was 'repatriated' to the Bareilly Central Prison on 28 March 1945, where 'there is much more of the typical jail atmosphere, that peculiar, slow, stagnant and rather oppressive air which we have got to know so well. There are high walls closing on us and iron bars and gates, and the noises of the Cos and warders at night as they keep watch or count the prisoners in the different barracks.' He read books, did a good deal of spinning, and took regular exercise. Elsewhere, he cleaned and washed his cell, took to digging, played about with the fresh earth, watched the seedlings peep out from its surface, or watched the migratory flights from Mansarovar in Tibet, or the new generation of birds coming out of their nests.[29] He wrote:

Life grows harder for all of us and the soft days of the past already belong to an age that is gone. When will they return? No one knows. Or will they return? We must adapt ourselves to life as it is and hunger for what is not. Physical risk and suffering are often all petty compared to the troubles and tempests of the mind. And whether life is soft or hard, one can always get something out of it—but to enjoy life ultimately one must decide not to count the cost.[30]

A French saying goes that 'on the eve of the revolution, revolution seems the most probable thing', an idea Raghupati Sahay 'Firaq' (Firaq Gorakhpuri), the Urdu poet, expressed in a couplet:

'Mark the march of revolution, Firaq, How slow it seems, and yet how fast!'[31]

In mid-November, the campaign's second stage began with the arrest of the CWC, AICC members, and the Congress representatives in the central and provincial legislatures. The third stage opened in January 1941 was with a marked increase in the number of satyagrahis. This is because Gandhi lifted his struggle to a high moral plane, above the entanglements and local factions and priorities that had dogged the Congress party. There was an alternative force as well, that is, the communist parties, which were the characteristic and dominant forms of the revolutionary movement. While producing schisms and heresies of political importance, they also communicated their enthusiasm to the mill workers, the jute workers, and other sections of the working classes.

The 1942 campaign required aggression, defiance, daring, and challenge. Linlithgow, the viceroy in 1942, described it as 'by far the most serious rebellion since 1857, the gravity and extent of which we have concealed from the world for reasons of military security'.[32] The Communist League in Bengal, who opposed collaboration with the government in the war effort, advised peasants to withhold food from the forces, seamen to decline work except in coastal waters, and dockers not to handle war material.[33]

There is a tale, perhaps apocryphal yet poignant, that upon being released from prison, Jawaharlal Nehru went directly to a large meeting, stood up, and said quite unaffectedly, 'As I was saying....' He felt that the best of works became useless and even harmful the moment satyagrahis avoided jail.[34] And so he was in Ahmadnagar Fort Prison, 'rooted in the same spot, with the same few individuals to see, the same limited environment, the same routine from time to time'. Jawaharlal Nehru erred on this side than on the side of caution. In those stirring times, he sent for roses to mark the New Years' Eve, and went about humming 'Auld Lang Sine'. A fellow prisoner commented: 'What an Englishman he is at heart! And what a tragic irony that he should draw on himself the wrath of the British imperialists every now and again, and find himself immobilized at this crucial moment of history.'[35] In a lighter vein, he did not see women for exactly 785 days—not even from a distance. He began to wonder—what are women like? How do they look—how do they talk and sit and walk? He found answers only after he and the other prisoners were allowed interviews after nearly two and a quarter years.

As always, he fretted a little, thinking of 'the big things and brave ventures' that had filled his mind. But he continued to look at the world in the face with calm and clear eyes. Like Oscar Wilde, whose trial opened on 3 April 1895 at the Old Bailey, he had continued to live in his mind beyond the gaol, experiencing nature and life as if for the first time, rejoining in all he could see, smell, hear, taste, and touch.[36] For two years, seven months and eighteen days, he existed 'like some plant or vegetables rooted to the ground', before being uprooted, transferred, and transplanted in some other barren and stony soil.[37] Political prisoners had no idea of their destination till their arrival at the spot. Nor did they know where and when they were repatriated to the various provinces or detained. As G.B. Pant complained, 'Strict secrecy is observed in the matter of transfer of political prisoners, and where prominent leaders are concerned, all such proposals are guarded more jealously than intricate secrets.'[38]

Jawaharlal Nehru did not live in the expectation of release.[39] On the contrary, he accepted the tyrannies of prison life as a duty and obligation. Was it worthwhile? On a personal level, the days he was allowed interviews with loved ones were the red-letter days in jail. Jawaharlal Nehru waited for them, though he sometimes felt weary and lonely after the interview. The man from the Criminal Investigation Department (CID) at the interviews, with paper and pencil, dampened his enthusiasm. He gave up the interviews because of the treatment meted out to his mother and Kamala in the Allahabad gaol. He could, however, write to Bapuji, Motilal Nehru, Nan, Kamala, Betty (Krishna Hutheesing), and Indira one letter a fortnight. Writing to the near and dear ones mattered, as they did to his co-prisoner, G.B. Pant. The future chief minister of the United Provinces wrote:

A letter no doubt speaks, as ever, but it is not merely a lifeless mouth-piece. It revives numberless memories, paints lovely scenes in vivid colours and for the moment lifts out of the slough of oppressive drudgery. However, patience has its reward and satisfaction after a series of disappointments—the merit of accumulated joy. Doubts and misgivings generated during the period of suspense, nevertheless, vanish in an instant on the receipt of a reassuring letter, the gloom disappears, the weight is completely taken off and one finds that no scar is left behind.[40]

Jail life changed the basic parameters of life and there were hardly any new images and definitions to live a new fully acceptable identity. Like everyone else who lived an existence full of abnormality in that haunted world, Jawaharlal Nehru viewed outside happenings as through a glass, with phantom and almost unreal figures moving hither and thither,[41] and the ghosts of the dead yesteryears rising up, bringing poignant memories.[42] He felt unsettled by the double lives— the ordered and circumscribed physical existence and the free life of the spirit, with its dreams and visions, faith and desires;[43] this thought occupied him during the time he walked up and down in his cell, five measured paces this way, and five measured paces back.

Jawaharlal Nehru led a life of languid ease rather than one of rush and bustle. He collected fine stones of all manners of colours, built a museum, and planted thirty or forty kinds of seeds in the otherwise bare quadrangle.[44] If Gandhi had known, he would have shared what he said to Mirabehn: 'Your affinity for bird, beast, trees and stone is your greatest support. They are never-failing friends and companions.'[45]

Gandhi had advised a close disciple with the words, 'light the fire of yoga and consume yourself in it'.[46] Tormented by the inability of his body to keep pace with his mind and desires, Jawaharlal Nehru, too, fought the growing lethargy he felt with yoga. One of the asanas he performed was to stand on his head for a few minutes every day, a practice he continued until the last years of his life. Ansar Harvani described it thus:

> In the morning, he used to do his Yoga exercises. After that he used to have his bath. Then all of us used to have our breakfast, together. Then he used to read newspapers. Then he used to sit down and read his books and do his writing work. Then lunch. After lunch, he never had rest. After that also, he used to read and write. Then at about 5 o'clock, he used to have again a bath. Then he used to play badminton.... In jail, he was rather a bad sportsman. Whenever he lost a point, he used to throw away his racket and shout too. After that, since electricity was not there we used to be supplied only [a] kerosene lamp in which it was

not possible to do night reading—he used to sit down and talk to us and discuss various political, social economic problems.[47]

Jawaharlal Nehru longed to be let out, but realized the value of patience.[48] He did not complain against the vagaries of life nor did he allow himself to become a victim of its pranks.[49] Instead, he wanted to mould the future. An empty conceit probably, but nevertheless good for the soul.[50] He believed that freedom was the ultimate crown of all his sacrifices.[51] Sarojini Naidu remarked on his fiftieth birthday, on 14 November 1939, that he would transmute sorrow, suffering, sacrifice, anguish, and strife 'into the very substance of ecstasy and victory—and freedom.'[52]

Like Rosa Luxembourg, Jawaharlal Nehru realized that it was not worth applying moral standards to the great elemental forces that manifested themselves in a hurricane, a flood, or an eclipse of the sun. These had to be accepted as data for investigation, as subjects of study. Given his own sense of ideas and movements in history, he followed them without losing sight of the main trend to conclude that someday India and the world may be transformed.[53] That's when he saw the stars better and the rays of the morning sun reaching him sooner than those in the valleys.[54]

Meanwhile, the Nehru folk began to come out of prison. The first was Vijaya Lakshmi Pandit, who was allowed out in March 1943 for thirty days on parole due to illness. Chandralekha was freed thereafter. Krishna Hutheesing met her sister. She and Nayantara rode in on a tonga to Anand Bhawan. She writes: 'The tall gates stood open, but the house seemed dim and cheerless. Nan was subdued, her face drawn and thin with wrinkles I had never seen before.' Vijaya Lakshmi went back to prison in April, got out again briefly, and was in and then out again in June; after that she did not go back.[55] On 14 January 1944, she lost her husband, Ranjit. Chandralekha and Nayantara, aged sixteen, did not know; they had left for America in May 1943.

By the time Jawaharlal Nehru and other CWC members were set free on 14 June 1945, the great Bengal famine had claimed three million victims. Intercommunity violence had become more widespread, with politicians of all hues using the situation to their advantage. And the Muslim League acquired salience in Indian politics. Its leader Jinnah was unyielding in his claim that the choice of the Muslim members of the Executive Council should be his, a condition which the Congress refused to accept. But, aided first by Linlithgow and later by his successor, Wavell, he moved from strength to strength to earn his prized trophy, Pakistan.

Jawaharlal Nehru accepted this reality within a month of Mountbatten's arrival in India on 22 March 1947. Even though partition painfully negated a lifetime's effort, he told Azad that it was unavoidable and that it would not be wise to oppose it. While Karachi celebrated, Delhi was, by contrast, in the 'dark, brooding, pock-marked with refugees, immobile with shock'.[56] In an orgy of slaughter, thousands upon thousands were killed, mutilated, raped, and abducted. Nayantara recalled a drive with her uncle: 'The road was lined at intervals with people who signalled the car to a halt. Some talked, some quietly cried. Some were agitated, some beseeching. They, too, were now part of [uncle's] daily routine.'[57] Yet the prime minister made his tryst with destiny. He stated:

> Long years ago we made a tryst with destiny, and now the time comes when we shall redeem our pledge, not wholly or in full measure, but very substantially. At the stroke of the midnight hour, when the world sleeps India will awake to life and freedom. A moment comes, which comes but rarely in history, when we step out from the old to the new, when an age ends, and when the soul of a nation, long suppressed, finds utterance. It is fitting that in this solemn moment we take the pledge of dedication to the service of India and her people and to the still larger cause of humanity.[58]

In *You Never Can Tell* (1899), Bernard Shaw heralded the new age through Mrs Clando, the imagined authoress of The Twentieth-Century

Treatises' on creeds, conduct, motherhood, parents and children, as well as on cooking and clothing. Likewise, while watching the Republic Day parade in 1955, Jawaharlal Nehru, who stole the limelight well before any one could imagine, had 'a sense of fulfillment in the air and of confidence in our destiny'.[59] This was a bold claim, of the sort that angered many and led them to call him an intolerable egoist.

Notes

1. Pandit, *Prison Days*, p. 93.
2. C. Rajagopalachari, *Jail Diary: A Day-to-Day Record of Life in Vellore Jail in 1921* (Bombay: Bharatiya Vidya Bhavan, 1922), p. iv.
3. Vishwa Nath Datta, *Maulana Azad* (Delhi: Manohar, 1990), p. 121.
4. *SWJN*, p. 323.
5. J. Nehru, *Discovery of India*, pp. 20–1.
6. Ali Sardar Jafri, *My Journey: Selected Urdu Poems*, translated by Bedar Bakht and Kathleen Grant Jaegar (New Delhi: Sterling,1999), p. 84.
7. Sachs, *Jail Diary of Albie Sachs*, p. 148.
8. J. Nehru, *An Autobiography*, p. 347.
9. 25 April 1930, *SWJN*, vol. 4, p. 330.
10. Gopal, *Jawaharlal Nehru: A Biography*, vol. 1, p. 143.
11. Gopal, *Jawaharlal Nehru: A Biography*, vol. 1, p. 584.
12. J. Nehru, *An Autobiography*, 348.
13. Sachs, *Jail Diary of Albie Sachs*, p. 151.
14. Statement to the Press, 31 May 1945, 26 April 1944, Nanda, *Selected Works of Govind Ballabh Pant*, vol. 10, p. 346; Mahmud, 'In and Out of Prison', p. 179.
15. 28 May 1930, *SWJN*, vol. 4, p. 353.
16. Statement on Meerut Prisoners, 22 May 1929, *SWJN*, vol. 3, p. 343. See also Hajrah Begum, Oral History Transcripts (613), pp. 36–7, NMML.
17. On the Indian Civil Liberties Union, *SWJN*, vol. 7, pp. 425–9.
18. Biweekly Bulletin, 4 May 1937, file no. G8, AICC papers.
19. Gopal, *Jawaharlal Nehru: A Biography*, vol. 1, p. 173.
20. Nehru, *An Autobiography*, p. 348.
21. J. Nehru, *Glimpses of World History*, p. 474.

22. J. Nehru, *Glimpses of World History*, p. 56.

23. Gupta, *They Lived Dangerously*, p. 55.

24. Mishra, *Living in an Era*, p. 51.

25. N. Sahgal, *Civilizing a Savage World*, p. 4.

26. *Harijan*, 7 April 1946.

27. *SWJN*, vol. 9, p. 244.

28. To J. Nehru, 24 October 1940, *CWMG*, vol. 73, p. 127

29. 17 August 1942, Pandit, *Prison Days*, p. 16.

30. J. Nehru to Krishna Nehru, 2 December 1940, Hutheesing, *Nehru's Letters to His Sister*, p. 67.

31. K.C. Kanda, ed., *Firaq Gorakhpuri: Selected Poetry* (Delhi: Sterling Publishers Pvt. Ltd, 2000), p. 29.

32. Telegram to Winston Churchill, 31 August 1942, in *India: The Transfer of Power, 1942–7*, vol. 2, 'Quit India 30 April–21 September 1942', edited by Nicholas Mansergh and E.W.R. Lumby (London: H.M.S.O, 1970), p. 853.

33. Home Department, Political, file no. 226, 1942 (Internal).

34. Syed Mahmud, 'Agrarian Programme for the UP', in *A Nationalist Muslim and Indian Politics: Selected Letters of Syed Mahmud*, edited by V.N. Datta and B.E. Cleghorn (Macmillan: New Delhi, 1974), p. 106.

35. 1 January 1943, Raghavan, *Sarvepalli Gopal*, p. 312.

36. Richard Ellmann, *Oscar Wilde* (London: Hamish Hamilton1987), p. 496.

37. J. Nehru to Indira Nehru, 27 March 1945, S. Gandhi, *Two Alone, Two Together*, p. 473; *SWJN*, vol. 13, p. 596.

38. On Jawaharlal Nehru's transfer to Almora Jail, 31 May 1945, Nanda, *Selected Works of Govind Ballabh Pant*, vol. 10, p. 344.

39. J. Nehru to Krishna, 19 April 1945, Hutheesing, *Nehru's Letters to His Sister*, p. 181.

40. G.B. Pant to Chandra Datt Pande, 12 June 1943, Nanda, *Selected Works of Govind Ballabh Pant*, vol. 10, p. 83.

41. 25 September 1935, *SWJN*, vol. 7, p. 26.

42. J. Nehru, *An Autobiography*, p. 598.

43. 'Prison Days', *SWJN*, vol. 8, p. 877.

44. 30 November 1944, G.N.S. Raghavan, ed., *M. Asaf Ali's Memoirs: The Emergence of Modern India* (Delhi: Ajanta, 1194), p. 309.

45.   M.K. Gandhi to Mirabehn, 21 September 1940, *CWMG*, vol. 73, p. 40.

46.   M.K. Gandhi to Premabehen Kantak, 28 October 1940, *CWMG*, vol. 73, p. 136.

47.   Ansar Harvani, Oral History Transcript (596), NMML, and his *Before Freedom and After* (New Delhi: Gian Publishing House, 1989).

48.   J. Nehru to Krishna, 1 March 1934, Hutheesing, *Nehru's Letters to His Sister*, p. 42.

49.   J. Nehru to Krishna, 27 December 1942, Hutheesing, *Nehru's Letters to His Sister*, p. 101.

50.   J. Nehru to Krishna, 10 November 1942, *Nehru's Letters to His Sister*, p. 95.

51.   J. Nehru to Krishna, 13 November 1937, Hutheesing, *Nehru's Letters to His Sister*, p. 255.

52.   J. Nehru to Krishna, Diwali 1939, Hutheesing, *Nehru's Letters to His Sister*, p. 407.

53.   Waters, *Rosa Luxemburg Speaks*, p. 337.

54.   Prison Diary, 1 September 1922, *SWJN*, vol. 1, p. 334.

55.   Hutheesing, *We Nehrus*, p. 168.

56.   N. Sahgal, *From Fear Set Free*, p. 11.

57.   N. Sahgal, *From Fear Set Free*, p. 46.

58.   *SWJN*, vol. 3, p. 135.

59.   Raghavan, *Sarvepalli Gopal*, p. 175.

7   *Prison and Family*

It is more blessed to be imprisoned for the sake of one's ideals than to imprison other people, incongruously, in the name of the same ideals. Nehru lived to have both experiences.

—Arnold J. Toynbee[1]

If ink and pen are snatched from me, shall I
Who have dipped my finger in my heart's blood complain—
Or if they seal my tongue, when I have made
A mouth of every round link of my chain?

—Faiz Ahmad Faiz[2]

Jawaharlal Nehru received from his kith and kin what he valued most—ethics and patriotic stimulus. Often, he would use them to hang his own reflections and maxims. Given the importance he attached to his relations, we devote this and the following sections to his relationship with the men and women who mattered most to him.

Books of Jawaharlal Nehru open with evidence of his fidelity to his family. When his sister's little children saw him in jail, it was more than his emotions could stand. He was upset by that touch of home life, after the long yearning for human contact. He treated the help no differently. Munshi Mubarak Ali remained a favourite mentor to whom he would relate all the tales of history and mythology that would hold imagination spellbound.[3] At some point during the Second World War, he gave a pay hike to the domestic help because their responsibilities had increased when he went to prison![4]

The birth of a new member reminded Jawaharlal Nehru of his childhood, which was not only a happy one but one crowned with promise and achievement. He was taught to regard the history of India as inseparable from the destiny of his family, and he came to look upon his family history as part and parcel of the progress for freedom. The birth of a child 'is an unending panorama of human life with its sweet and bitterness, its ups and down.'[5] He was in the Naini Central Prison when he selected the name of Rajivratna, his grandson, from lists that were sent to him.[6] Again, he thought he'd preserve the family lineage. He wrote:

> To some extent you cannot get rid of the family tradition, for it will pursue you and, whether you want to or not, it will give you a certain public position which you have done nothing to deserve. This is unfortunate but you will have to put up with it. After all, it is not a bad thing to have a good family tradition. It helps looking up, it reminds us that we have to keep a torch burning and that we cannot cheapen ourselves or vulgarize ourselves…. If your grandfather's example strengthens and inspires you in any way, that is your good fortune. If your feelings towards your father or mother also help you in that way, well and good.[7]

As Che Guevara (1928–1967) said: 'At the risk of seeming ridiculous, let me say that the true revolutionary is guided by a great feeling of love. It is impossible to think of a genuine revolutionary lacking this quality.'[8] This applies to Jawaharlal Nehru. There were no traces of ambition in early life, and after his first imprisonment he did not forget his family duties. Family disputes were endemic, but his affectionate nature appears again and again in his letters. He judged his father as a tower of strength. Trying to judge him not as his son but independently of it, he believed in his greatness. Wondering if he had repaid his love and care, he felt ashamed at his record. On Motilal's *barsi* (death anniversary), almost all of Jawaharlal's latest memories of him were jail memories, and being again in prison, his mind went back to his father again.[9] His loss made it difficult for him to settle down nicely as he had done in the past. The historian Ravinder Kumar sums it up well:

> The bond of affection between Motilal and Jawaharlal was characterized by a blend of admiration, esteem and regard on the part of Jawaharlal; and a deeply tempered love, parental and solicitous, on the part of Motilal. Yet in the texture of his personality, no less than in the cast of his features, the young Jawaharlal drew as much upon as his mother as he drew upon his father. Particularly did Jawaharlal inherit his sensitive eyes, the eyes of a Hamlet, introspective and soulful, searching and questioning, from the gentle Swarup Rani, who in a quiet and unobtrusive manner, filled the Nehru household with the warm presence of a devoted wife and a loving mother.[10]

The Nehru Women in Bondage

Women's emancipation was, in its principal outlines, part of the Independence struggle. Gandhi saw them 'not as objects of reform and humanitarianism, but as self-conscious arbiters of their own destiny',[11] and showed to a growing generation a picture of a new life through action-oriented policies.[12] He could have done more, but went ahead of most in a society where the education of sons was a prime consideration and the woman's place was considered to be the home. Gandhi changed not only their status but encouraged them, without disturbing patriarchy, to contribute as equals in the fight for Swaraj. Swimming the waters of tradition was good, but to drown in them was suicidal.

Women from the middle classes answered Gandhi's call with patriotic fervour. Some of them detected the smell of thunder in the air and anticipated mass arrests. The Salt Satyagraha brought out tens and thousands of women from their seclusion and showed that they could serve the country on equal terms with men. It gave them a dignity they never enjoyed before.[13] Sarojini Naidu, who combined her widely acclaimed poetry with wisdom, prepared herself in her Bombay house for her eventual arrest. The bell rang at 4 a.m. The police came in. Her hunch proved right. She and others were led into prison on 9 August 1942. For Beverley Nichols, an otherwise unsympathetic observer of Indian political trends, it was 'more interesting to consider her merely as a cultured, charming woman, swept into gaol as the result of her convictions.'[14] Appalled by the government's ignorance of conditions, opinions, and aspirations, she found the British blind and drunk with the arrogance of power.[15]

Defying well-established convention, Aruna Ganguly married a Muslim lawyer, M. Asaf Ali. She participated in the Salt Satyagraha and, in the early 1930s, worked with the Women's League affiliated with the All India Women's Conference (AIWC). For the period of the Quit India campaign, she went underground, stood out as a gutsy fighter, and captured the popular imagination.[16] Similarly, Mridula Sarabhai, daughter of the industrialist Ambalal Sarabhai, along with her three aunts, Anasuya, Nirmala, and Indumati, spent several years in jail. She and Anis Kidwai displayed unsurpassed nerve in rehabilitating refugees and in the rescuing of abducted women. Gandhi, the 'Little Man' worked his magic on them too. Anis Kidwai came to Gandhi, who was in the capital with his spirit in action. She came to drown her grief—her husband was killed in Mussoorie—in the hope that she might stumble on some clue to the future. Gandhi motivated her and many other women, inspiring them to be not appendages to anyone but strong individuals moving forward with dynamic urges.

'Causes save one', a woman told Gretta Cousins (who established AIWC in 1927). This was particularly true of women, whose line of least resistance is self-sacrifice. 'See the women of India', Jawaharlal Nehru wrote triumphantly, 'how proudly they marched ahead of all in the struggle! Gentle and yet brave and indomitable, see how they set the pace for others.'[17] They did not naturally move towards fighting for their own freedom, but achieved empowerment by throwing themselves into a 'cause'. 'Certainly,' Jawaharlal Nehru stated, 'the way hundreds and thousands of them [women] shed their veils and, leaving their sheltered homes, came into the street and the marketplace to fight side by side in the struggle with their brothers ... was something that could hardly be believed by those who did not see it.'[18]

Her great-aunt Bibima taught Nayantara that if Lord Krishna was on her side, it did not matter if the armies of the world were on the other side. This assurance had a ringing romance for her.[19] One day, the Nehrus were enjoying a rich dark cake, chocolate through and through, with chocolate swirls on top. Just then, policemen arrived to arrest Motilal Nehru. The household kissed him goodbye and watched him leave. They ate their chocolate cake and, in the infant minds, prison became in a mysterious way associated with chocolate cake.[20] Where there were no cakes, people made do with garlands, and carried the prison-goer to jail amidst shouts of 'Jai'.[21] Prison had turned into 'a temple and the way thereto into a path of pilgrimage'.[22] Vijaya Lakshmi Pandit described another episode thus:

The story of the arrest [of Chandralekha] is the usual comic opera affair—police, armed guards, C.I.D. men and the usual paraphernalia went to Anand Bhawan about 9 p.m. yesterday. The girls had gone out with friends to a picnic at Ram Bagh. The Inspector asked for Lekha and was informed that she was out. They waited and meanwhile produced a warrant for the search of her room. When this was over and nothing incriminating found, Lekha was still not back so they went away. This morning the arrest took place at 8 o'clock. Lekha informs us that although she was seething with excitement, she was determined to appear casual and actually ate an extra piece of toast for breakfast just to make the police wait and show them that she regarded this event

as of no special importance! Obviously an attempt to imitate Mamaji
(Jawaharlal Nehru).[23]

Edward Thompson, who prided himself on his ability to discern and
interpret Tagore's thought and feelings, remarked, 'You Nehrus have
been very lucky in many ways, and lucky most of all in your charming
and splendid women.'[24] He was right. Much earlier, Motilal Nehru
saw their energy, courage, and ability, spoke of them with affectionate
pride, and encouraged them to take part in public life.

The Nehru women were quick to assert that the 'cause' for which
they fought was related to the attainment of progress or emancipation.[25] Who can supply the impetus for greater understanding and
magnanimity? Asked Rameshwari, Motilal Nehru's niece-in-law and
editor of *Stri Darpan* (Mirror of Beauty/Womanhood). Once she
wrote to Jawaharlal Nehru, then at Harrow, telling him not to waste
his time in foreign countries but to come back home and work to
throw out the foreign rulers from its soil; the letter reached Rev. Joseph
Wood, the headmaster.[26] She looked up to Gandhi as 'the personifica-
tion of the spirit of the ancient Dharma'.[27] Without being lured into
accepting office, she took command of the Harijan Sewak Sangh
in October 1932, worked for the eradication of untouchability, and
promoted truth-force and moral striving. She founded an industrial
home for the education of Dalit girls near the Okhla station in Delhi.
Rameshwari and Lado Rani, mother of Manmohini Zutshi, joined the
Allahabad Ladies' Branch of the Hindu Marriage Reform League.[28]
In 1935, Rameshwari toured Travancore in support of temple entry.
The Royal Proclamation followed, and the temples were thrown open
to Dalits. This was a miracle in a state where even the shadow of a
Dalit was considered to pollute a caste Hindu. During the course of a
month, she and Thakkar Baba travelled widely to spread the message
of the removal of untouchability.[29]

Jawaharlal Nehru's mother adapted to a new mode of living without
any sign of distress or reluctance, [30] though she was, all said and done,

'weak, uneducated, querulous, prone to undervalue the telling of truth, and dominated by her child-widow sister, Bibi'.[31] On 8 April 1932, she suffered injuries because of police action. Shiv Dutt Upadhyaya (1899–1984), who served as personal secretary to the Nehrus and was imprisoned several times, saw this happen. Jawaharlal Nehru, then lodged in Bareilly District Jail, could neither imagine his mother being beaten repeatedly with heavy canes, bleeding on the dusty road, nor could he tolerate an affront or an insult to her in the lock-up. Towards the end of August 1933 he stayed by her bedside until she recovered.

In 1906, Swarup Rani went around town looking for a 'faultless' bride for her son. The search ended with a girl who boasted of the typically fair skin of Brahmins of Kashmiri descent. Her grandfather had been adviser to the royal families of Jaipur, Jodhpur, and Rewa. And when she gave birth to a child on 19 November 1917, the family munshi prayed, 'May Allah's blessings go with the child, who should be a worthy heir to Jawahar as Jawahar has proved a worthy son to you, and may the child illuminate the name of Jawaharlal Nehru.' Not a grandson, as munshiji thought, but a granddaughter was born. 'This girl is going to be worth more than a thousand grandsons', the grandfather prophesied.

Born in a social environ much humbler than that of her father-in-law, Kamala Nehru suffered silently at the hands of her unkind mother-in-law, her child-widow sister Bibi—who had been 'so warped by her misfortune that she could not bear to see anybody happy'[32]—and the 'acid-tongued' Vijaya Lakshmi Pandit.[33] If Kamala suggested a meal to the butler, it was liable to be countermanded; if tickets were to be bought for an English movie, *Bhabhi* was left out because she knew no English.[34] In this way, she had to suffer all kinds of indignities. She could not air her complaints. Instead, she'd lie in bed in the verandah outside her room, quite alone and very lonely. Jawaharlal Nehru talked of his wife's patience, forbearance, and courage,[35] but he was never there to comfort her. Indira quarrelled for her mother and felt emotionally nearer to her maternal rather than paternal family.[36] She recalled years later:

Many people knew the part which was played by my grandfather and my father. But, in my opinion, a more important part was played by my mother. When my father wanted to join Gandhiji and to change the whole way of life ... the whole family was against it. It was only my mother's courageous and persistent support and encouragement that enabled him to take this step which made such a difference to our family and the history of modern India.[37]

Kamala was a novice of sorts when she first entered the Nehru household. She struggled to adjust herself to the big dinners, the quick loud voices of the many British guests, and the unusual camaraderie between her husband and his sister Vijaya Lakshmi. Even though the odds did not favour Kamala, she met her domestic responsibilities stoically without striking an evocative association with the jewel of the Nehru clan. She parted with her jewellery, willingly tossed her silks and fineries into the fire, and took to wearing coarse khadi. Jawaharlal Nehru did not regret any of her sacrifices, for he knew Gandhi's saying that 'man falls from the pursuit of the ideal of plain living and high thinking the moment he wants to multiply his daily needs'.[38]

Besides these voluntary sacrifices, Kamala spent over three weeks in jail from 1 January to 26 January 1931. She was, first of all, in the Allahabad District Jail before her transfer to the Lucknow Female Jail took place. Here Motilal Nehru made sure that all her needs were taken care of. With pride and happiness Jawaharlal Nehru noted that while Kamala suffered in jail, he too agonized in Naini Prison. He missed her rather badly.[39]

Kamala had to spend over a year at Montana in Switzerland, a well-known town along with Davos and Laysin that specialized in treating pulmonary tuberculosis patients. Her health deteriorated in September 1934. The doctor felt that her husband's presence would make her cheerful.[40] There was something inhuman in the situation which kept a political prisoner who had not done an act of violence only a very short distance away from his dying wife without any opportunity of seeing her or being with her.[41] C.F. Andrews, one of

Gandhi's close British associates, tried securing Jawaharlal Nehru's unconditional release. However, this did not bear fruit. Jawaharlal was finally released on 4 September 1935 on compassionate grounds and went to see his wife.

Raja Rao, the novelist, met him in Germany's Black Forest. This is how he describes the final moments of their conversation:

> I rose quietly. I made a profound *namaskar* to Kamala Nehru. She seemed so like a figure from the *Ramayana* or the *Mahabharata*—simple, wise, dedicated, timeless. To her, acceptance seemed the very breath of beauty. She lay unafraid of the darkness of the clouds, the solitude of the hills, the cruelty of Hitlerite mankind. For one to be—was to glow. One could not imagine darkness when her silence spoke.[42]

Rajni Palme Dutt (1896–1974), the Marxist intellectual, had met Jawaharlal Nehru in 1907 when both were members of the Cambridge Majlis.[43] They came across each other yet again in 1936 at the Lausanne sanatorium. Here, Dutt carried the impression that Kamala was a 'wonderful woman', who gave her husband much of his inspiration and breadth of outlook.[44] She died on 28 February 1936; her ashes were poured into the bosom of the swift-flowing Ganga. Jawaharlal Nehru plunged into an abyss of remorse. 'How many of our forbears', he remarked, 'she [Ganga] had carried thus to the sea, how many of those who follow us will take that last journey in the embrace of her water.' In 1962, a plaque was put outside the house where Kamala stayed.

Jawaharlal Nehru, who relived the feelings he had endured previously, lamented that two long prison terms of two years each had come between them just when their need for each other was the greatest, just when they had come so near each other especially when he would read out to her a chapter or two from his unpublished autobiography. He dedicated it to her. He has left a touching portrait of her, a gentle, uncomplaining woman. But this belated gesture could hardly heal the wounds of Kamala's family, who could not have forgotten that

Jawaharlal Nehru's political engagements made him to some extent blind to the great tides of emotion and outbursts of passion.

The Two Sisters

Jawaharlal Nehru's love for children was intense, and they returned his love. Nayantara Sahgal wrote, 'For me and my sisters, growing up in Anand Bhawan, he was a special shining being.'[45] One of the most exciting moments of Krishna Hutheesing's childhood was the day she met her brother, eighteen years older, in June 1912 when he came home from Cambridge. The bond between them grew with the years.[46] He listened to *choti beti* (youngest daughter) and others, respected their views instead of brushing them aside, and paid attention to their hardships. From time to time, he advised her on personal and political matters. On her birthday on 19 October 1930, he asked her to buy books, 'the belated but loving gift of a somewhat absent minded brother who thinks often of his little sister'.[47] Out of the books, he wanted her to construct a magic city full of dream castles and flowering gardens and running brooks where beauty and happiness dwell'.[48] He gave his sister away at her wedding during a brief spell out of jail in October 1933, but could not afford the traditional trousseau, let alone the 'Nehru Wedding Camp' that Motilal Nehru had arranged for his own wedding in 1916. Yet he declined all offers of help. G.D. Birla discreetly offered Jawaharlal Nehru a monthly stipend, which he turned down. He was furious that any capitalist could presume to place him on his payroll.[49] The father was equally adamant; he would not permit any child or grandchild of his to depend for maintenance on any other person.

Later, when it came to dividing his father's property assets, he assured Krishna that she had as much right, indeed more, to the property as he did.[50] In his eloquent will, he recorded: 'In the course of a life which has had its share of trial and difficulty, the love and tender care for me of both my sisters ... has been of the greatest solace to me.' Soon after Krishna came out of prison, she received a note from him.

It said, 'I understand that you are getting caskets and addresses. What exploits are they meant to celebrate? Surely, a few hours in jail do not deserve an epic. Anyway, don't get a swelled head or perhaps it is better to have a swelled head than no head at all.'[51]

Jawaharlal Nehru thought prison was the best of universities, if only one knew how to take its courses. Seeing themselves as people of their times,[52] the Nehru women courted arrest voluntarily, accepted imprisonment gladly, and treated jail-going as a gala occasion, not a sombre one. Uma Nehru—wife of Jawaharlal's cousin Shamlal—was at the forefront of the civil disobedience campaign in Allahabad. Her efforts produced the results she wanted: the Ewing Christian College, the Crosthwaite Girls College, and the Muir College experienced picketing or closure. 'We were excited and enthusiastic about being taken to prison', writes Manmohini. 'We felt as if a great honour had been conferred on us. We shouted slogans and sang national songs while waiting for the formalities to be completed. In fact, the three of us, my sisters and I, dearly hoped to be imprisoned three times so we would be termed "habitual offenders".'[53]

Nayantara was too young to go to jail, but she was old enough to notice that the 'rich tapestry of life that had been woven by its grown-up occupants through the years lay over like a peaceful, protective mantle and we discovered we were not lonely.'[54] She saw her mother being taken away, and cried for her, always in secret. Months of separation did not do her good, but it helped the family to be more united and to be imbued with a deep sense of unity and common ideals. 'So childhood, despite its unhappy moments … had an enchanted quality.'[55]

Once in jail, Chandralekha and her mother devoured George Bernard Shaw (1856–1950) and a modern comedy called 'Drawing Room' by Thomas Browne (1605–1682) that indicated some things in common with their own family, and they had a good many laughs over it. Their lives were accompanied by a great deal of laughter and mutual back-slapping. Jail-goers were no silent sufferers but pilgrims armed with the song 'Raghupati Raghava Raja Ram'. Despite the dreary monotony and harshness, they did not give up. Thus, when Jawaharlal and Sadiq Ali (1910–2001) broke the salt law, Kamala revealed remarkable courage. Krishna Hutheesing together with the first batch of satyagrahis manufactured salt in the Allahabad University area, comprising the mohallas of Lawrenceganj, adjoining Colonelganj and Katra, and lit a bonfire of foreign cloth in the market.[56] She describes the popular enthusiasm:

> The streets were crowded and thousands turned up to see the salt being made. I have seldom seen such enormous crowds. It is believed that there were 20 thousand people or even more. For miles you could see nothing but heads of the thousands there. On the way the procession was stopped every now and then and people came and garlanded us and put tika and chandan on our foreheads.[57]

Krishna was arrested; an unknown person paid the fine of fifty rupees inflicted on her on 11 November. Motilal Nehru was outraged: 'If my information is true the unknown person has done the greatest conceivable disservice to me, to my daughter and to the country.'[58]

'You are a brave little darling', Motilal Nehru had complimented Vijaya Lakshmi Pandit. 'I was remarking last night at the dinner table that you alone of my children have inherited my spirit.' It was this fusion of professional commitment and family pride that he bequeathed to his children. 'Three cheers for jail', Bhai (Jawaharlal) complimented Vijaya Lakshmi when she waited in the dead of night to be taken away. Jawaharlal Nehru had great affection for his self-willed and proud sister.[59] He encouraged her to be strong-willed and to grow in mind, and in outlook, in self-assurance. He advised her to grow and learn, be flexible in mind and body, and 'yet always with that hard steel-like something which tempers us and keeps us straight and anchored, and gives us a sense of real values.'[60]

19 November 1942 was Bhai Duj (festival in which sisters pray for a long and happy life for their brothers). The sister reciprocated the love with the remark: 'Out of the many good things fate gave me at

my birth, one of the best was surely my brother. To have known and loved him and been so near to him would have been ample justification for having been born.'[61] Her daughter Nayantara was no less ecstatic: 'I do not think there was anything unusual or sentimental about our admiration for him [Mamu]. He was quite simply the most wonderful person we knew, and children have an unerring instinct for singling out wonderful people for their devotion.'[62]

Vijaya Lakshmi Pandit had three rounds of imprisonment. The first round was difficult, but she stood like a soldier during the individual satyagraha in 1941.[63] She expected more sorrow and suffering in August 1942; it was better, she thought, for her to not see dates and count days. She waited for the post, for the one letter she wanted—'maybe it was news of a child far away from us—a friend from whom we have been parted—money on which many things depended—or just a love letter'.[64] She missed her daughter Rita's birthday for the third time. At such times, she felt torn in two—between her duty to the children and the other duty of serving the country.

She had to make do with the rations of the poorest quality and mixed with grit and dirt, tiny stones and even an odd spider or two thrown in for good weight.[65] She went through the ordeal, day after day, with the 'chains of sound ... strangling [her] with their dissonance'.[66] She longed for solitude so that she had nothing to do with a whole barrack full of talking, quarrelling women. The sight of a solitary plane far overhead symbolized freedom for her. Often Vijaya Lakshmi and 'her fellow-prisoners had watched one with longing as it flew on its way, its red and green tail lights winking against the night sky. Out there had been liberty and space unlimited. Thinking of this, her spirits rose within her, as the plane left the ground'.[67]

Ranjit Pandit's death in 'one of the worst prisons'—Bareilly District Jail—was a great blow to Vijaya Lakshmi Pandit. A barrister-turned-satyagrahi, he had settled in Allahabad and lived at 9 Kanpur (Cawnpore) Road. His daughter, Rita Vitasta, was born in this house. He had married Swarup on 10 May 1921, who changed not only her last name, but also her own personal name, becoming Vijaya Lakshmi. Her brother called her 'Nan'. Inspired by Gandhi's example, Ranjit spurned favours from the 'petty gauleiters'.[68] A man of fastidious scholarship and a lover of art, he started work on the English translation of *Mudrarakshasa* or the Signet Ring, a Sanskrit play by Vishakhadatta, written in about 400 AD.[69]

While Vijaya Lakshmi mourned Ranjit Pandit's death, she did not forget the Congress leaders who were afflicted with various ailments all the way through their incarceration. For example, Vallabhbhai Patel suffered from a spastic colon; doctors diagnosed G.B. Pant with giddiness of the head, pain in the spine, and double hernia; Maulana Azad lost weight; although Syed Mahmud, Jawaharlal Nehru's protégé, had a list of ailments, he still observed fast for the whole month of Ramzan. Jawaharlal Nehru prepared his 'Iftar'—egg, toast, and tea.[70] Troubled by illness and intense heat, M.N. Roy stopped spinning.[71] Earlier, he had stolen the limelight with his propaganda and the Comintern (Communist International) leaders commended his efforts.[72] Jawaharlal Nehru's own failing health in March–April 1934 concerned his family. He lost weight, and felt lonely and cut off from the world. Ailments in jail made the loneliness greater. Motilal Nehru's death added to his loneliness, as also to the burden of running a household.[73] A restless Jawaharlal Nehru was oppressed by the news of Kamala's illness and angry that Indu had not written to him. The death of his wife added to his woes; hence, some of his correspondence reflects a hopeless drift, sterility, and general dereliction. 'The old exuberance is much less now,' he wrote in April 1944, 'the almost uncontrollable impulses have toned down, and passions and feeling are more in check.'[74]

What I wish to extract from these examples is that the close confinement affected the nerves of the leaders. Something else also occurred. There was no respite, no relief from isolation. The political prisoners spent the day performing various chores, but the nights were dark and grim. Every hour was a burden and a horror. The political prisoner played the warmth and sincerity of their homes against a cold and uncertain jail world, where there was no freshness and fragrance or the cool smell of grass and soft earth. Even dreaming of Swaraj was difficult in confinement. 'Locks and bars and walls. Locks and locks and locks', Jawaharlal Nehru wrote on 9 March 1934. 'There are four solid locks between me (and every other prisoner) and the fresh air outside the prison. How I shall hate all locks in future!'[75]

Indira Priyadarshini: Making of a Rebel

Jawaharlal Nehru wrote to his daughter on 28 March 1932: 'You are a lucky girl. Born in the month and year of the great revolution which ushered in a new era in Russia, you are now a witness to a revolution in your own country, and soon you may be an actor in it.'[76] Motilal Nehru expected Indu to grow up to be worthy of the family name. She did not disappoint. When the police started throwing furniture and carpets out of Anand Bhawan, the three-year-old furiously confronted them. This was a familiar scene to all victims of repression, whether in Allahabad, Italy, Russia, or Germany, which Alexander Solzhenitsyn describes in *The Gulag Archipelago*: 'The traditional image of arrest is ... what happens afterward, when the poor victim has been taken away. It is an alien, brutal, and crushing force totally dominating the apartment for hours on end, a breaking, ripping open, pulling from the walls, emptying things from wardrobes and desks onto the floor.'[77]

As Indira matured, she developed a strong sense of duty to her father and her country. She was arrested because she and some other women organized a political meeting. A scuffle between a section of the audience and the police took place; Indira was pulled about and bruised and had her clothes torn. On 11 September 1942, she and Ramkali Devi, Mahadevi Chaube, Lakshmibai Bapat, and two young girls—Vidyavati and Govindi Devi—shared the dreadfulness of prison life with Vijaya Lakshmi Pandit and Chandralekha. She named her dormitory 'chimborazo'; Lekha called hers 'Bien Venue.' She celebrated her twenty-fifth birthday on 19 November 1942. When she was released on 13 May 1943, freedom was 'like coming out of a dark passage'. She was dazzled by 'the rush of life, the many hues and textures, the scale of sounds and the range of ideas'.[78]

Indira Gandhi's childhood memories began with the searching of homes and persons, the arrests of and visiting her father and other members of the family in prison. One visitor to Anand Bhawan remembered a grave-faced little girl saying politely to him, 'I'm sorry, but my grandfather, father and Mummy are all in prison'.[79] No other family was so involved in the freedom struggle and its hardships.[80] They aroused respect, interest, and curiosity. Thousands came to Anand Bhawan to get a glimpse of them. The inmates felt good because of the public expression of goodwill, though they did not find it easy to adjust to anti-government chanting and public processions.[81]

One missed many things in prison, but perhaps most of all, Jawaharlal Nehru missed Indu, which means moon, or Indira. He wanted to see his daughter quietly, normally and with a feeling of freedom and leisure.[82] He wanted to talk to her, whether face to face or by letter.[83] His first letter on her thirteenth birthday offered 'the air and the mind and spirit, such as a good fairy might have bestowed on you— things that even the high walls of prison cannot stop'.[84] He placed vivid images of the past before her, one after another, to make her sense how the world had changed, step by step, and developed and progressed, and sometimes apparently gone back.[85] He suggested how best she could develop the extrovert sides of her personality and find oases of friendly feeling and sometimes of adventure outside Allahabad.[86] He ended up composing 176 letters, running into 1,849 foolscap pages to her alone. 'What a mountain of letters I have written! And what a lot of good swadeshi ink I have spread out on swadeshi paper!'[87] He pinned the pages and put them neatly in a stack, not knowing when Indu would read them.

Born to a world of 'storm and trouble',[88] Indira was lonesome without her father. This made her shy, reticent, and glum in her youth, and led her to see life in a solemn perspective,'cast in an austere mould, shorn of lightness, as if lightness were a weakness, a trap to be avoided'.[89] A concerned father urged her to get rid of 'melancholy and its brood'. In 1931, he had her admitted to the Pupil's Own School in Poona, and thereafter, to Santiniketan, a place where Tagore's 'spirit seemed to roam and hover over one and follow one with a loving though deep watchfulness'.[90] Here, too, the young Indira lapsed into her usual feeling of isolation. She felt alone even when she was surrounded by crowds, their chattering and playing, their rowdiness and noise.

In Oxford, Indira felt comfortable with radical and left-wing Indian students at Somerville College, Oxford (1937–41). In London, Krishna Menon drew her into socialist and anti-imperialist work, and encouraged her to acquire new skills. By this time, she had a close friend in Feroze Gandhi, who was educated in Allahabad where his father Jahangir Gandhi had set up a liquor and provision business. They were married on 26 March 1942, despite the strong opposition to their intercommunity marriage.

Indira could not ignore the tumult around her—the political visitors storming in, protest rallies, and arrests. Reading about Joan of Arc by night, she lectured the servants by day and, in between, founded the Vanar Sena (meaning monkey army) a children's army to carry messages in and out of jail, and she was even seen drilling the children. 'What is the position of your monkey army?' Motilal Nehru wrote from jail. 'I suggest the wearing of a tail by every member of it the length of which should be in proportion to the rank of the wearer.'[91] She looked at her aunt Krishna Hutheesing solemnly, and said, 'I'm practically being Joan of Arc. I have just been reading about her, and someday I am going to lead my people to freedom just as Joan of Arc did.'[92] She returned the embroidered frock her aunt brought from Paris, and set fire to the 'foreign doll'.[93]

The strong patriotic fervour did not leave her. In December 1929, Indira felt part of the excitement while reading the Independence

Resolution at Lahore. Her father's speech itself unfolded a great picture of nationalism spreading over India and Asia. He inherited the doctrine which some of his predecessors had preached, that the formation of large aggregates was the key to India's stability. On 20 September 1932, Indira held prayers when Gandhi fasted.

Indira tasted prison life as well. The magistrate had marked a cross on her card which meant that she would have no privileges whatsoever. She could neither write to nor receive letters from her father. Yet she marshalled her inner resources to face the grim realities of life. She depicted a 'lovely dream...walking on a deep path'.

> I had a feeling that it was suspended in the air although there was noth-ing to show it positively. And in a perfect circle all round far away as if there was no obstacle to prevent me seeing the whole horizon at the same time-there was a chain of mountains. All sorts of mountains; high towering into the sky besides smaller ones, ragged and smooth, snow covered and bare. And on a single peak in front of me there was a dazzlingly beautiful light. It seemed like a spotlight from above although the sky was pitched dark, neither sun, nor moon nor stars. It was awe-inspiring. I was looking at it and walking on and on when the road became narrow and covered with deep snow like a mountain pass. I woke up feeling exhilarated and fresh, as if I had been to the Mont Blanc or the Matterhorn at least.[94]

Indira made merry on Vasanta Panchami and Holi, and wore a new sari on Nauroz.[95] She and Chandralekha saved up their rations to host a party in the 'Blue Drawing Room'.[96] They could not decide whether to write the menu in French or not. They polished and repolished their silver, which consisted of three bent forks and a single dull knife. Once, Vijaya Lakshmi regaled them with how Diwali was celebrated in the old Anand Bhawan and how Motilal Nehru used to give her an *ashrafi* (gold coin) to gamble with. 'Locked up in the jail barrack,' recounts Chandralekha, 'and sitting on the floor in our crumpled khadi saris, listening to the tales of grand happenings by the dim light of a lantern was like peeping into the exotic world of Scheherezade.'[97]

After lock-up, they read plays; Nan watched and listened. They even held a party to celebrate Indira's birthday on 19 November 1942. When they were unexpectedly liberated on 13 May 1943, Indira shed a few tears. She was growing to be a Nehru worthy of the name.[98] She possessed exceptional courage and initiative, and the family support stood her in good stead in confronting a turbulent world. After her father's death in 1964, she demonstrated amazing stamina and stay-ing power. Like Kamala, who faced police lathis without batting an eyelid, Indira fought her way up through 'a morass of contemptuous, too familiar elite, and in so doing developed a contempt for the class of politicians and bureaucrats who considered themselves, more or less, the true heirs of power'.[99]

Christian Toller, who met Indira in London in August 1936, described her as 'a little flower which the wind might blow away so easily'.[100] The fact of the matter was that she was not afraid of the wind. When the opportune moment arrived, she dealt with the 'syndi-cate', a bunch of right-wingers, decisively with the help of her advisers, and her two sons, Sanjay and Rajiv, gave her strength. However, her aunt and cousins could not stomach her unexpected rise to power and made friends with Indira Gandhi's enemies. The proclamation of the Emergency in 1975 was the last straw. Indira Gandhi could neither forgive Vijaya Lakshmi Pandit for linking up with Jagjivan Ram, who had done a volte face, nor did she approve of Nayantara signing up with Jayaprakash Narayan.

In a life so full of tragedy and triumph, Indira Gandhi, like her father, bequeathed a mixed but vibrant legacy to her party and the nation. Drawing a fair balance sheet of her achievements and short-comings is not possible. At the same time, there is no denying that she consolidated her father's inheritance, raised the country's profile in the comity of nations, and infused dynamism into the Congress party in her early days before it became a tool in the hands of a coterie.

She began her term energetically, selflessly, and was motivated by the mission to serve the nation. But the bureaucracy's stranglehold and intra-party factionalism jettisoned her plans. Her own mistakes were numerous; she did not allow dissent, and she did not tolerate regional Congress leaders with a large following. But her monumental folly was to impose the Emergency: it was a reckless and an indefensible act to undermine the constitution. The electorate knew it and voted her out of power. By the time she bounced back in 1977, her credibility had not been restored. Civil society still remembered the dark days of the Emergency.

On the face of it, the Nehru clan was fairly well-knit, but in reality the tensions brewed until they exploded. To begin with, Bibi Amma (Swarup Rani's sister) created a cleavage between Kamala, the young bride, and Vijaya Lakshmi Pandit. Kamala kept the lid on, though the young Indira complained bitterly of her mother's ill-treatment. Kamala's death in Lausanne on 28 February 1936 led to increased bitterness in the Nehru household. Vijaya Lakshmi Pandit's decision to move out of Anand Bhawan in October 1943 upset her brother. The publication of her book *Prison Days* did not go down well with him either. 'It is rather thin', he remarked. Indira Gandhi reacted much more strongly: 'I feel that she has missed out much—the enjoyment we took in little things, the sad cases of many convicts, the anguish of not having news of you, and so many incidents, interesting or exciting or humiliating. I think she has made our jail life sound dull—it wasn't that for me.'[101]

Vijaya Lakshmi Pandit enjoyed the fruits of office after Independence, but her frustrations, which had deepened over the decades, came out in the open when Indira Gandhi imposed the Emergency in 1975. She thought that the Congress would pass on the mantle of leadership to her after her brother died in 1964, but that could not have happened. She thought herself to be the inheritor of her brother's legacy, but Indira left her in no doubt that she was the sole custodian of her father's inheritance.

The relations between *phupi* (aunt) and Indu soured: it impacted Nayantara and Krishna as well. Later, the rift between Sonia Gandhi and Maneka Gandhi, the widow of Sanjay Gandhi, who died in an accident, split the Nehru clan irrevocably. Today, the family feud extends to the political domain. While Sonia Gandhi and her son Rahul lead the Congress, Maneka Gandhi, a minister in the Narendra Modi government, and her son, a member of parliament, stay put in the Bharatiya Janata Party (BJP). This may not have happened if the family had mended its fences and adhered to the Nehruvian legacy.

Notes

1.   Arnold J. Toynbee as quoted in *Nehru: A Contemporary's Estimate* by Walter Russell Crocker (Delhi: Oxford University Press, 1966), p. 118. The later part of the quote refers to Sheikh Abdullah's imprisonment for the Kashmir Conspiracy Case under Nehru's prime ministership.

2.   Faiz Ahmad Faiz quoted in Hasan, *India Partitioned*, vol. 1, p. 86.

3.   Vasudev, *Indira Gandhi*, p. 16.

4.   Brecher, *Nehru: A Political Biography*, p. 4.

5.   Gopal, *Jawaharlal Nehru: An Anthology*, p. 630.

6.   In Sanskrit, 'Rajiv' means 'lotus', as does 'Kamala', the name of Jawaharlal's wife. 'Ratna' means 'jewel', one of the meanings of 'Jawahar'.

7.   Mushirul Hasan, *The Nehrus: Personal Histories* (London: Mercury Books, 2006), p. 19.

8.   Waters, *Rosa Luxemburg Speaks*, p. 332.

9.   25 February 1931, *SWJN*, vol. 5, p. 361.

10.   Kumar, 'Introduction', *SWMN*, vol. 1, p. 5.

11.   Madhu Kishwar, 'Gandhi on Women', *Economic and Political Weekly* 20, no. 40 (October 1985): 1698.

12.   Chattopadhyay, *Inner Recesses Outer Spaces*, p. 47.

13.   M.K. Gandhi, 'Swaraj through Women', *Harijan*, 2 December 1939.

14.   Beverly Nichols, *Verdict on India* (London: Book Traders, 1944), p. 151.

15.   Nichols, *Verdict on India*, p. 147.

16.   Verinder Grover and Ranjana Arora, eds, *Aruna Asaf Ali: A Biography of Her Vision and Ideas* (Delhi: Deep & Deep Publications, 1999).

17.   J. Nehru, *Glimpses of World History*, p. 8.

18.   J. Nehru, *Glimpses of World History*, p. 729.

19.   N. Sahgal, *Civilizing a Savage World*, p. 6.

20.   N. Sahgal, *Prison and Chocolate Cake*, pp. 21–2.

21.   He was sentenced to a year's imprisonment and fined one hundred rupees by Fategarh's district magistrate. (Moti Lal Bhargava, *Ganesh Shankar Vidyarthi* [Publications Division, Ministry of Information and Broadcasting, Government of India, 1988], pp. 65–6.)

22.   N. Sahgal, *Prison and Chocolate Cake*, p. 71.

23.   Pandit, *Prison Days*, p. 53.

24.   Edward Thompson to Jawaharlal, 24 November 1936, J. Nehru, *Bunch of Old Letters*, p. 205.

25.   Margaret E. Cousins, *Indian Womanhood Today* (Allahabad: Kitabistan, 1941), p. 58.

26.   B.K. Nehru, *Nice Guys Finish Second*, p. 19.

27.   Rameshwari Nehru, *Gandhi Is My Star: Speeches and Writings of Smt. Rameshwari Nehru* (Patna: Pustak Bhandar, 1950), pp. 89, 199; Sushila Nayar and Kamla Mankekar, eds, *Women Pioneers in India's Renaissance: As I Remember Her* (Delhi: National Book Trust, 2002).

28.   M.Z. Sahgal, *An Indian Freedom Fighter*, p. xiv.

29.   *Harijan*, 18 March 1939.

30.   Hutheesing, *We Nehrus*, pp. 5–6.

31.   B.K. Nehru, *Nice Guys Finish Second*, p. 78.

32.   B.K. Nehru, *Nice Guys Finish Second*, p. 78.

33.   Gupte, *Mother India*, pp. 129–31. Vijaya Lakshmi denied having ill-treated Kamala and blamed Indira for spreading this canard and harbouring ill-will against her on this score. 'If Mrs Pandit's denials are usually disbelieved it is because too many friends and acquaintances of the family witnessed the taunts Kamala had to endure.' (Inder Malhotra, *Indira Gandhi: A Personal and Political Biography* [London: Holder & Stoughton, 1989], p. 29.)

34.   Adams and Whitehead, *Dynasty*, p. 39.

35.   Aruna Asaf Ali and G.N.S. Raghavan, *Private Face of a Public Person: A Study of Jawaharlal Nehru* (New Delhi: Radiant Publishers, 1989), p. 131.

36.   'You are also very fortunate in having a very brave and wonderful little woman for your Mummie, and if you are ever in doubt or in trouble you cannot have a better friend.' (J. Nehru, *Glimpses of World History*, p. 3.)

37.   Malhotra, *Indira Gandhi*, p. 36.

38.   *Harijan*, 1 January1940, *CWMG*, vol. 73, p. 94.

39.   J. Nehru, *Glimpses of World History*, p. 7.

40.   Jivraj Mehta to Home Member, 20 September 1934, Home Department, Political, file no. 38/7, 1934.

41.   Andrews to Hallet, 21 September 1934, Home Department, Political file no. 38/7, 1934.

42.   Raja Rao, *The Meaning of India* (New Delhi: Vision Books, 1996), p. 42.

43.   The Cambridge Majlis was founded around 1891 for Indian students at the university, and named after the Persian word for assembly. Indian students at Cambridge could reason and practise debates at this debating organization. It was also a place to socialize in and discuss political matters.

44.   Rajni Palme Dutt, Oral History Transcript (141), NMML.

45.   N. Sahgal, *Civilizing a Savage World*, p. 15.

46.   Hutheesing, 'Introduction', *Nehru's Letters to His Sister*, p. 8.

47.   Zakaria, *A Study of Nehru*, p. 148.

48.   November 1930, *SWJN*, vol. 4, p. 422.

49.   Shashi Tharoor, *Nehru: The Invention of India* (New Delhi: Penguin, 2003), pp. 97–8.

50.   J. Nehru to Krishna, October 1931, Hutheesing, *Nehru's Letters to His Sister*, p. 17.

51.   Hutheesing, *With No Regrets*, p. 62.

52.   N. Sahgal, *Civilizing a Savaged World*, p. 3.

53.   M.Z. Sahgal, *An Indian Freedom Fighter*, p. 73.

54.   Nayantara Sahgal, 'Life with Uncle', Zakaria, *A Study of Nehru*, p. 155.

55.   N. Sahgal, *Prison and Chocolate*, p. 21.

56.   Bhargava, *Hundred Years of Allahabad University*, p. 213.

57.   Krishna to Deen Dayal Bhargava, 13 April 1930, file no. 176, Misc., AICC papers.

58.   *SWMN*, vol. 7, p. 356.

59.   Describing the occasion of Vijaya Lakshmi's birth, Jawaharlal wrote in his *Autobiography*: 'A domestic event, however, just then absorbed my attention. This was the birth of a little sister. I had long nourished a secret grievance at not having brothers or sisters when everybody seemed to have

them, and the prospect of having a baby brother or sister all to myself was exhilarating. Father was then in Europe. I remember waiting anxiously for the events. One of the doctors came and told me of it and added, presumably as a joke, that I must be glad that it was not a boy, who would have taken a share in my patrimony. I felt bitter and angry at the thought that anyone should imagine that I could harbour such a vile notion.' (Jawaharlal Nehru, *Before Freedom: Letters to His Sister*, edited by Nayantara Sahgal [New Delhi: HarperCollins, 2000], p. 10.)

60. 10 April 1945, J. Nehru, *Before Freedom*, p. 470.

61. 10 November 1942, Pandit, *Prison Days*, p. 91.

62. N. Sahgal, 'Life with Uncle', Zakaria, *A Study of Nehru*, p. 155.

63. Mehta, *Freedom's Child*, p. 54; 21 December 1942, Pandit, *Prison Days*, p. 105; 25 August 1942, Pandit, *Prison Days*, p. 41.

64. 16 August 1942, Pandit, *Prison Days*, p. 12.

65. 21 April 1943, Pandit, *Prison Days*, p. 115.

66. Ernst Toller quoted in *Struggle for Independence: Vijaya Lakshmi Pandit* by S.R. Bakshi (Delhi: Anmol Publications, 1992), p. 81.

67. N. Sahgal, *From Fear Set Free*, p. 15.

68. 18 November 1942, Pandit, *Prison Days*, p. 94.

69. 3 May 1943, Pandit, *Prison Days*, pp. 119–20.

70. 2 January 1944, Datta and Cleghorn, *A Nationalist Muslim and Indian Politics*, p. 234; Syed Mahmud, 'In and Out of Prison', Zakaria, *A Study of Nehru*, p. 176.

71. 8 August 1932, M.N. Roy, *Fragments of a Prisoner's Diary: Crime and Karma: Cats and Women* (Calcutta: Renaissance Publishers Private Ltd, 1950), p. 31.

72. Home Department, Political, file no. 11, 1923, NAI.

73. J. Nehru to Kamala Nehru, 19 July 1935, *SWJN*, vol. 12, p. 686.

74. Rabindra Chandra Dutt, *Socialism of Jawaharlal Nehru* (New Delhi: Abhinav Publications, 1981), p. 170.

75. Zakaria, *A Study of Nehru*, p. 498.

76. J. Nehru, *Glimpses of World History*, p. 59.

77. Solzhenitsyn, *Gulag Archipelago*, p. 5.

78. Kishor Gandhi, *India's Date with Destiny: Ranbir Singh Chowdhary: Felicitation Volume* (Delhi: Allied Publishers, 2006), p. lxxxv.

79. Hutheesing, *We Nehrus*, p.137.

80.   Gupte, *Mother India*, p. 206.

81.   N. Sahgal, 'Life with Uncle', in Zakaria, *A Study of Nehru*, p. 139.

82.   24 February, 1945, S. Gandhi, *Two Alone, Two Together*, p. 467.

83.   Lamb, *The Nehrus in India*, p. 112.

84.   J. Nehru, *Glimpses of World History*, p. 1.

85.   J. Nehru, *Glimpses of World History*, p. 172.

86.   24 March 1945, *SWJN*, vol. 13, p. 591.

87.   J. Nehru, *Glimpses of World History*, p. 494.

88.   Katherine Frank, *Indira: The Life of Indira Gandhi* (Delhi: HarperCollins, 2001), p. 14.

89.   Nayantara Sahgal, *Indira Gandhi, Her Road to Power* (New York: F. Ungar, 1982), p. 19.

90.   S. Gandhi, *Two Alone, Two Together*, p. xiv.

91.   Circular letter to Anand Bhawan, 16 July 1930, *SWMN*, vol. 7, p. 256.

92.   Hutheesing, *We Nehrus*, p. 55.

93.   Indira Gandhi, *The Speeches and Reminiscences of Indira Gandhi* (London, 1975), p. 14.

94.   Hasan, *The Nehrus*, p. 228.

95.   To Darling Papu (from Naini Central Prison), 19 April 1943; S. Gandhi, *Two Alone, Two Together*, p. 355.

96.   One half of Indira Gandhi's cell was covered in a blue sheet from home and was renamed the 'Blue Drawing Room'. N. Sahgal, *Indira Gandhi*, p. 17.

97.   Mehta, *Freedom's Child*, p. 33.

98.   S. Gandhi, *Two Alone, Two Together*, p. 17.

99.   Gail Omvedt, *We Will Smash This Prison* (New Delhi: Orient Longman Ltd, 1979), p. 125.

100.   To Nehru, 27 August 1936, Oesterheld, *Jawaharlal Nehru, Ernst Toller*, p. 109.

101.   Indira Gandhi to Jawaharlal, 3 June 1945, S. Gandhi, *Two Alone, Two Together*, p. 486.

8   *Friends in Chains*

We are little men serving a great cause, but because the cause is great,
something of that greatness falls upon us also.

— Jawaharlal Nehru[1]

In a world in which everything had seemed alarmingly unstable,
uncertain, and impermanent, it was a delight for Jawaharlal Nehru
to strike friendships. 'Friendship flourishes on common ideals and
endeavours. Without them there can be no friendship', he told his
Cambridge buddy Syed Mahmud.[2] He dedicated *The Discovery
of India* to his 'colleagues and co-prisoners in the Ahmadnagar Fort
prison camp from August 9, 1942 to March 28, 1943'.[3] While thinking
of friends and their loyalty, he mulled over the low points in the anti-
colonial struggle: destructive jealousies, hatreds and ambitions, which
were previously kept hidden and unexpressed, and the mounting
caste friction and inter-community tension. All this is sufficient to

give a pretty good idea of the considerable diversity of opinions in the nationalist movement.

A mixed group of prisoners who were herded together spoke in glowing terms of Jawaharlal Nehru's kindness and consideration, in matters vital and trivial. Many of his companions have testified to his remarkable resilience and his zest for mental and manual activities. 'His varied interests and vitality', stated Acharya Kripalani, 'were a source of strength and entertainment to our enforced communal existence.'[4] Jawaharlal Nehru, of course, acknowledged his friends:

> The world seems a very dark, dismal and dreary place, full of people with wrong urges or no urge at all, living their lives trivially and without any significance…. I feel overwhelmed, not so much by the great problems facing us but rather by the affection and comradeship of friends who expect so much from me. A sense of utter humility seized me in the face of this faith and trust.[5]

Prison was not a pleasant place to live in even for a short period, much less for long years. It was, moreover, irritating for a group of persons of entirely different habits and tastes, to be forced into living together. Yet Jawaharlal Nehru felt privileged living in close contact with some men of outstanding ability and culture. Unlike Oscar Wilde who did not value friends, he maintained his personal friendships.[6] Hence, letters came from friends who shared his dreams, or from those who followed him to the public platform and the prison.[7]

Jawaharlal Nehru and Azad were Gandhi's chief lieutenants in the 1930s and 1940s. They shared a great deal with each other, though the Maulana's thoughts were elusive and could not be condensed into anyone's political programme. In short, they did not lend themselves to formulation. In the Ahmadnagar Fort Prison, they came to know each other a little better, but their differences remained. They were, after all, the products of different worlds and had grown up in wholly different mental climates. The differences between them surfaced in the prison, where they exchanged notes with other co-prisoners on the current political situation. At one such meeting, Azad discussed the events in 1942. His interpretation drew sharp reactions from Vallabhbhai Patel.[8] On 18 September 1942, Jawaharlal Nehru recorded, 'Maulana is an extraordinarily interesting companion.... I wish I could profit more by this enforced companionship.'[9] In yet another entry, he talks of his fund of knowledge, but also takes note of his limited writings.[10]

The Nehrus revered Tagore, the nation's pride, the symbol of its reawakening. Although Tagore did not go to jail, he did renounce the knighthood after the bloodbath at the Jallianwala Bagh.[11] People loved him before, but after that they adored him, and his melodious tunes haunted them for many nights and days.[12] In 1937, Tagore pleaded for a changed mindset of the people to move to a new era of Hindu–Muslim relationship. He noted: 'In the manner in which Europe emerged from the middle ages and entered the modern era through the pursuit of truth and by expanding the frontiers of knowledge, Hindus and Muslims will have to venture forth from the walls hemming them in.'[13] In addition, he tried balancing the affirmation of separate identities and a sense of the universal human community, and, using his extraordinary imagination and breadth of vision, he sought to identify areas of East–West cooperation.

In the solitude of the Dehradun Jail, Jawaharlal Nehru's ideas and attitudes helped to strengthen his emotional bond with Tagore. After Independence, during a debate in the Lok Sabha over the linguistic reorganization of states, he informed the House that he had sent Indira to Santiniketan so that she could imbibe Bengal's culture. But it is in his tribute to Tagore on his birth centenary that one gets a sense of the reasons that prompted him to do so. The Viswa Bharati exemplified the values that he himself held dearly: the confluence of nationalism and internationalism, tradition and modernity, the importance of developing the spirit over sheer material gains, the necessity of breaking down the narrow barriers of caste, race, and creed. He said,

> I have a fear that in this year of Gurudeva's birth centenary his message and ideals might be swept away in the flood of words and eloquence

and that we may imagine that we have done our duty by him. That is a dangerous delusion which comes over us often. I should like you specially here at Santiniketan and the Visva Bharati to remember that the test of your homage is not what you may say about him but the way you live, the way you grow, and the way you act up to his message.[14]

From the Golden Threshold

'The Golden Threshold', Sarojini Naidu's home in Hyderabad, was a spacious bungalow with a walled-in compound. As in Anand Bhawan, it had a lovely garden with fully grown trees. On 11 May 1925, Sarojini Naidu shared with Jawaharlal Nehru the pleasure of sunbirds and honeybirds making music in the garden among the flowering gulmohars and scarlet roses. She attracted and inspired other strong and independent minds, who turned the house into 'an oasis of stimulating personalities, talk and activity'. 'Why don't you too go on strike and hide here?' she once suggested to Jawaharlal Nehru.[15]

The Nehrus grew more and more to admire Sarojini Naidu and to think of her as a rich and rare being. An outspoken opponent of religious rituals and superstitions, Motilal Nehru did not harp on trifles and eschewed religious controversies. Sarojini Naidu shared his 'modern' sensibilities, and his spacious and unprejudiced viewpoint on past and present, and, combined with him, added a cosmopolitan thrust to Congress activities. They were both faithful to their wider political interests, and, while their politics shifted somewhat, their vigour was unabated to the end. What is more, they strove for dignity in public life. Right through the Home Rule protests and Rowlatt Satyagraha, Sarojini Naidu bore the hardships with much stoicism and humour. Once seen, she could not be forgotten because of her verbal ingenuity and powerful oratory. Most either warmed up to her instantly or were spellbound by her talent and vitality. Her exuberance was such that she would put all her strength into whatever she said. To speak was as easy for her as it was for a fish to swim. Though deflected from the highway of poetry by her engagement in politics, her three books—*The Golden*

Threshold (1905), *The Bird of Time* (1912), and, later, *The Broken Wing* (1917)—received acclaim in India and England.

In early 1913, Sarojini Naidu attended a Muslim League meeting. Gokhale had told her that Jinnah 'has true stuff in him, and that freedom from all sectarian prejudice which will make him the best ambassador of Hindu–Muslim unity'.[16] In 1915, she honoured Jinnah from the Congress platform in her poem 'Awake', and a year later, following the Lucknow Pact in December 1916, she called him the ambassador of Hindu–Muslim unity. She trusted his searching and quintessentially 'secular' mind, and relied on his credentials to close the breach with Congress.[17] When the Nehru Report was drafted in August 1928, Motilal Nehru sought Sarojini Naidu's intervention in bringing Jinnah back for talks.[18] Years later, she spoke of Jinnah as of Lucifer, a fallen angel, one who had once promised to be 'a great leader of Indian freedom, but had instead, cast himself out of the Congress heaven'.[19]

Sarojini Naidu's almost wayward impatience apart, Jawaharlal Nehru was touched by her intellectual serenity in a crisis. She reciprocated by expressing her abiding faith in his sincerity and passion for liberty.[20] Reminding him that 'liberty is the ultimate crown of all your sacrifice', she assured him that 'you will not walk alone'.[21] 'A man of destiny born to be alone in the midst of crowds, deeply loved but little understood',[22] she was confident that Jawaharlal Nehru would transmute sorrow, suffering, sacrifice, anguish, and strife into the very substance of ecstasy and victory—and freedom. On 14 November 1945, her telegram to Anand Bhawan read: 'Our hearts turn to love today towards one [Jawaharlal Nehru] whose prison is the nation's sanctuary'.[23]

The Nightingale's voice was stilled on 2 March 1949. As in life, she would have faced death with a light heart and with a song on the lips and smile on the face. Jawaharlal affirmed that 'just as the Father of the Nation had infused moral grandeur and greatness into the struggle, Sarojini Naidu gave it artistry and poetry'.[24] She saw herself as an

individual whose experiences, opinions, and inner feelings had a right
to be heard, and were certainly worth hearing. She wrote poetry—the
poetry of love and pleasure, laughter and tears. She talked of things
with Gandhi—who called her Bharat Kokila (Nightingale of India)—
which she would never have thought of discussing with any other man.
There was something very beautiful in the relationship they developed;
so closely and constantly were they linked together. Endowed as he
was with the liveliest sensibility to feminine influence, 'his life of self-
discipline and self-development, and, as he aptly called it, self-abandon,
enabled him to weld together in his own person the masculine and
feminine qualities into a single whole, free from tension'.[25] Gandhi
admitted that he deliberately surrounded himself with women to
prove that his mastery over 'lust' was not achieved by avoiding them.[26]

Sarojini Naidu exhibited the perceptiveness of a poet and its corol-
lary, the fine sense of humour and irony. The Indian bourgeoisie was in
many cases Western through and through; but Jawaharlal, who waited
for years for his 'discovery' to take place, respected Sarojini Naidu's
adaptation to and acceptance of traditions. Besides her speeches that
were 'all nationalism and patriotism',[27] she built bridges of cooperation,
harmony, concord, and tolerance, a necessity for human survival.[28]
Her approach became an essential foundation for a strong secular
democracy and, even more, a necessary part of a multicultural society.
Like Jawaharlal, she exerted herself to recognizing the 'Western' point
of view and approaches in the concrete world of nation-building.

Aligarh's Second Generation

'Awful creature I must have been then with my "education" and "snob-
bishness"', Jawaharlal Nehru once remarked. That he was not. He valued
constancy in friendship. Meeting friends in or out of jail bolstered his
spirits. Among the former Aligarh graduates, Jawaharlal Nehru had
warm feelings towards Mohamed Ali. 'A bond of affection and mutual
appreciation tied us to each other', he remarked. He was attracted by

his earnestness, his energy, and keen intelligence.[29] It was a misfortune
for India that Mohamed Ali left the country for Europe in the summer
of 1928. A great effort was then made to solve the communal problem.
If Mohamed Ali had been there then it is conceivable that matters
would have shaped differently. But his outpourings against the Nehru
Report and civil disobedience disappointed Jawaharlal Nehru. They
met on the occasion of the Lahore Congress in December 1929, after
which Jawaharlal Nehru reacted angrily to Mohamed Ali signing the
'Delhi Manifesto' with a bunch of politically reactionary Muslims.
This led him to suggest that India's Muslims could do nothing more
disastrous for their own interests than to keep away from the freedom movement.[30] He was equally disappointed when Mohamed
Ali attended the Round Table Conference at a time when the Civil
Disobedience Movement was in full swing. However, when it came to
naming a street or park in Allahabad after Ali, Nehru readily agreed.[31]
He received the news of his death in Naini Prison.

Anand Bhawan sheltered aspiring lawyers, journalists, and teachers.
It attracted well-to-do Muslims as well: A.M. Khwaja (1885–1962),
Jawaharlal's contemporary in Cambridge, T.A.K. Sherwani and
Chaudhry Khaliquzzaman, secretaries of the Swaraj Party from its
inception in January 1923, and Syed Mahmud. Each one of them
learned from him and drew themselves up to a higher plane than was
their own. In jail, Jawaharlal Nehru thought of a long pilgrimage with
Khaliquzzaman that would take them to Kashmir, Ladakh, and Tibet,
to the Mansarovar Lake and Mount Kailas, and to the famous cities of
Central Asia, Afghanistan, Iran, Arabia, and the West.[32] He narrated
how Khaliq neither had a beard nor a moustache. To a maulvi who
gently reminded him for not observing *sunnat* (a practice observed by
the Prophet), Khaliq said with great fervour, 'Don't say anything at all
about a beard. I have the greatest possible respect for it, therefore I
have allowed it to grow in my heart.'[33]

In the late 1930s, no accommodation of thought or feeling was
possible between Jawaharlal Nehru and Khaliquzzaman. The impasse

was complete over the coalition issue in 1937, and by the decision of the latter to shift his loyalties to the Muslim League. Like several educated Muslims, Khaliquzzaman believed, with all the intensity of his romantic faith, in salvation from Islam; and salvation could only come through Pakistan.

Syed Mahmud had met Jawaharlal Nehru, 'a charming young man', in Cambridge on 14 November 1909. Like many other contemporaries, he was charmed by the 'Jewel of India', the 'embodiment of sacrifice'. Quite early in public life, he had said to his mentor on his birthday, 'I am painfully conscious of the worthlessness of my devotion, but then, my boy, just like a dog I have nothing else or better in my possession to give my master—a thought which sometimes makes me bitter and sad.'[34] 'Why are you so emotional or rather why do you exhibit your emotion so much', Jawaharlal Nehru once told him. 'Surely emotion should not be cheapened, it is too valuable a commodity.'[35] Mahmud was not altogether a blind sentimentalist; he believed, as others did, that Nehru alone possessed the splendid vision of India. The facts may, to the objective historian, appear commonplace; but in the eyes of contemporaries, they had a vital and peculiar significance.

Mahmud's single-minded devotion inspired in Jawaharlal Nehru the most sincere and respectable emotions of gratitude and friendship. But he was uneasy with some of his political ideas. 'Mahmud irritates me', Jawaharlal Nehru noted in his prison diary, 'probably because I like him and want him to pull himself up.'[36] He also felt that Mahmud was indecisive on social matters. On the issue of his daughters observing purdah and not being educated, Kamala Nehru rebuked Mahmud: 'Your profession and practice are different. Is it correct? I took you as a frank and independent minded person, but you have proved just the opposite.'[37]

The Frontier Gandhi

In the North-West Frontier Province (NWFP), Khan Abdul Ghaffar Khan tamed the fiery and rebellious spirit of his followers only to use their energies creatively to build an anti-British ideology. Without being a revolutionary or an innovative reformer, he transformed them. He never talked down to them, knowing what they could understand and phrasing his arguments accordingly. He did not throw his weight about, but established the principle, which the League fiercely contested, that nationalism was compatible with Islam and that Indian citizenry did not come in conflict with the concept of ummah. *Qaum* (nation, and not community) and ummah were indivisible.

Jawaharlal Nehru's attachment to the serene and amiable Ghaffar Khan took the form of a dream; in the heat of a summer afternoon, he saw him being attacked and himself fighting to defend him. He woke up in an exhausted state, 'feeling very miserable'. Further, 'that surprised me, for in my waking state I was not liable to such emotional outbursts'.[38] Mahatma Gandhi spoke at a prayer meeting in early January 1932 on fear in man's minds—fear of death and fear of loss of material possession. 'A man of prayer and self-purification, he said, will shed the fear of death and embrace death as a boon companion and will regard all earthly possessions as fleeting and of no account'.[39] The 'Frontier Gandhi', as Ghaffar Khan was called, did just that. One can safely link him with the whole dark body of subterranean forces and energies that were geared up to wage jihad against foreign rule. Officials declined to deal with 'a fanatic or an honest fanatic, whose fanaticism got the better of him'.[40] On 'first principle', one of them asserted, 'it seems to me that government must maintain its position as the final and authoritative arbiter and must not submit to being placed on trial before any independent individual or organisation—however eminent'.[41] Mahatma Gandhi committed himself very deeply on the side of the innocence and nonviolence of the Red Shirts.[42] C.F. Andrews (1871–1940) tried to soften the official stance towards them, but the government failed to realize how much Ghaffar Khan had done to imbue the concept of nonviolence into the Frontier people. In this respect, as also in many other respects, the 'Frontier Gandhi' was, undoubtedly, one of the makers of history.[43] Andrews met the Home Member in December 1934 to explain that he and his

Red Shirt followers were misrepresented as a dangerously violent force akin to Russian communism.

In Hazaribagh Jail, Ghaffar Khan had no access to letters—he spent more than forty years of his life in detention, having been first arrested in 1914. Visitors were kept out on the excuse that they'd conspire, if together, against the civil administration. Naturally, Ghaffar Khan felt miserable,[44] but followed Gandhi in eschewing the favours offered to him by the jailors.[45] He thought always of his children and felt anxious—one of his sons studied in the United States, two others at school in Dehradun, and a daughter went to a convent in Muree. He confided in Ansari:

> I live alone in a third class barrack. I am closed up at night time. Nobody can come to me, nor can I go to see any body. There is neither volley-ball nor badminton nor rules nor regulations nor a letter nor interview in spite of the fact that I am a state prisoner. Administer [sic] justice yourself. I consider 'C' class prisoners better off than myself. In my opinion this law had been constituted for taking revenge. What should I write more? If I do so, perhaps you would be deprived of this letter and so consider this 'A grain from the heap.' But well, we too have a God who might be seeing our oppressedness [sic] and we are also seeing what He will do. I am quite healthy. Morning and evening I take good exercise in walking. I have formed a small beautiful garden by which my time passes well. Perhaps you may appreciate my garden if you see it. It is bigger and better than that of Zafar Ali Khan. You should pray for me and I will pray for you.[46]

The Bihar and Orissa government allowed his brother Khan Sahib (1883–1958) to join him in the Naini Prison on 2 June 1932.[47] 'The blood of the martyr is the deed of the church'—this eternal law prevailed in the case of the 'Frontier Gandhi'. Legends of all kinds quickly crystallized around the grinding prison labour imposed on him. He would have cited Ghalib to the effect:

Where's the second step of desire, O God?
The desert of possibilities was only a footprint.

'On the summit of deep, universal tumultuous movements', ran Ranke's last dictated words, 'appear natures cast in a gigantic mould, which rivet the attention of the centuries. General tendencies do not alone decide; great personalities are always necessary to make them effective.'[48] We have dealt with a number of great personalities, who had a certain romance in life and a certain vision to nurture. They did not fear imprisonment or death; instead they defied British laws and challenged the raison d'être of British rule. In much the same vein, Jawaharlal Nehru told the judge at his trial in Gorakhpur on 3 November 1940:

> It is a small matter what happens to me in this trial or subsequently. Individuals count for little; they come and go, as I shall go when my time is up. Seven times I have been tried and convicted by British authority in India, and many years of my life are buried within prison walls. An eighth time or a ninth time, and a few more years, makes little difference.[49]

Likewise, at the trial in the court of E. de V. Moss in 1942, he offered no defence; it was the government itself that was on trial, he said. Indeed, it was the judge himself on trial. We can hardly overestimate the impact of this state of mind: it got rid of whatever scepticism and despair that afflicted the mind of the political actors.

Prison is a place where each day was like a year, a year whose days were long, wrote Oscar Wilde. Being oppressed, ill-treated, and brutalized, the inmates felt sad, abandoned, and weary. Some of them, though, lived with their thoughts, dreams, and ideas, and having long, dreary months and years ahead of them, they all the same wanted to live. They lived with one thought, one desire—to further the cause of liberty, and, without drawing any hard and sharp lines, their personal and political identities were continuously shaped and restructured to generate resentment towards British rule. One had to accept everything as it came both in social and private life with a smile. Rosa Luxemburg, the revolutionary whose life spanned a great historical epoch until her murder in Berlin in 1919, lived with the conviction that things will take the right turn before one passes through a period of terrible human suffering.[50] In the subcontinent, audacious men and women were grinding corn or working on 'oil presses' in sweltering heat. Rajaji saw so many cheerfully toiling away like men 'to the manner born', who had accepted hard labour as an alternative for merely giving security.[51] He saw Sesha Reddy and the two brave Nellore youths with broomstick in hand sweeping the grounds in front of his cell saying, 'Are we not scavengers?' In Vellore Jail, he exchanged notes with fellow non-cooperators. 'Of Shafiqur Rahman [Kidwai] of Aligarh, what shall I say', he noted in his diary. 'I count it as a privilege to know such a man—I have not known a better young man or a more self-restrained, a more truly God-fearing, finer or noble soul.'[52] Another entry mentions: 'I am very glad that the superintendent's promise to look after Shafiq's health has borne fruit. He will get two eggs and a pint of milk besides chappaties.'[53]

Gandhi had promised Swaraj within a year. One of the non-cooperators learnt somewhere that it had come and depended on three years' good conduct.[54] Jawaharlal Nehru was determined to break through and demolish all the prison walls that 'encompass our bodies and mind, and function as a free nation'.

Notes

1. Quoted in Moraes, *Jawaharlal Nehru*, p. 357.
2. *SWJN*, vol. 2, p. 314.
3. It is difficult to say who first had the idea of using the fort as a prison, but during the First World War the British had hidden here detainees whose whereabouts had, for a variety of reasons, to be kept secret. The prisoners lived in blind casemates whose narrow windows just below the ceiling were now completely bricked up. The casemates gave onto an inner courtyard, 50 metres from wall to wall, with bare cracked ground and a single stunted tree with withered leaves hidden in one corner.
4. Moraes, *Jawaharlal Nehru*, p. 84.
5. Gopal, *Jawaharlal Nehru—A Biography*, vol. 2, p. 27.

6.   E.P. Thompson, Oral History Transcript (689), NMML.

7.   An official wrote of a largish collection of literature mostly addressed to Jawaharlal and suggested forwarding of the stuff to the addresses, except in individual cases where the book or magazine concerned was objectionable. Home Department, Political (1), file no. 156.

8.   19 March 1942, *SWJN*, pp. 585–6.

9.   *SWJN*, vol. 13, p. 15.

10.   *SWJN*, vol. 13 pp. 38–9.

11.   Fakrul Alam and Radha Chakravarty, eds, *The Essential Tagore* (Cambridge, Massachusetts: Belknap and Harvard University Press), p. 99.

12.   Mazumdar, *Memoirs of an Indian Woman*, p. 169.

13.   Alam and Chakravarty, *The Essential Tagore*, p. 182.

14.   Jawaharlal Nehru, *Jawaharlal Nehru's Speeches*, vol. 4 (Publications Division, Ministry of Information and Broadcasting, Government of India, 1983), p. 444.

15.   J. Nehru, *Bunch of Old Letters*, p. 42.

16.   Stanley A. Wolpert, *Jinnah of Pakistan* (Delhi: Oxford University Press, 1984), p. 35.

17.   Kanji Dwarkadas, *India's Fight for Freedom, 1913–1937: An Eyewitness Story* (Bombay: Popular Prakashan, 1966), pp. 63–4.

18.   Ansari to Jawaharlal, 29 March 1928, AICC papers (G-60); Motilal to Thakurdas, 28, 29 April 1928, Thakurdas Papers (71), NMML.

19.   Wolpert, *Jinnah of Pakistan* p. 289.

20.   Sarojini Naidu to Jawaharlal, 29 September 1929, *Bunch of Old Letters*, p. 75.

21.   Sarojini Naidu to Jawaharlal, 13 November 1937, *Bunch of Old Letters*, p. 255.

22.   Sarojini Naidu to Jawaharlal, Diwali 1939, *Bunch of Old Letters*, p. 407.

23.   14 November 1944, S. Gandhi, *Two Alone, Two Together*, p. 457.

24.   Edib, *Inside India*, p. 28.

25.   Horace Gundry Alexander, *Consider India: An Essay in Values* (Bombay: Asia Publishing House, 1961), p. 58.

26.   Louis Fischer, *The Life of Mahatma Gandhi* (New York: Harper and Row Publishers, 1983 edition), p. 440.

27.   J. Nehru, *An Autobiography*, p. 35.

28.   J. Nehru, *An Autobiography*, p. 594.

29.   J. Nehru, *An Autobiography*, p. 117.

30.   'Prison Diary', 30 April 1930, *SWJN*, vol. 4, p. 335.

31.   To Chairman Municipal Board, (before) 14 March 1931, *SWJN*, vol. 4, p. 588. J. Nehru, *An Autobiography*, p. 117.

32.   Nanda, *The Nehrus*, pp. 213–14.

33.   J. Nehru, *An Autobiography*, p. 117.

34.   Syed Mahmud to Nehru, 13 November 1924, Datta and Cleghorn, *A Nationalist Muslim and Indian Politics*, p. 51.

35.   J. Nehru to Mahmud, 21 March 1927, Datta and Cleghorn, *A Nationalist Muslim and Indian Politics*, p. 48.

36.   16 October 1942, *SWJN*, vol. 13, p. 25.

37.   Kamala Nehru to Mahmud, 21 June 1927, *SWMN*, vol. 13, p. 77.

38.   Gopalkrishna Gandhi, *Of a Certain Age: Twenty Life Sketches* (Delhi: Penguin Books India, 2011), p. 50.

39.   3 January 1932, *CWMG*, vol. 48, p. 489.

40.   Dinanath Gopal Tendulkar, *Abdul Ghaffar Khan* (Delhi: Gandhi Peace Foundation, 1967), p. 198.

41.   Home Department, Political, File no. 11/14, 1934.

42.   Byname of Khudai Khidmatgar, started by Abdul Ghaffar Khan in support of the Indian National Congress.

43.   He was arrested on 24 December 1931.

44.   He felt strongly that he had not been allowed to receive any letters and apparently all letters from him were with the inspector general of police, NWFP.

45.   Mohammad Yunus, *Letters from Prison* (New Delhi: Vikas Publishing House, 1969), p. 15.

46.   4 February 1932. The police intercepted the letter. (Police Home Department Political, file no. 31/107, 1932.) Maulana Zafar Ali Khan, a poet and a journalist from Lahore, was one of the early victims of the government's repressive policy. On 12 January 1914, the Punjab government forfeited the security of the zamindar, and in December that year, restricted him to his village near Sialkot. This was followed in May 1915 by the arrests of the Ali brothers, and Azad and Hasrat Mohani. In December 1916, Maulana Mahmud Hasan and his four companions of Deoband were arrested for

their part in the 'Silk Letter Conspiracy' (*Tehrik-e Reshmi Rumal*), a scheme Ubaidullah Sindhi and his chief disciple, Mahmud Hasan devised to destroy British rule.

47.   Home Department, Political, file no. 30/70, 1932.

48.   G.P. Gooch, *History and Historians in the Nineteenth Century* (Boston: Beacon Press, 1959), p. 95.

49.   J. Nehru, *The Unity of India*, p. 399.

50.   Waters, *Rosa Luxemburg Speaks*.

51.   25 December 1921, Rajagopalachari, *Jail Diary*, p. 8. He was locked up in Vellore's Central Jail from 21 December 1921 until 20 March 1922.

52.   S.R. Kidwai, 'Shafiqur Rahman Kidwai', in *Dilli Wale*, edited by Dr Salahuddin (Delhi: Urdu Academy, 1986), p. 239.

53.   Rajagopalachari to Shafiqur Rahman Kidwai, 17 March 1952, in Riaz-ur-Rahman Kidwai, *Biographical Sketch of Kidwais of Avadh: With Special Reference to Barabanki Families* (Aligarh: Kitab Ghar Publishers, 1987), p. 166.

54.   25 December 1921, Rajagopalachari, *Jail Diary*, p. 8.

9 Writing History in a Cell

The most effective pose is one in which there seems to be the least of posing, and Jawahar had learned well to act without the paint and powder of an actor.... What is behind that mask of his? ... What will to power? He has the power in him to do great good for India or great injury.... Men like Jawaharlal, with all their capacity for great and good work, are unsafe in a democracy.

—Jawaharlal Nehru[1]

The French political theorist Alexis Tocqueville (1805–1859) talked about the part played in French political thinking by men of letters. In the second half of the nineteenth century, Bengal witnessed a 'renaissance' to which literary men, reformers, and journalists contributed their bit. In this context, the historian Sabyasachi Bhattacharya has talked of a new 'Bengali Patriotism' and the vernacularization of politics.[2] Literary works in Urdu and Hindi in the 1920s and 1930s had a striking impact in raising mass awakening.

'A room without books is like a body without soul', wrote Marcus Tullius Cicero.[3] Indeed, the man who does not read has no advantage over the man who cannot read, wrote Mark Twain (1835–1910).[4] Jawaharlal Nehru was a voracious reader: between 21 May 1922 till 29 January 1923 alone, he read fifty-five books. Oscar Wilde's *The Ballad of Reading Goal* had a magical sway over him; Plato's *Republic* stimulated him; *To the Lighthouse* by Virginia Woolf opened his eyes to many scenes of life; he found an echo of his moods and inner conflict in some of Ernst Toller's *Letters from Prison* and his *Seven Plays*.[5] While the sisters had Miss Hooper as their governess, Jawaharlal Nehru's tutor, Ferdinand T. Brooks, a theosophist, had introduced him to the English classics.

Jawaharlal Nehru perused Beatrice Webb (1858–1943), a Fabian socialist, and Sidney Webb (1859–1947). He delved into philosophy, and turned the pages of history to sharpen his understanding of the ideas and movements that stood apart as catalysts for momentous changes. In so doing, he looked through other people's writings to understand how simple, ordinary men and women became heroes, and how their strivings made history stirring and epoch-making. Prison had made a man of him, he told the Socialist leader Acharya Narendra Deva (1889–1956) when they were in jail for the last time in 1942.[6] Putting pen to paper was an antidote to isolation. The British superintendent of prison complained: 'I cannot understand your passion for reading. I finished all my reading at the age of twelve.'[7]

Benjamin Disraeli (1804–1881), the British statesman, wrote about the Dutch philosopher Hugo Grotius (1583–1645): 'Other men condemned to exile or captivity, if they survive, despair; the man of letters may reckon those days as the sweetest of his life.'[8] This applies to Jawaharlal Nehru, who imagined books lined up, 'row after row, with the wisdom of ages locked up in them, serene and untroubled in a changing and distracted world, looking down silently on the mortals that come and go'.[9] About *Prison Days and other Poems* by S.H. Vatsyayan (1911–1987), he commented: 'Something of that dreaming comes out in these poems, something of that yearning when the arms stretched out in search for what was not and clutched at empty space…. There was always a sorrow to hope for, a tomorrow which might bring deliverance.'[10] Without comparing his own role with the famous jail-birds—such as Miguel de Cervantes (1547–1616) and John Bunyan (1628–1688)—he lived in the world of ideas and bequeathed to contemporary discourse a method and a model, 'the model of growth and progress and of the possibility of an infinite advance for man'.[11] He shared with tens and thousands of prisoners the changing moods of exaltations and depressions, of intense activity and enforced leisure. To buttress the idea that man is not just a simple individual but a crowd of thoughts and ideas, he cited Ghalib's couplet.

Man is himself
A tumultuous world of thought
A company all around I feel
Even if I am all alone![12]

Why did Jawaharlal Nehru write? Who did he write for? For himself or for others? He wrote to regenerate his generation, to render them capable of following Gandhi's nonviolent Satyagraha, and to put before them the tangled web of current affairs in Russia, Germany, England, America, Japan, China, France, Spain, Italy, and Central Europe. It was a tangled web no doubt, difficult to unravel and difficult even to see as a whole. Yet he presented the many-coloured life of other ages and countries to enrich the reader's understanding, analyzed the ebb and flow of the old civilizations, and took up ideas in their full flow. The superimposed loneliness empowered him to turn to himself for fellowship and guidance, and arrange his thoughts and evolve his political creed undisturbed by external influences. It affected the whole gamut of his emotions.

Felix Dzerzhinsky, the Soviet statesman, found it impossible to explain everything in a letter so that people could turn over in their mind all that the soul had undergone in the long and excruciating years of wandering.[13] Jawaharlal Nehru secured some space to contemplate and script his thoughts behind stone walls and iron bars. He had no archives to consult, and so he relied on his recollections and on bits of information that he could access. He disliked being called a writer, and yet, armed with a varied experience of affairs, writing became a congenial occupation. Sometimes he did not write for weeks, sometimes he wrote daily. The letters he wrote represented his moods and thoughts at the time of each event; they were also his escapes from gaol.[14]

The word 'intellectual' caused annoyance to Jawaharlal Nehru, but his writings transmit the enthusiasm and animation he felt for the discipline of history. In a reminiscent mood, he said, 'What I wrote may or may not be of value. But the writing of it was of tremendous value to me. You have to read and study and think.'[15] In fact, there is something uncanny about the way in which a self-taught and amateur historian like him explored the unbounded universe in full variety. True, his vision was far from settled, but it was being etched out in conjunction and contention with other voices.

Jawaharlal Nehru put down his thoughts in words that came with graceful spontaneity.[16] He did so because he was conscious of making history by taking part in the great Indian drama.[17] Reading history was good, but even more interesting and fascinating was to be of help in its making.[18] Thus,

'in the golden days to come when the history of our times and our country comes to be written, the present will occupy a glorious chapter. And shall we not think of the good old days? Shall we not remember the great men who showed us the way, and filled us with the fire of faith? In the words of [George] Meredith (changing but one word Italia for India):

We who have seen India in the throes
Half-risen but to be hurled to the ground, and now,
Like a ripe field of wheat where once drove plough,
All bounteous as she is fair, we think
Of those who blew the breath of life into her frame.[19]

The point is admirably made, and there are in such interventions vigour and a conviction that sweeps the reader along. One is not required to pause and consider subtleties, contradictions, or an illusion of pulsating life.

Jawaharlal Nehru talked of a whole people becoming full of faith for a great cause, and brought to the fore their treasures of knowledge, learning, heroism, and devotion. He looked at the entire world with a fresh eye and gave a balanced view of man's life on many continents. His was a global view—not an Asian view any more than it was a European one.[20] With this eclectic approach, he called for the breakdown of national histories and the construction of a more relevant world history as a means to understand the global exchange of ideas in the past and the necessity of exchange for a better future.[21] He wanted books not for specialists alone but also for the general, interested lay reader in a popular and accessible mode. He wanted books on the daily lives of ordinary men and women who lived in the past (family budgets from hundreds of years ago, he suggests, could show us how life was organized in that age!). And he wanted Asia's history to be read as widely as possible so that the readers should think of all the countries and all the peoples, and not merely of one little country.[22] Reading Meredith Townsend's *Asia and Europe* in Cambridge had convinced him of 'a disposition to believe that Asia belongs of right to the Asiatics, and that any event which brings that right nearer to realization is to all Asiatics a pleasurable experience.'[23]

With his historical appreciation of conflicts between nation states, Jawaharlal Nehru denounced narrow-minded nationalism and envisioned, instead, a world free of ceaseless warfare. Asia and Europe were mere geographical expressions, and the problems confronting them were 'world problems'. They should explore the new social ideas of equality and visualize a future that would be free of any form of political domination. He reiterated his view in the inaugural address of the Asian History Congress in 1961. 'In a seismic shift of perspective from the Western point of view', writes Nayantara Sahgal, 'my uncle wrote an alternative version of history while interned in different prisons between 1930 and 1933.'[24]

Gandhi, who lived through the negative images of Indians in South Africa, highlighted the intractability of ethnocentrism. The meeting of the East and West was possible only when the latter threw overboard modern civilization almost in its entirety.[25] Tagore related the new nationalist stirrings in India to the Boer War in South Africa, and the collective colonial encroachments on China's independence and sovereignty.[26] Yet, as a major proponent of cultural diversity, he always stood for East–West cooperation.

Jawaharlal Nehru's thinking centred round an incessant dialogue and synthesis of ideas amongst cultures and civilizations. In May 1905, he had heard joyously the news of the decisive Japanese victory over Russia in the strait of Tsushima. The fourteen-year-old mused of Indian freedom and Asiatic freedom from the thralldom of Europe, and dreamt of brave deeds; of how, sword in hand, he would fight for India and help in freeing her. In the summer of 1939, the Kuominatang government invited him to China. At the end of the visit he hoped that India and China will work together for their own good and the good of the world.

Jawaharlal Nehru dealt with the ideals and aspirations of liberal nationalism in Turkey and in the Middle East. In this respect, he and Halide Edib, the Turkish revolutionary, had a great deal in common. Both articulated Asian voices, and chronicled and derived strength from their past. Both talked of understanding other people's sufferings and rejected a narrow, negative, and destructive nationalism. Both repudiated chauvinism and imperialism, and claimed that the selfish and materialistic philosophy of the latter part of the nineteenth century brought disasters in the form of the World War.[27] Whatever differences of opinion one may hold with their conclusions, one is struck by their quest for knowledge, their extensive knowledge, their inclusive vision, and their objective analysis. Jawaharlal Nehru was a romantic in many respects, but emphatically never in politics.

Jawaharlal Nehru emphasized India's shared heritage with Turkey to such an extent that the differences in the antecedents were overshadowed by close similarities in the sequel. He recognized Turkey's war of liberation, and attributed the Committee of Union's triumph to the iron determination of its members.[28] With his ability to look at societies with an eye neither jaundiced nor morbid, he drew comparisons between India and Turkey, recovered his own voice, his own enthusiasm, and his own strong arm at people's service. On his fiftieth birthday, his article in the *Modern Review* illuminates his own sense of leading a critical mission:

> From the far North to Cape Comorin, he has gone like some triumphant Caesar, passing by leaving a trail of glory and a legend behind him. Is all this for him just a passing fancy which amuses him? ... Is it his will to power ... that is driving him from crowd to crowd and making him whisper to himself, 'I drew these tides of men into my hands and wrote my will across the sky in stars'? [*Seven Pillars of Wisdom* by T.E. Lawrence][29]

Jawaharlal Nehru was asked what he was heir to, and answered that he was heir to all that humanity had achieved over tens of thousands of years. He had inherited all that humanity had thought, felt, suffered, and taken joy in; to its cries of triumph and its bitter agonies of defeat; to that astonishing adventure that had begun long ago yet still continued and beckoned to man. Besides commenting on the wisdom of India's great inexhaustible spiritual heritage, he talked of the vital necessity to apply it intelligently and reasonably to the present and the future.[30] His vision was hardly ever trapped in the exclusivist, cultural-logical mode; far from it, it was supremely inclusive and driven by a belief in the existence, even the necessity of cultures constantly interacting with each other, of cultures working on and transforming the other and their own through a live contact.

Writings

In the memorandum on the United Province's land tenure system Jawaharlal Nehru steered the course over an unchartered sea, and it was designed to shake off the hegemony of the landlords and the moneylenders. 'Whither India', another important piece of writing, covered a multitude of selfish interests, local narrowness, and class privilege. These questions of radically transforming social relations and economic structures belong to the very heart of Jawaharlal Nehru's story and explain to us why he became the icon of the Left in the middle and late 1930s. The younger Congressmen were inspired by the contents of such writings and formed the Congress Socialist Party, with Jawaharlal Nehru as their acknowledged spiritual godfather. UP's chief secretary wondered what might be its impact and how far Congress was prepared to go on the road to Communism.[31]

In other writings, Jawaharlal Nehru roused enthusiasm in ideas which, quite apart from their economic aspect, contemplated the overthrow of the Raj. He raised issues of poverty, of people in distress, who faced infinitely worse difficulties than the of the comfortable bourgeois, and led a muddied existence. His conviction that their condition was mirrored in the colonial institutions struck notes of a thoughtful response. He sought to understand what lay behind the eyes that stared at him. Glimpses came to him that illumined his vision and made him realize the immensity of their problems. Those teething troubles absorbed not only the past experiences and ignominious failures, but also outlined his impulses for a new life. He wanted India to be in pursuit of transition, regeneration, and transformation and not be in the throes of a conflict. At the same time, his dialectic of change and development was strongly rooted in past accomplishments. He learnt lessons from the history of a generation, indeed the interpretation of a whole liberation struggle,[32] and he, therefore, wanted his countrymen to adjust to a new scheme of things.[33] Indira Gandhi realized, after becoming prime minister, that her father's letters helped to form her mind in a way that no other education did because they helped her to see things in perspective.[34]

Jawaharlal Nehru's feelings in jail were unbridled and his frustration intense. Perhaps he wanted the violence outside to be an outlet for his confinement. But the frail old man in loincloth told him not to be troubled by the outside world but to read, write, or learn any handicraft. Jawaharlal Nehru heeded his advice and put his thoughts in writing.[35] A friend describes a group of young women sitting at his feet while he told them about his life in jail, how to just see the sky helped pass the time, and how he had to wrack his brains to remember history.[36] He wrote only when he had the urge to do so. Talking to Ramakrishna, who had received a UNESCO prize, in Bhopal, he described to him:

> I was in jail for one year, but the thought never came into my mind that I should write. Slowly I began to think about it. I thought over it for several months, and then began a study to see if it was worthwhile. I made notes, as has always been my custom. Gradually, I got the urge to write, and then I sat down and in about four-and-a-half months of continuous writing, wrote *Discovery of India*.[37]

Even though decades of research and discussion have overthrown or modified many of the generalizations in *Glimpses of World History*, and it is not a standard text book, it still makes an impression of sustained intellectual power. Received with a chorus of admiration,[38] it has become standard reading in India, Africa, Europe, and the United States. Is it a better survey of world story than H.G. Well's *Outline of History*? A reviewer in *The American Current History* thought so.[39] Fenner Brockway (1888–1988), a friend of India, mentioned that his daughter learnt more from *Glimpses* than any other history book she studied at school.[40] Marie Seton found the letters to be 'wonderful'. This is what Seton writes:

> Jawaharlal Nehru looked surprised and asked: 'You mean to say you read the whole of it?'
> 'Yes, the one thousand pages.'
> 'I never knew anybody did,' said Jawaharlal Nehru. 'You really did?'
> 'I really did. I learnt a great deal from it. It was like learning history anew—where things fitted into the whole.'
> He still looked slightly surprised. Then he said softy: 'I'm glad you learnt something from it. It surprises me.[41]

Maina wa Kinyatti of Kenya wanted *Glimpses of World History* to be sent to the Kamiti Prison. He knew that the prison censorship would definitely not allow him to read the book because it would be classified as 'politics' and 'dangerous', but he was confident of smuggling in the book: 'The prison system is based on lies and brutalities, one therefore must be smart and brave enough to beat it.'[42]

When passages from the *Glimpses of World History* were read out to Gandhi, he felt like translating them.[43] G.B. Pant, a co-prisoner in the Ahmadnagar Fort Prison, found the letters 'extremely interesting and instructive'.[44] Since then, new editions have succeeded one another. Besides public men, lawyers, and judges thought highly of them,[45] and few works of the time require so little adaptation to satisfy students today. Wrote Michael Brecher: 'His feel for the flow of human history, his sensitivity to the many facets of social evolution, his capacity to weave together a wide range of knowledge in a meaningful pattern give to this book qualities of a high order.'[46] To Norman Cousins, editor of *Saturday Review* in New York, 'the letters constituted something of a liberal university education, ranging as they did over the whole of the human historical record'. They embraced, besides the national and continental civilization, the creative thrust and splendor of mankind.[47]

Written in elegant prose poised between the critical and the sentimental, no historian or generalist can take the book lightly, or ignore the author's intimate acquaintance with philosophy and literature, no less than history. Even though Nehru cast his net wide, his breadth of view and patient learning is impressive. A lover of words and phrases which he expressed intelligently and in ordered sequence, his approach to life was compounded by buoyancy and optimism, and a humorous tolerance towards life's foibles and even its trials. He was sensitive to the artist's perception of feeling that a novelist or a painter has.[48]

The letters identify the milestones in world history, the creative thrust and splendour of mankind, the theory and practice of statecraft, the multiple influences of events, and the fate of societies that have been constructed in a narrow and superficial spirit. We thus come across 'a mighty procession of living men and women and children in every age and every clime, different from us and yet very like us, with much the same human virtues and human feelings. History is not a magic show, but there is plenty of magic in it for those who have eyes to see'.[49] This is well-documented in *Discovery of India*, which also reveals the author's own dilemmas in reconciling his Westernized world view with his understanding of India. Writers without a global vision celebrated the unbridgeable chasm between the 'East' and the 'West', but Jawaharlal Nehru saw the unities across cultures and civilization. In this respect, he was one with Gandhi who wanted to do away with national borders and bring the people of the East and the West on a common platform.

According to Leopold von Ranke (1795–1886), historiography followed the great impulses of public life. Jawaharlal Nehru agreed, adding that the history of one country had to be connected with the stirring and epoch-making past events in other parts of the world.[50] With this point of view in mind, he appreciated the role of leaders who made the masses do great deeds—Lenin, who made his people write a noble and never to be forgotten chapter in history; Giuseppe Garibaldi (1807–1882) and the Italian Risorgimento; Cavour (1810–1861), the first prime minister of Italy; Giuseppe Mazzini (1805–1872); and Mustafa Kemal Ataturk (1881–1938) whose triumph electrified the subcontinent. Hearing the news of the latter's triumph, Jawaharlal Nehru and his co-prisoners in the Lucknow District Gaol decorated their barracks with such odds and ends as they could gather.[51] The Turkish leader became the lustrous example worthy of being emulated by those struggling against an alien imperialist.

Much ink and paper has been expended on discussing Gandhi's life. Jawaharlal Nehru was the first among his colleagues to make sense of his rather complex range of ideas, and to explain the secret behind his hold over the masses. 'Bapuji lies in prison', he writes, 'but the magic of his message steals into the hearts of India's millions, and men and women, and even little children, come out of their little shells and become soldiers of freedom.'[52] Politics was a chaotic and contaminated pursuit, but Gandhi moved the millions like a thunderbolt, and illumined the minds of many. Crowds of ten and twenty thousand gathered just in the hope of seeing and hearing the man who brought freely into the open his amazing powers to stimulate and stir the dream of Swaraj.[53] Some of this even crept inside the goal. 'Swaraj is coming!' said the ordinary convicts expectantly; they waited impatiently for it. The warders, who came in contact with the bazaar gossip, expected Swaraj to come in the near future.

The Non-Cooperation Movement had raised the prospect of a better world guided by astute statesmen. But these expectations were not fulfilled. The masses felt cheated; the leaders had a profound sense of betrayal. Disenchanted with political regression,[54] Jawaharlal Nehru wondered: 'Were a remote village and a mob of excited peasants in an out-of-the-way place going to put an end, for some time at least, to our struggle for freedom? If this was the inevitable consequence of a sporadic act of violence, then there was something lacking in the philosophy and technique of nonviolent struggle.'[55] At the same time, Gandhi's political heir understood, to borrow a quote from Lenin, that 'nothing is final; we must learn from circumstances', and from the grandeur of the Gandhian revolution. Others had no reason to defend what they regarded as Gandhi's reckless and ill-considered decision to betray the masses. For example, Munshi Premchand (1880–1936) gave up his career in the education department, only to find that new India's spirit and the pulse of its new life were non-existent.[56] Manmathnath Gupta, the revolutionary in Varanasi, felt reduced to the position of an ordinary convict.[57]

A running thread is discernible within Jawaharlal Nehru's clear, emphatic, neat outlook.[58] Owing to his awareness of the continuity between the past, the present, and his hopes and vision for the future, he tried to reveal the wealth India possessed in chronicles. At the same time, he did not want the greatness of the civilization to be a burden. He brought to light the 'demonstration of human intellectual capacity',[59] and then let the reader draw any conclusion that he liked. In this respect, it is hard to find much fault with his general conception of ideas and their execution or to deny the limitations of an otherwise wide canvas. Even though *Glimpses of World History* has its shortcomings—the coverage of Latin America and the African continent south of the Mediterranean fringe are non-existent—it serves as an excellent source for examining the formation of Jawaharlal Nehru's liberal and Marxist ideas.

The Great Rebellion

A great deal has been written about the 'Mutiny' or the 'First War of Independence' in 1857 in letters, diaries, memoirs, reminiscences, poems, novels, travelogues, newspapers, government documents, military histories, and scholarly accounts. Books, including reprints of earlier editions, were let loose on the public in the 125th year, indicating the avid interest that the incident continues to evoke. They detail the perils, dangers, and events of the year. On earlier occasions, too, the revolt served to legitimize radicalism. Thus, the proponents of Swadeshi in 1907 determined to celebrate the Golden Jubilee of the revolt on 10 May 1907 by starting a procession from the Katra locality and proceeding through Colonelganj.[60]

Why did such a violent upheaval take place, and why did it peter out so quickly? Was it simply a sepoy mutiny, a people's resistance, a civil rebellion, the dying groans of an obsolete autocracy, or an attempt to turn back the clock of history to feudal isolation and tyranny? Was it little more than the spark that touched off a smouldering mass of combustible material? Was it the Indian War of Independence?[61] Or 'the last flicker of feudal India'?[62]

To answer these questions, I return to Jawaharlal Nehru, who understood the events about which he wrote with fervour and in somewhat glowing colours. For a man whose mind had been formed in the anti-imperialist climate of early industrial, competitive capitalism, the 1857 upsurge became an important symbol of a protracted struggle against

British colonialism. In addition, he read in the pages of stone and brick and mortar what his ancestors did in the old, old times. He understood that the cry of 'independence' covered a multitude of regional, local, and class interests. Unlike some of the British historians who represented one side as villains and the other as virtue, wisdom and heroism personified, he probed behind the appearance of events and contextualized the 1857 upsurge in the light of latter-day anti-colonial movements in Asia and Africa.

The 1857 stir left behind a bitter legacy. Poets and writers exemplify this. Mirza Asadullah Ghalib, the best amongst them, recorded his painful experience of living in Shahjahanabad; Altaf Hussain Hali (1837–1914), another well-known literary figure, was so overwhelmed by the dark terror of the times that he abandoned Delhi in search of a safe haven. Jawaharlal Nehru's ancestors experienced many vicissitudes of fortune right through the unsettled times that followed. Their *jagir* (landholding) dwindled and vanished away.[63] Forced by their circumstances, they were among the numerous fugitives who fled to Agra. Motilal's munshi, Mubarak Ali, whose own family in Badaun had suffered at the hands of the British, narrated to Jawaharlal Nehru his story. Jawaharlal Nehru described how the world of his ancestors darkened after the British occupation of Delhi:

> The family, having lost nearly all it possessed, joined the numerous fugitives who were leaving the old imperial city and went to Agra. My father was not born then but my two uncles were already young men and possessed some knowledge of English. This knowledge saved the younger of the two uncles, as well as some other members of the family, from a sudden and ignominious end. He was journeying from Delhi with some family members, among whom was his young sister, a little girl who was very fair, as some Kashmiri children are. Some English soldiers met them on the way and they suspected this little aunt of mine to be an English girl and accused my uncle of kidnapping her. From an accusation, to summary justice and punishment, was usually a matter of minutes in those days, and my uncles and others of the family might well have found themselves hanging on the nearest tree.

Fortunately for them, my uncle's knowledge of English delayed matters a little and then someone who knew him passed that way and rescued him and the others.[64]

From among those who fled Delhi, the tales of Ramchander, the mathematician teaching at Delhi College, and Altaf Hussain Hali, the literary giant, are well known. But little or no attention has been paid to the plight of many other fugitives and their pangs of hunger and thirst. Gangadhar, then only thirty years old, is one of them. He found a safe haven in Agra, once the seat of the Mughal emperors and renowned for its Taj Mahal. He appeared to be doing well until his star set as suddenly as it rose. He died in February 1861, barely four years after leaving Delhi and only three months after his wife gave birth to Motilal Nehru on 6 May. His premature death came as a bombshell, but Nandlal and Bansidhar, the other two elder sons, although still in their teens, shouldered family responsibilities and looked after their young brother. Between Nandlal and Motilal, there 'grew up a knot of affection, a happy blend of the filial and the fraternal, of which the Hindu joint family, with all its faults, furnishes probably the best example'.[65] Nandlal served Rajputana's Kheri state as its diwan until 1870. Patient and hardworking, he sometimes misleadingly gave others the impression of being a laborious plodder on the first acquaintance. That he was not. It is true that he worked, quietly, steadily, placidly, but did so with unfailing thoroughness.

Pandit Ajudhia Nath Kunzru's family, too, moved from place to place until his father settled in Allahabad. A leading pleader in Allahabad in the 1880s, his father had settled at the site of the Sadr Diwani Adalat, which became the high court in 1866. A year later, the high court moved to Allahabad. That is when Ajudhia Nath opted to live in Allahabad. Bishambhar Nath was enrolled in Delhi College when he became a part of a Kashmiri group that included Motilal, Katju, Dharm Narain Haksar, Sarup Narain Haksar—the great-grandfather of P.N. Haksar, the renowned civil servant—and Ram Kishen. There was, then, Tej Bahadur Sapru, whose grandfather had become one of the first Indian deputy collectors. Jawaharlal Nehru has recorded how he had great hopes that Sapru would give them a lead: 'He was emotional and could occasionally be carried by enthusiasm. Compared to him my father seemed cold-bloodedness itself.'[66] As a law member of the viceroy's council under Reading and then in the UP and Imperial Legislative Councils between 1912 and 1922, he remained 'an Asquithian-type Liberal until his dying day'.[67]

Jawaharlal Nehru attributed the people's anger during the 1857 Rebellion to the ignorance and rapacity of officers, and the bitterness of feudal chiefs.[68] He linked colonialism with racism, observing how the combination had corrupted Britain's public life and made her forget the lessons of her own history and literature.[69] He compared Jesus preaching nonviolence and ahimsa with his loud-voiced followers of today, with their imperialism and armaments and wars and worship of wealth. 'The Sermon on the Mount and modern European and American Christianity—how amazingly dissimilar they are!' he observed.[70] He denounced the British for spreading terror, for shooting down people in cold blood, for hanging thousands from the wayside trees, and for destroying prosperous villages.[71] Making a special mention of General Neill,[72] a Madras officer who converted every tree by the roadside from Allahabad to Kanpur into a gibbet, he detailed the horrors:

> It is all a terrible and most painful story, and I hardly dare tell you all the bitter truth. If Nana Sahab had behaved barbarously and treacherously, many an English officer exceeded his barbarity a hundred-fold. If mobs of mutinous Indian soldiers, without officers or leaders, had been guilty of cruel and Rebellioning deeds, the trained British soldiers, led by their officers, exceeded them in cruelty and barbarity. I do not want to compare the two. It is a sorry business on both sides, but our perverted histories tell us a lot about the treachery and cruelty on the Indian side, and hardly mention the other side. It is also well to remember that the cruelty of a mob is nothing compared to the cruelty of an organized government when it begins to behave like a mob. Even today, if you go

to many of the villages in our province, you will find that the people have still got a vivid and ghastly memory of the horrors that befell them during the crushing of the Rebellion.[73]

Later, Jawaharlal Nehru invoked Buddha Purnima to remind his audience of the virtue of eschewing nonviolence and reconciliation. He disapproved of extremism and of bombs being thrown on English officers; instead, he returned to Gandhi 'to remind ourselves that unless we see reason and defeat violence, it will bring ruin to mankind'.[74] The Gandhian way had acquired greater relevance in the atomic age with its potential for unimaginable violence.[75] Indeed, he considered the stirring of a fierce hatred towards the enemy to be inconsistent with the Indian tradition so that saints and seers, poets and writers, dancers and musicians could challenge the might of the British empire without invoking the war symbols. Often, they could soothe frayed tempers. Thus Gandhi launched a satyagraha without calling for savage reprisals.

Jawaharlal Nehru did not want the past to be a burden on a community or the nation. As opposed to the British who glorified their heroes—there were 50,700 recipients of the Indian Mutiny Medal alone[76]—he did not believe in sighing for the past. He wanted the ghastly and horrible picture showing man at its worst to be forgotten, or remembered in a detached impersonal way. According to him, 'So long as the connecting links and reminders are present, and the spirit behind those events survives and shows itself, that memory also will endure and influence our people. Attempts to suppress that picture do not destroy it but drive it deeper in the mind. Only by dealing with it normally can its effect be lessened.'[77] It was hateful to have to refer to this past history, but the spirit behind those events did not end with them.[78]

Great men had something in them that inspired a whole people and make them do great deeds. In *Glimpses of World History*, he discussed the role of Lakshmi Bai (1828–1858), the young and impulsive Rani of Jhansi,[79] and of 'fine guerrilla leaders' like Firoz Shah and Tantya Tope

(1814–1859).[80] He talked of 'a whole people [becoming] full of faith for a great cause, and then even simple, ordinary men and women [becoming] heroes, and history [becoming] stirring and epoch-making.'[81]

If the 1857 revolt was the last flicker of feudal India, why did it fail? Jawaharlal Nehru blamed the feudal chiefs for their disunity and their desire to preserve their own privileges.[82] Without any clear signs of a constructive ideal, the 'mutinous rabble' created that very condition of anarchy that had offered the East India Company the excuse to gain a stronghold in India in the first place. Historians agree that modern nationalism had yet to come; India had still to go through much sorrow and travail before learning the lesson that would give her real freedom.[83]

The 1857 revolt had some bright spots: one of them was that Hindus and Muslims shared the fruits of victory and the disappointment of defeat.[84] G.R. Forrest, author of the military operations, warned that one of the lessons of the Rebellion is that Hindus and Muslims could be united against the British.[85] The Lucknow proclamation of 5–17 July pleaded for unity against the 'inhuman and ungodly Christians'. Those who wrote it were in all likelihood inspired by Maulvi Ahmadullah Shah, a Sufi who led both the Hindu and Muslim sepoys at the battle of Chinhat, a village on the Fyzabad road. Every other proclamation mentioned Hindus and Muslims and their respective religions in the same breath; Bahadur Shah, the Mughal emperor, emphasized the standard of the Prophet of Islam and the standard of Mahavir, the founder of Jainism.

Hindus and Muslims acted in unity from the time a detachment of the 34th Native Infantry marched into Behrampore, 116 miles north of Calcutta, until death, desolation, and despair afflicted Delhi and Lucknow. The prevalent spirit of harmony was manifested in the rebels hailing Birjis Qadr as Lord Krishna, and in Bahadur Shah celebrating Holi at Mehrauli (Kottab-sahib). When some zealots erected the green standard of holy war at the Jama Masjid on 19 May 1857, the emperor ordered its removal. By the beat of drums, he decreed the death penalty for those sacrificing cows and goats in Bakr-Id.

How different was the reality! Hardly had the dust of the revolution settled, Hindu–Muslim dissension surfaced. The later generations have had their memory refreshed by the Partition of India. Today one will not look at Jawaharlal Nehru's account for a faithful representation of later-nineteenth-century men and conditions, but one can still enjoy it as an eloquent and earnest testimony of liberal idealism.

People often speak of 'the verdict of history', the 'philosophy of history', and the 'science of history'. G.P. Gooch, the historian, declared that there is no agreed verdict, no agreed philosophy, only 'a welter of conflicts'. 'We continue our eager and never-ending search for truth', he added, 'but the sphinx smiles at us and keeps her secrets'. He went on to ask, are there or will there ever be final answers to the questions prompted by our study of the human endeavours? 'If so', he answered, 'they have not yet been found.'[86] Jawaharlal Nehru would have agreed with this formulation. What Nehru offered was the barest outline of the 1857 revolt and just fleeting glimpses of India's colonial past.

The Self in Nationalism

The autobiographies of Jawaharlal Nehru and his German writer and dramatist friend Ernst Toller (1893–1939) came out almost simultaneously and, since both had suffered jail terms, the two books were frequently reviewed together.[87] Ernst Toller, who read 'one of the finest autobiographies', was proud of this linking together: 'I often think the people who have been in prison form an invisible brotherhood based on suffering and on the greater imagination of heart which the prison develops.'[88] Jawaharlal Nehru agreed, adding, 'When I read your beautiful Letters from Prison again and again they brought pictures of my own moods and thoughts in prison to me and your book occasionally became a mirror of myself.'[89] He recommended Toller's *The Machine Wreckers* to Gandhi, and to his sister Krishna. 'It is a strangely moving book and Toller is such a loveable creature', he wrote from Dehradun District Jail on 1 June 1934. He read *Seven*

Plays in Almora District Jail and was moved by their intensity. 'We were attracted to each other', he said, remembering Toller.[90]

Breathing Tagore's spirit and tracing the person of Gandhi through the ages as the dominant factor in India's life and thought, Jawaharlal Nehru's *Autobiography* remains an indispensable companion for students.[91] It is an exaggeration to suggest that with the *Autobiography*, Nehru established for himself 'a permanent position in the world of letters',[92] but it is fair to claim that it was probably the most revealing thing he ever produced (written almost entirely in prison from June 1931 to February 1935). It bears the mark of a passionate, albeit humane, nationalism.[93] Others have also put pen to paper writing on their life and times,[94] but Jawaharlal Nehru's autobiography glows with patriotic feelings. There is no concealment of facts. As for the 'self', the influences are too subtle, too diffused, to be easily identified or measured. Jawaharlal loved India tenderly, and, in the words of Monod, to him that loved, much may be forgiven.[95]

Even though autobiographical confessions cannot be regarded as accurate descriptions of a consistent life, Jawaharlal Nehru's narrative is out of the ordinary precisely for its tropes and figures of thought, without which he would not have turned the real events of life into a narrative and transformed them from a chronicle into a story. He recognized the role of nationalist ideas, and paid attention to the popular upsurge that transformed the face of the rural world in parts of Awadh. He applied his mind to literature and manners, explored culture and its rich manifestations, and held together the alternate and complementary themes by an underlying devotion to objective writing. Hence, Tagore discerned in him 'a deep current of humanity which overpasses the tangle of facts and leads us to the person who is greater than his deeds, and truer than his surroundings'. Jawaharlal Nehru was touched by Tagore's commendation.[96]

Although Partha Chatterjee, the political scientist, dismissed the *Autobiography* and *The Discovery of India* as 'rambling, bristling with the most obvious contradictions, and gristly overwritten',[97] he conceded that their author spelt out clearly the key ideological elements and relations of nationalist thought at its moment of arrival.[98] Others have commented on their subtle, complex, discriminating, infinitely cultivated nature that is suffused with intellectual passion, their rationality, breadth of learning, and the fluent lucidity of expression.[99] *Discovery* is by no means Jawaharlal Nehru's greatest contribution to history, but it is a substantial work nevertheless and a much better book than its reputation would suggest.

By March 1937, the *Autobiography* had already gone into several editions in England (Krishna Menon earned £12 15s. 7d. as editor).[100] The younger readers devoured rather than read it, and there was nothing to criticize and nothing to desire. They found in its spirit and substance a romantic pensiveness and gentle melancholy. 'Rafiq Zakaria, the author-politician, wrote, 'There was something so moving about the narration of the story of our hopes and aspirations in its pages that no Indian who read it could escape its magical effects. There was something so regal about the personality of the author who emerged out of its pages with such power and grace that the spell it cast was overwhelming. It drew the readers to the author as a duck to the water.'[101] The union of prophecy and autobiography released energies that were to flow into them.[102] M.V. Kamath, a journalist, read the autobiography avidly in 1936. He was then all of fifteen but by then Jawaharlal Nehru had become for him, as for his generation, an icon.[103]

The freedom movement would have lacked the vital intellectual and aesthetic dimension without Jawaharlal Nehru. It was he who saved it from aggressive philistines getting the upper hand.[104] One is regaled by the literary quality of his words, and their clear and honest exposition. Now you hear him delighted, now solemn, now youthful and energetic, full of hopes for his country, and now piqued at the delays in the fruition of his ideas. It is a voice that we shall gain much by returning to more often, though many others who stood outside the Congress camp found him wanting in his analysis and interpretation.

At this stage, it would be necessary to enumerate the historical inac-
curacies of the author. Still more would be needed to show that his
theories did not explain hundreds of the most important facts pertain-
ing to the nationalist movement. 'We must choose our allies once for
all, for they stick to us even when we might be glad to be rid of them',
Tagore wrote to C.F. Andrews.[105] Jawaharlal Nehru failed to compre-
hend those who opposed him, and his fundamental error, for which
he invited the ire of the socialists and communists and the Muslim
League, was to make the Congress the sole custodian of national interests. He criticized the communists for being on the other side of the
barricades at the time of the 1942 revolution. With his exaggerated
sensitivity to ridicule, the communist cartoonists riled him by inflating
his figure to portray him as a bloated plutocrat.[106]

He was harsh on the Liberals, though their outlook was largely
ecumenical. One such Liberal was Sapru. Religious or political funda-
mentalism had no place in Sapru's world which was made up of law,
literature, and politics. His drawing room, with its parallelograms of
light, was full of Urdu and Persian books. He read, recited, and repro-
duced the verses of Mir Taqi Mir, Ghalib, Shaikh Saadi, and Hafiz
Shirazi. His equanimity was bottomless, as was his lack of ambition,
and he assumed that everyone else was like him. Sapru resembled the
Nehrus in his pride, quickness of temper, and in an urbanity deriving as
much from an Indo-Persian background as from a punctilious adher-
ence to the forms of late Victorian politesse.[107] He was a formidable
mediator, acceptable to, as it turned out at the All-Parties Conference,
both Muslim and Hindu leaders.

In Sapru's view, no one was mean-spirited, not even his worst
detractors in the Congress who despairingly referred to his devotion
to the Raj. But Jawaharlal Nehru reprimanded him and the Liberals
for their British love of fair play and tolerance.[108] He chastised them
as 'old women—weeping and howling and feeling terribly oppressed
about everything.' At some stage in UP's no-tax campaign, he feared
that they were ranged against his group.[109] The Liberals, in turn,

countered his audacious contentions. Thus, Sapru refused to align himself with Jawaharlal Nehru's non-party, non-sectarian civil liberties union. Generally speaking, he did not approve of his contrasting the patriotism of the masses with the coldness and opportunism of Liberals. Jawaharlal Nehru once wrote that life and politics were much too complex to think of in straight lines, but his attitude confirmed the widespread impression that he was reluctant to even heed the clamour of the secular formations. Likewise, his negotiations with Jinnah did not reflect his mood to cooperate or compromise with him. Quoting Lenin, who had said that 'to march forward without compromise, without turning from the path' was 'intellectual childishness and not the serious tactics of a revolutionary class', Jawaharlal Nehru surmised: 'Compromises there are bound to be, and we should not worry too much about them.'[110] The reality to which Syed Abdullah Brelvi, editor of *Bombay Chronicle*, drew his attention was that he gave too little attention to the communal question as a fundamental constraint on future progress. Jawaharlal Nehru agreed; in the political lull of 1933, he admitted that the diversion of public attention to the positive economic and political side of the struggle had not made any impact on the problem.[111] The other reality, due to which scores of public figures rebuked Jawaharlal Nehru, was his dogged refusal to form a coalition government in UP in 1937.

Jinnah belonged to a eclectic yet religiously structured and defined world. In Bombay, his admirers were drawn from an arena that was being gradually secularized by educational institutions, law courts, travel, and the transmission of knowledge. They extolled his personal integrity, professional skills, and commitment to self-government and, in later years, Swaraj. Once catapulted to the national leadership, for which he had all the necessary skills, he quickly developed a following among his natural allies—the 'moderates'. In the Legislative Assembly, he and Motilal Nehru refused to sign the Majority Report of the Reforms Enquiry Committee, and were hardly ever swayed by the outpourings of the Hindu and

Muslim hardliners. Hence, a section of the Congress pinned their faith in Jinnah when the Nehru Committee Report got down to the business of drafting a constitution for India.

Jinnah was stationed in London and Paris nursing his ailing wife. Motilal Nehru bemoaned his absence.[112] M.A. Ansari, the Congress President in 1927, felt that Jinnah was 'the only man to deliver the goods on behalf of the Muslim League'.[113] Again, when Motilal Nehru heard of Jinnah's return to Bombay in October, he wrote excitedly: 'So much depends on Jinnah that I have a mind to go to Bombay to receive him. If I have the necessary funds within the next few days I hope to create a strong opinion amongst the Mussalmans to greet Jinnah on his arrival. Therefore, please lose no time to raise as much money as you can for this great enterprise.'[114] This bond snapped when the Congress High Command turned down Jinnah's advice on Hindu–Muslim relations.

Jawaharlal Nehru presumed that Jinnah desired to prevent radical changes not because of a Hindu majority but because the radical elements would put an end to semi-feudal privileges.[115] Probably, it was reasoning of this kind that consciously or unconsciously determined his tactics. Needless to say, such reasoning was fallacious. Instead of charting all the peaks and troughs of the past, Jawaharlal Nehru dedicated space only to those events that enhanced his ability to distinguish between the 'progressive' Congress and the 'reactionary' League. He understood the reality of power politics, but not how it affected the minorities. His admirers seem to suggest that he was too honourable—or, perhaps, too conventional—to deal with the rising aspirations of the Muslim middle classes, though the fact of the matter is that Muslim nationalism was a bitter pill that he could not swallow. He was shocked by it, and was vaguely conscious of its abnormality, and in the end he allowed the situation to drift in the hope that it would right itself. It is said that a man can be judged by how he uses his power. Inferior minds misuse the scraps of authority that chance or folly provides them with.

Jinnah's idea of sovereignty was at fundamental variance with Congress' notion of an indivisible and non-negotiable sovereignty for independent India. The sharing of sovereignty between the Hindu majority and Muslim minority groups was unacceptable to the Congress advocating composite nationalism based on an indivisible sovereign central authority.[116] Jawaharlal Nehru disliked Jinnah: he thought his reading did not extend beyond the daily newspaper and that he had not a single intelligent or enlightened idea in his head.[117] He compared the ardour of the masses with the coldness and the conservative minds of the Muslim upper classes. His irritation was legitimate but inopportune. As a result, India had to pay a heavy price for avoiding a constructive engagement with Jinnah, who beguiled the masses with unexpected and, for the most part, welcome success.[118]

Finally, Jawaharlal Nehru preferred to look right through the nasty and brutal aspects of Indian life and tended to rationalize social and cultural practices. The truth is that he failed to translate his concern for the poor and the oppressed into action. In the United Provinces and Bihar, the two most populous states with a high percentage of poor people, he turned a blind eye to the nexus between the landlords, the bureaucrats and the Congress politicians. He tried to hunt with the hounds and run with the hares. He grasped the retarding character of the Congress party, but did not struggle against it. He always predicted that the masses would speak out against the will of the Congress apparatus. That did not happen. Similarly, the prime minister allowed the obscurantist elements and the right-wingers to have a field day in the party. Secularism was on everybody's lips, but there were serious contradictions between the rhetoric and reality.

In 1953, the Nehru addressed a press conference in Burma. One of the pressmen asked him: 'When you wrote *Glimpses of World History*, you seemed to be a die-hard revolutionary. You seem to have changed now.'

Jawaharlal Nehru replied,

> I think that ... this is a rather unintelligent question, if I may say so.
> And yet it is perhaps valid. There is nothing so conservative as a die-
> hard revolutionary. Revolution is a process of dynamic change. It does
> not mean noise in the streets and the breaking of heads. It means a
> strong economic change. These days, when the state is so strong, no
> revolutionary rabble can subvert it. Perhaps it's age, but more than age,
> it is because times have changed so much that we can't judge everything
> by what Marx and Lenin had said several years ago.[119]

Voyage of Discovery

A friend describes how a group of young women were sitting at Nehru's
feet while he told them about his life in jail; he told them how just to
see the sky helped pass the time and how he had to wrack his brains
to remember history when he wrote his *The Discovery of India*.[120]
Written in Ahmadnagar Fort Prison from April to September 1944,
it is Jawaharlal Nehru's mental voyage of exploration. He brings

> not just political ambition but all of the intellectual means at his
> command—journalistic reportage, anthropological fieldwork, electoral
> campaigning, the intimate and affectionate tutelage of Gandhi and
> Tagore, the reading of literature, the writing of history, and spells of
> deep personal reflection, especially over the ten years or so that he was
> locked up in jail in the course of his career—to construct India as an
> object that he and his compatriots can relate to in some fundamental
> way.[121]

Discovery is a hymn to the glories of India. He mapped the
metaphysical and philosophic approach to life, and paid tribute to
the countless sages who laid down their lives performing penance.
Probably, he attributed to them more historical substance than they
possessed. In other respects, he idealized ancient India as a world

apart, independent of and superior to the rest of the civilizations, toning down the barbarism of the caste system and throwing the warm colours of fancy around in his narrative. At the same time, with his eyes set on India's infinite charm, variety, and oneness, Jawaharlal Nehru worked ceaselessly for a synthesis, drawing on the best, and breaking with the worst.[122] He consciously followed Gandhi and Tagore in the direction of the universal.[123] Consequently, India appears in *Discovery* as a space of ceaseless cultural mixing, and the past seems to be a celebration of the soiling effects of cultural miscegenation and accretion.[124] While the romantic in Jawaharlal Nehru drew on the old and new interpretations to buttress ecumenical and universalistic points of view, some other Indian writers did so from a rather narrow perspective.[125]

Discovery suggested a departure into new modes of feeling and thought, necessarily admitting the knowledge of the European Renaissance, with a view to absorbing the lessons of the third industrial revolution and asking, now, what is the destiny of man.[126] Endowed with a prodigious literary gift, the author's intellectual style is self-consciously dispassionate and philosophical. Reading him is, therefore, a very distinctive experience, different in all kinds of ways from reading Gandhi, Tagore, and B.R. Ambedkar.[127] While reproducing the atmosphere of the middle ages and providing a tableaux rather than a record of events, his account of the twentieth century is humane and sympathetic towards the torment of the colonized, which it breathes throughout. He conducts the reader through the labyrinth of the colonial era, narrates the most complex events, and recreates portraits of outstanding fellow countrymen. By and large, his writings make public the spirit and substance of his many-sidedness, the deep-seated urge to freedom, and the negative response to the concomitants and consequences of colonial rule. He quoted Ghalib's famous couplet to the effect: 'If we are to be punished for the sins we have committed, at least we should be praised for our yearning for the sins we have not committed.'[128]

As for Nehru's idea of India, Tagore summed it up in the following words:

Where the mind is without fear and the head is held high,
Where knowledge is free
Where the world has not been broken up into
    fragments by narrow domestic walls;
Where words come out from the depth of truth;
Where tireless striving stretches its arms towards
    perfection;
Where the clear stream of reason has not lost its
    way into the dreary desert sand of habit;
Where the mind is led forward by thee into
    ever-widening thought and action—
    Into that heaven of freedom, my Father,
    Let my country awake.[129]

Like Anatole France in *The Gods Are Athirst*, Jawaharlal Nehru seems to be saying: 'Behold out of these personalities, out of these trivial commonplaces, arise, when the hour is ripe, the most titanic events and the most monumental gestures of history.'[130] He has made on all this the most penetrating and the most balanced comments:

The years I have spent in prison! Sitting alone, wrapped in my thoughts, how many seasons I have seen go by, following each other into oblivion! How many moons I have watched wax and wane, and the pageant of the stars moving along inexorably and majestically! How many yesterdays of my youth lie buried here; and sometimes I see the ghosts of these dead yesterdays rise up, bring poignant memories, and whispering to me: Was it worthwhile? There is no hesitation about the answer. If I were given the chance to go through my life again, with my present knowledge and experience added, I would no doubt try to make many changes in my personal life; I would endeavour to improve in many ways on what I had previously done, but my major decisions in public affairs would remain untouched. Indeed, I would not vary them, for they are stronger than myself, and a force beyond my control drove me to them.... This year too will pass, and I shall go out—and then? I do not know, but I have a feeling that a chapter of my life is over and another chapter will begin. What this is going to be I cannot clearly guess. The leaves of the book of life are closed.[131]

In his epilogue, Jawaharlal Nehru talked about the egotistical narrative of his adventures through life until 14 February 1935 in the Almora District Jail. There are strong elements of that, but some scholars have also sensed the weakness in his writings both theoretically and practically; indeed, nowadays it is a fashion to treat them with derision. I believe an objective appraisal is called for. The fact is, he provides a number of insights into India's past and present, even though he laboured under the disability of writing subject to the censors of an alien power and had no access to his library in Anand Bhawan. People read and responded to his books according to what they wanted to find. Halide Edib, the Turkish author, considered them to be 'extremely well thought-out and objective summaries of historical force.[132] Paying her generous compliments to a remarkably skilled craftsman, she probably had Jawaharlal Nehru in mind in formulating the view that 'ideas and wisdom change the destinies of men gradually, but it is the dynamic and volcanic temperaments of men of destiny which make the sudden and dramatic episodes in history'.[133]

The Triumph of Integrity

With a parliamentary government in place, Jawaharlal Nehru's fortunes were at their zenith in the mid-1950s. Despite the horrors of Partition, the democratic fabric rested on pluralist and secular thoughts and principles. With the colonial hangover over, poets and writers welcomed the removal of blinders and chains on eyes and hearts. They had much to look forward to, more so with the country's leadership in the hands of a reliable guide. Jawaharlal Nehru walked 'steadfastly along that steep and perilous' path that was his destiny, but his image suffered a setback after the Chinese invasion of 1962. Much earlier, of course, his sympathizers and supporters had found that he was a poor judge of people, that he was not averse to flattery, and that he was intolerant of criticism. His political adversaries, between the extreme right and the extreme left, attributed all ills to his mistakes. They were right, except they had themselves frustrated his social and economic goals. Hence, the blazing rocket of the 1950s became the fallen sticks of the 1950s.[134] 'It seems doubtful', Marie Seton remarked, 'if Jawaharlal Nehru ever fully grasped the full import of the conservative and self-interested motives underlying Indian society.'[135] He did not, because he had too much faith in his colleagues.

With all his shakiness, hesitancies, and weak spot, the intelligentsia's perception was that Jawaharlal Nehru kept the country together, established secular ideals, propelled it forward with the thrust of science and modernity, healed some of the wounds of Partition, and stood before the world as the prime minister of an independent nation. What endeared him to his contemporaries was that the life of the people, which flows in a dark current beneath political events, attracted his attention—the circumstances, sorrows and joys of millions of humble men and women. Even if his personal misfortunes had a melodramatic tinge, there was always a constant element of moral austerity to serve as a counterweight.

Jawaharlal Nehru died in 1964. 'I loved him', Syed Mahmud told Marie Seton two months after the prime minister's death. 'Both of us wept over the communal troubles in the country. I know it was that which killed him. I think he was trying to find some solution with Pakistan.'[136] The problem of national unity remained unsolved, and this was a constant source of weakness, to which in the end Gandhi and Jawaharlal Nehru succumbed.

India has changed. There is a tendency to cavalierly push our own past, to set aside our traditions and ingrained beliefs. The Congress party is in total disarray after its electoral defeat in the 2014 general elections; as a result, a non-Congress government occupies the reins of office in Delhi and in several other states. That government is obsessed with the idea of change and development to the extent of not caring any longer about preserving our heritage. Their outlook is akin to the mentality which Benedetto Croce described under the name of 'anti-historicism'—'That feeling,' as Croce defined it, 'that true history is only about to begin, and that we are at last escaping from the bonds of false history and struggling into freedom and space.'[137] Even if new idols must replace the old icons in the temples of modern India, we are duty-bound not to be blinded by narrow prejudices or short-term political gains.

When Fernand Braudel thought of the individual, he was inclined to see him imprisoned within a destiny in which he himself had little hand, fixed in a landscape in which the infinite perspectives of the long term stretch into the distance both behind him and before. In historical analysis as he saw it, the long run always won in the end.[138] Jawaharlal Nehru would have agreed with this formulation. He had, after all, noted in his diary that it was easy to allow the mind to wander rather aimlessly in known grooves, but that had a 'fatal fascination' for the past. Moreover, it satisfied his conceit to imagine that he could mould this as it emerged from the slime and mud of the present, as a potter with his clay.[139]

It is true that Jawaharlal Nehru was the unconscious instrument of destiny for a challenging work, but he probably did not fathom the meaning of his own enterprises. He could not overcome the many swamps and marshes and muddy places, and often lived in a world of thought and imagination. In his later years, he was in the habit of blaming others for avoiding action, but the coterie around him did not remind him that he was himself guilty of inaction in certain spheres of public life. This failing, notwithstanding, Jawaharlal Nehru's place in history seems assured for the reasons best summed up by the historian Romila Thapar:

> Jawaharlal Nehru was in some ways a threshold maker, casting a glance
> at the past, summing up the moments of time and providing a sliver of
> the feel for future times. From the perspective of the present … it does

seem almost a fantasy that we once had a Prime Minister who, without being a historian, was nevertheless receptive to the rational underpinning of a historical perspective, who used this understanding to draw India into movements of significant historical mutation; and who, in appreciating the political culture of India, was responsive to the idea that if historical action is to be applauded it must carry the imprint of ethics.[140]

Notes

1. Jawaharlal Nehru under the pseudonym 'Chanakya', *Modern Review*, 1936.

2. Sabyasachi Bhattacharya, *The Redefining Moments in Bengal, 1920–1947* (New Delhi: Oxford University Press, 2014).

3. Marcus Tullius Cicero was a Roman philosopher, politician, lawyer, orator, political theorist, consul, and constitutionalist. He came from a wealthy municipal family of the Roman equestrian order, and is widely considered as one of Rome's greatest orators and prose stylists.

4. Samuel Langhorne Clemens, better known by his pen name Mark Twain, was an American author and humorist. He wrote *The Adventures of Tom Sawyer* and its sequel, *Adventures of Huckleberry Finn*, the latter often called 'the Great American Novel'.

5. Oesterheld, *Jawaharlal Nehru, Ernst Toller*, p. 72.

6. Moraes, *Jawaharlal Nehru*, p. 91.

7. Moraes, *Jawaharlal Nehru*, p. 96.

8. Moraes, *Jawaharlal Nehru*, p. 949.

9. 'A Dialogue with Jawaharlal by Mohamed H. Heikal', file no. 1097, Misc., AICC papers.

10. J. Nehru, 'Prison Days', *SWJN*, vol. 8, p. 877. Sachchidananda Hirananda Vatsyayan, popularly known by his pen-name Ajneya, was a pioneer of modern trends not only in the realm of Hindi poetry, but also fiction, criticism, and journalism. He was one of the most prominent exponents of *Nayi Kavita* (New Poetry) and *Prayog* (Experiments) in modern Hindi literature, and started the Hindi newsweekly, *Dinamaan*.

11. J. Nehru, *Glimpses of World History*, p. 953.

12. S. Gandhi, *Two Alone, Two Together*, p. 362.

13.   Felix Dzerzhinsky to A.E. Bulhak, 15 April 1919, in his *Prison Diary and Letters* (Moscow: Foreign Languages Publishing House1959), p. 293.

14.   J. Nehru, *Glimpses of World History*, p. 476.

15.   Khusro Faramurz Rustamji, *I Was Nehru's Shadow: From the Diaries of K.F. Rustamji*, edited by P.V. Rajgopal (New Delhi: Wisdom Free, 2006), p. 220.

16.   Hiren Mukherjee, *The Gentle Colossus: Study of Jawaharlal* (Delhi: Oxford University Press, 1968), p. 35.

17.   J. Nehru, *Glimpses of World History*, p. 2.

18.   J. Nehru, *Glimpses of World History*, p. 4.

19.   J. Nehru, *An Autobiography*.

20.   Lamb, *The Nehrus of India*, p. 114.

21.   Michele L. Langford, 'Deconstructing Glimpses of World History: An Analysis of Jawaharlal Nehru's Letters to his Daughter' (PhD diss., Miami University, 2005).

22.   J. Nehru, *Glimpses of World History*, p. 9.

23.   This was at the Inter-Asian Relations Conference in March 1947, J. Nehru, *Glimpses of World History*, p. 294.

24.   N. Sahgal, *Civilizing a Savage World*, p. 8.

25.   Gandhi to Wybergh, 10 May 1910, Anthony J. Parel, *Gandhi: Hind Swaraj and other Writings* (Cambridge: Cambridge University Press, 1997), p. 145.

26.   Bhabani Sengupta, 'The "Radical" Mind of Calcutta', in *The Calcutta Psyche*, edited by Geeti Sen (New Delhi: Rupa & Co., 1990).

27.   Halide Edib Adıvar, *The Turkish Ordeal: Being the Further Memoirs of Halidé Edib* (New York: Century Company, 1928), pp. 327, 328.

28.   J. Nehru, *Glimpses of World History*, p. 703.

29.   On the article and its interpretation, see Benjamin Zachariah, *Nehru* (London: Routledge, 2004), pp. 88–9.

30.   A. Gorev and V. Zimyanin, *Jawaharlal Nehru* (Moscow: Progress Publishers, 1982), pp. 226–7.

31.   Home Department, Political, file no. 4/8, 1933.

32.   Mulk Raj Anand, 'Self-Actualization in the Writings of Nehru', in *Jawaharlal Nehru: Centenary Volume*, edited by Sheila Dikshit et al. (New Delhi: Oxford University Press, 1989), p. 7.

33.   J. Nehru to Nan (from Ahmadnagar Fort), 27 February 1945, J. Nehru, *Before Freedom*, p. 361.

34.   Malhotra, *Indira Gandhi*, p. 40.

35.   'A Dialogue with Jawaharlal by Mohamed H. Heikal', file no. 1097, Misc., AICC papers.

36.   Tara Ali Baig, *Portraits of an Era* (New Delhi: Roli Books Pvt. Ltd, 1982), p. 80.

37.   Rustamji, *I Was Nehru's Shadow*, p. 220.

38.   It consists of letters to Indira written in different prisons between October 1930 and August 1933. They were gathered together before Jawaharlal's arrest on 12 February 1934 and published by Vijaya Lakshmi Pandit. A revised version appeared in 1939.

39.   J. Nehru to Indira, 7–8 May 1943, S. Gandhi, *Two Alone, Two Together*, p. 362.

40.   Lord Brockway, Oral History Transcript (18), NMML.

41.   Seton, *Panditji*, p. 440.

42.   22 November 1983, Maina wa Kinyatti, *Mother Kenya*.

43.   2 November 1943, Sushila Nayyar, *Mahatma Gandhi's Last Imprisonment: The Inside Story* (Delhi: Har-Anand Publications, 1996), p. 309.

44.   G.B. Pant to Lakshmi Pant and K.C. Pant, 26 April 1944, Nanda, *Selected Works of Govind Ballabh Pant*, vol. 10, p. 229.

45.   Husain B. Tyabji, Oral History Transcript (266), NMML.

46.   Brecher, *Nehru: A Political Biography*, p. 163.

47.   Natwar Singh, ed., *The Legacy of Nehru* (Jawaharlal Nehru Memorial Fund: Delhi, 1996), p. 34.

48.   Begum Iftikharuddin, Oral History Transcript (53), NMML; Humayun Kabir,'Artist in Public Life', in Zakaria, *A Study of Nehru*, pp. 392–3.

49.   J. Nehru, *Glimpses of World History*, p. 951.

50.   J. Nehru, *Glimpses of World History*, p. 4.

51.   J. Nehru, *Glimpses of World History*, p. 704.

52.   J. Nehru, *Glimpses of World History*, p. 3.

53.   28 July 1930, *SWJN*, vol. 4, p. 370.

54.   This is how Rajaji also felt. 18 February 1922, Rajagopalachari, *Jail Diary*, p. 71. 'In Yeravda jail, when all the politicals were placed in the

European yard for a day, we told him how angry people were for his suspension of the Bardoli campaign of total non-cooperation and civil disobedience, on the plea that there was violence in Chauri Chaura. He quietly explained to us that, if he had not done what he did, the whole movement would have gone on wrong lines and gone beyond control. He confidently declared that what had been achieved in a single year of the movement would not have been possible by normal methods of agitation for thirty years. Without doubt, the seeds of future campaigns were really sown by the movement in 1921–22.' (Moraji Desai, *The Story of My Life* [Madras: Macmillan India, 1974], p. 111.)

55.   Gupta, *They Lived Dangerously*, p. 280.

56.   He wrote in February 1923:'You ask me which party I support. I do not support either party. Because neither is at the moment doing any effective work. The party I am a member of is that party of the future which will devote itself to the political education of the lower classes.' (Premchand, *Rangbhumi: The Arena of Life*, translated by Christopher King with an Introduction by Alok Rai [New Delhi: Oxford University Press, 2010], p. viii.)

57.   Gupta, *They Lived Dangerously*, p. 55.

58.   Gopal, *Jawaharlal Nehru: A Biography*, vol. 1, p. 147.

59.   Norman Cousins, in Dikshit et al., *Jawaharlal Nehru: Centenary Volume*, p. 133.

60.   M. Nehru to J. Nehru, 9 April 1907, *SWMN*, vol. 1, p. 123.

61.   See V.D. Savarkar, *The Indian War of Independence* (London: n.p., 1909), for the Rebellion taking on the character of a war of independence. R.C. Majumdar contested this view. According to him, the 'mutiny' did not evoke any sense of national feeling at the time, nor was it regarded as a national war of independence till the rise of national consciousness at the close of the nineteenth century. R.C. Majumdar, *The Sepoy Mutiny and the Revolt of 1857* (Calcutta: Oriental Press Pvt. Ltd, 1957), p. 238.

62.   J. Nehru, *Glimpses of World History*, p. 415. Close to this is the following view: The Rebellion was 'against nationalism and modernity; it was an attempt to turn the clock of history back to feudal isolation and to feudal tyranny, to the handloom and the spinning wheel, and to primitive methods of transport and communication. The miseries and bloodshed of 1857–8 were not the birth pangs of a freedom movement but the dying groans of an obsolete autocracy'. (Lester Hutchinson, *The Empire of the Nabobs* [London: Allen & Unwin, 1937], p. 415.)

63. J. Nehru, *An Autobiography*, p. 2.

64. J. Nehru, *An Autobiography*, p. 2.

65. B.R. Nanda, *Gokhale, Gandhi and the Nehrus: Studies in Indian Nationalism* (London: Allen & Unwin, 1974), p. 86.

66. J. Nehru, *An Autobiography*, p. 34.

67. D.A. Low 'Tej Bahadur Sapru and the First Round Table Conference', in *Soundings in Modern South Asian History*, edited by D.A. Low (Berkeley: University of California Press 1968), p. 298.

68. J. Nehru, *Glimpses of World History*, p. 414.

69. J. Nehru, *Glimpses of World History*, p. 326.

70. J. Nehru, *Glimpses of World History*, p. 87.

71. Also mentions the 'barbarous behaviour' of some rebels, who sullied their cause by cruel massacres of the British.

72. He 'dimmed his glory by deeds of dark vengeance'. (Percival Spear, *The Oxford History of Modern India 1740-1947* [Oxford: Clarendon Press, 1965], p. 226.)

73. J. Nehru, *Glimpses of World History*, p. 415.

74. *SWJN*, vol. 38, p. 15.

75. *SWJN*, vol. 38, p. 14.

76. Pramod K. Nayyar, ed., *The Trial of Bahadur Shah Zafar* (New Delhi: Orient Blackswan, 2007), p. xxiii.

77. J. Nehru, *Discovery of India*, pp. 324–5.

78. J. Nehru, *Discovery of India*, pp. 324–5.

79. J. Nehru, *Glimpses of World History*, p. 415.

80. J. Nehru, *Discovery of India*, p. 324.

81. Gupte, *Mother India*.

82. J. Nehru, *Discovery of India*, p. 324.

83. J. Nehru, *Discovery of India*, p. 325.

84. Mushirul Hasan, ed., *Selected Works of Jawaharlal Nehru*, Second Series, vol. 39 (New Delhi: Oxford University Press, 2006), p. 7.

85. Quoted in Sashi Bhusan Chaudhuri, *Civil Rebellion in the Indian Mutinies, 1857–1859* (Calcutta: World Press, 1957), p. 282.

86. G.P. Gooch, *History and Historians of the Nineteenth Century* (Boston: Beacon Hill Press, 1959), p. i.

87. Ernst Toller, a German left-wing playwright, is known for his Expressionist plays. For six days in 1919, he served as President of the

Bavarian Soviet Republic. For this he was imprisoned for five years. During this time, he wrote several plays and poetry, which earned him international repute. He had been imprisoned in the fortress of Niederschönenfeld from February 1920; and until his release, he spent 149 days in solitary confinement and 24 days on hunger strike. The most famous of his later dramas, *Hoppla, We're Alive!* (*Hoppla, wir Leben!*), premiered in Berlin in 1925 and was directed by Erwin Piscator. After the Nazi rise to power, Toller was exiled from Germany in 1933 because of his work. In 1935, he co-directed the Manchester production of his play *Rake Out the Fires* (*Feuer aus den Kesseln*). In the face of financial struggles and the news that his brother and sister had been sent to a concentration camp in Germany, a depressed Toller committed suicide in May 1939.

88.   21 July 1936, Oesterheld, *Jawaharlal Nehru, Ernst Toller*, p. 109; Seton, *Panditji*, pp. 90, 100.

89.   10 August 1910, Oesterheld, *Jawaharlal Nehru, Ernst Toller*, p. 104.

90.   Oesterheld, *Jawaharlal Nehru, Ernst* Toller, p. 10.

91.   In his foreword to the second Hebrew edition of *Autobiography*, published in 1957, Jawaharlal Nehru himself recalled: 'This book was written when we in India were in the middle of our struggle for freedom. That struggle was long drawn out and it brought many experiences of joy and sorrow, of hope and despair. But the despair did not last long because of the inspiration that came to us from our leader, Mahatma Gandhi, and the deep delight of working for a cause that took us out of our little shells.... All of us are older now and our days of youth are long past. Yet, even now, when we face the troubles and torments that encompasses, something of that old memory of our leader gives us strength.'

92.   Humayun Kabir, 'Artist in Public Life', Zakaria, *A Study of Nehru*, p. 395.

93.   Nanda, *The Nehrus*, p. 362.

94.   Vijay Ramasawamy and Yogesh Sharma, eds, *Biography as History: Indian Perspective* (New Delhi: Sage, 2009); Udaya Kumar, 'Autobiography as a Way of Writing History: Personal Narratives from Kerala and the Inhabitation of Modernity', in *History in the Vernacular*, edited by Raziuddin Aquil and Partha Chatterjee (New Delhi: Permanent Black, 2005).

95.   C.F. Andrews advised Jawaharlal Nehru to publish his *Autobiography* with Allen & Unwin. On Krishna Menon's advice, however, Jawaharlal Nehru

approached John Lane at The Bodley Head. Unfortunately, the firm became bankrupt, and a consortium of publishers, led by Stanley Union, bought up the firm of Lane.

96. Zakaria, *A Study of Nehru*, p. 518.

97. Subhash Kashyap, on the other hand, considered the *Glimpses of World History* and *The Discovery of India* as 'classics'. Subhash Kashyap, 'Nehru: From Far and Near', in *Witness to History: Transition and Transformation for India, 1947–1964* (New Delhi: Oxford University Press, 2011), p. 42.

98. Partha Chatterjee, *Nationalist Thought and the Colonial World: A Derivative Discourse* (New Delhi: Oxford University Press, 1986), p. 132.

99. Tharoor, *Nehru*.

100. 'It is doubtful whether Nehru's intellectual status, or his political standing, would have been appreciated outside India but for Menon's efforts in publishing Nehru's writings as books and as pamphlets.' Seton, *Panditji*, p. 461.

101. Zakaria, *A Study of Nehru*, p. 4.

102. Anand, in Dikshit et al., *Jawaharlal Nehru: Centenary Volume*, p. 10.

103. H.V. Kamath, 'Jawaharlal Nehru as I Saw Him', in *Witness to History*, p. 154.

104. Dikshit et al., *Jawaharlal Nehru: Centenary Volume*, p. 430.

105. 5 March 1921, Alam and Chakravarty, *The Essential Tagore*, p. 101.

106. Moraes, *Jawaharlal Nehru*, p. 85.

107. Moraes, *Jawaharlal Nehru*, p. 134.

108. 'Am I a lunatic or is India full of lunatics that they can tolerate the Sastris and Saprus, not to mention those who grovel even more abjectly before the imperial power?' (18 June 1933, *SWJN*, vol. 5, p. 484.) Srinivas Sastri (1869–1946), who joined the Servants of India Society and succeeded Gokhale as President, poured scorn on the Liberal efforts to reach a deal with Irwin, the viceroy. (Gopal, *Jawaharlal: A Biography*, vol. 1, p. 145; Mansergh and Lumby, *Transfer of Power*, pp. 87–8.)

109. 31 May 1930, *SWJN*, vol. 4, p. 357. They visited the Nehrus in Naini Jail on 27 July 1930. Earlier, they met with Gandhi in Yeravda on 21–4 July.

110. J. Nehru *An Autobiography*, 594.

111. Milton Israel, 'Competing Images of Division and Unity in the Indian Nationalist Movement, 1920–30', in *Writers, Editors and Reformers:*

Social and Political Transformations of Maharashtra, edited by N.K. Wagle (New Delhi: Manohar, 1999), p. 93.

112.   M. Nehru to Thakurdas, 28 April 1928, P. Thakurdas Papers (71), NMML.

113.   Ansari to J. Nehru, 29 March 1928, AICC Papers (G-60).

114.   M. Nehru to Thakurdas, 29 September 1928, P. Thakurdas Papers (71), NMML.

115.   2 February 1942, Datta and Cleghorn, *A Nationalist Muslim and Indian Politics*, p. 219.

116.   Ayesha Jalal, *Democracy and Authoritarianism in South Asia: A Comparative and Historical Perspective* (Cambridge: Cambridge University Press, 1995), p. 15.

117.   Mahomedali Currim Chagla, *Roses in December: An Autobiography* (Bombay: Bharatiya Vidya Bhavan, 1974), p. 79.

118.   Linlithgow to Amery, 7 March 1942, Mansergh and Lumby, *Transfer of* Power, pp. 361–2.

119.   Rustamji, *I Was Nehru's Shadow*, p. 221.

120.   Baig, *Portraits of an Era*, p. 80.

121.   Vajpeyi, *Righteous Republic*, p. 182.

122.   J. Nehru to Betty, 10 November 1942, *SWJN*, vol. 3, p. 27.

123.   Albert Memmi, *The Colonizer and the Colonized* (Boston: Beacon Press, 1965), p. xxii.

124.   Sunil Khilnani, *The Idea of India* (London: Hamish Hamilton, 1997), p. 169.

125.   Dayanand Saraswati (1824–1883) and Swami Vivekananda (1863–1902) belong to this group.

126.   Anand, in Dikshit et al., *Jawaharlal Nehru: Centenary Volume*, p. 11.

127.   Vajpeyi, *Righteous Republic*, p. 170.

128.   J. Nehru to Indira, 7–8 May 1943, S. Gandhi, *Two Alone, Two Together*, p. 162.

129.   Anna Kurian, *Texts and Their Worlds I: Literature of India: An Introduction* (New Delhi: Foundation Books, 2006), p. 8.

130.   Quoted in Waters, *Rosa Luxembourg Speaks*, p. 337–8.

131.   J. Nehru, *An Autobiography*, p. 598.

132.   Edib, *Inside India*, p. 75.

133. Halide Edib, *The Turkish Ordeal: Being the Further Memoirs* (Westport, Connecticut: Hyperion Press, 1981), p. 141.

134. Percival Spear, *A History of India* (New Delhi: Penguin Books, 1965), p. 254.

135. Seton, *Panditji*, p. 91.

136. Seton, *Panditji*, p. 442.

137. Pieter Geyl, *Encounters in History* (Cleveland: Meridian Books, 1962), p. 338.

138. Fernand Braudel, *The Mediterranean and the Mediterranean World in the Age of Philip II* (London: Fontana Books, fourth impression, 1982), p. 1244.

139. 10 November 1942, *SWJN*, vol. 13, p. 27.

140. Romila Thapar, 'Nationalism and History', in Kamath, *Nehru Revisited*, p. 527.

Appendix

Table A.1 Jawaharlal Nehru in Jail

	Date of Imprisonment	Days	Place
1.	6 December 1921–3 March 1922	87	Lucknow District Jail
2.	11 May 1922–31 January 1923	265	Allahabad District Jail, Lucknow District Jail
3.	22 September 1923–4 October 1923	12	Nabha Jail (Nabha State)
4.	14 April 1930–11 October 1930	180	Naini Central Prison, Allahabad
5.	19 October 1930–26 January 1931		Naini Central Prison, Allahabad
6.	26 December 1931–30 August 1933	612	Naini Central Prison, Allahabad, Bareilly District Jail, Dehradun Jail, Naini Central Prison

(*Cont'd*)

Table A.1 (*Cont'd*)

	Date of Imprisonment	Days	Place
7.	12 February 1934– 4 September 1935	569	Alipur Central Jail, Calcutta, Dehradun Jail, Naini Central Prison, Allahabad, Almora Jail
8.	31 October 1940– 3 December 1941	398	Gorakhpur Jail, Dehradun Jail, Lucknow District Jail, Dehradun Jail
9.	9 August 1942– 15 June 1945	1040	Ahmadnagar Fort Prison, Bareilly Central Prison, Almora Jail,
		3262	(Nine years less twenty-three days)

Source: S. Gandhi, *Two Alone, Two Together*, xxxii–xxxiii.

Table A.2   The Week Out of Jail (11 October 1930 to 19 October 1930)

October 11

3.30 p.m. Released from Naini Central Prison.
Attended office and went round Allahabad immediately after.

October 12

8 a.m. Hoisted National Flag at Swaraj Bhawan. Issued short message to the country.
12 noon. Met Congress workers of Allahabad.
4 p.m. Taken out in procession by citizens.
7 p.m. Addressed a very large public meeting.

October 13

10.15 a.m. Left for Mussoorie. Wrote long circular letters to PCCs in the train. Met workers at principal stations and delivered short speeches to the assembled crowds.

October 14, 15, and 16

Spent in Mussoorie with the family; met prominent workers and deputations from various parts of the country. Issued messages to the men and women of the NWF and instructions about boycott of foreign cloth, statement on colours of the National Flag.

(*Cont'd*)

Table A.2   (*Cont'd*)

October 17

Left Mussoorie, addressed largely attended public meeting at Dehradun. Served with notice under Section 144 after his speech. Met workers of Dehradun. Left by the evening train.

October 18

Received municipal address at Lucknow. Met workers. Notice under Section 144 issued but not served. Left by car for Allahabad, meeting workers at Rae Bareli and Pratapgarh.

October 19

Addressed office and issued appeal to the public and mill owners for boycott of foreign cloth. Notice under Section 144 served. Presided at District Volunteers Conference. Received Pandit Motilal Nehru and family at Prayag Station at 5.30 p.m., attended meeting at Purshottamdas Park at 7 p.m., arrested under Section 124-A on his way from the meeting to Anand Bhawan. Jawaharlal made the following statement to a press representative immediately after his release on October 11:'I am very much alive and kicking. I hope to do my little bit to hasten the dissolution of the British Empire and take part in its final obsequies.'

Source: File no. 17, 1930, part 1, AICC Papers.

Index

About the Author

Mushirul Hasan is former Professor of History and Vice-Chancellor of Jamia Millia Islamia (2004–9). He has also served as the Director General of the National Archives of India (2010–13) and was appointed the Jawaharlal Nehru Fellow (2013–15). He has been a Visiting Professor at the Central European University, Budapest; the International Institute of Languages and Civilizations, Paris; the University of Virginia; the University of Rome; Fondation Maison des Sciences del' Homme, Paris; a Fellow at the Institute of Advanced Study, Shimla, and a Professorial Fellow at the Nehru Memorial Museum and Library, New Delhi. He was elected President of the Indian History Congress (Modern India) in 2002 and its General President in 2014. He was a recipient of the Padma Shri in 2007. He is the author of several books, including *Faith and Freedom: Gandhi in History* (2013), *A Moral Reckoning: Muslim Intellectuals in Nineteenth-Century Delhi*

(Oxford University Press, 2005), *From Pluralism to Separatism: Qasbas in Colonial Awadh* (Oxford University Press, 2004), *Legacy of a Divided Nation: India's Muslims since Independence* (Oxford University Press, 1997), *India's Partition: Process, Strategy, and Mobilization* (Oxford University Press, 1993), *India Partitioned: The Other Face of Freedom*, volumes 1 and 2 (Oxford University Press, 1995 and 1997), and *Roads to Freedom* (Oxford University Press, 2016) among others.